AF606930

Artemisia Gentileschi

Illuminating Women Artists: Renaissance and Baroque

The series *Illuminating Women Artists* launches at a critical moment in contemporary culture. It marks a significant intervention within the broader movement underway among scholars, museums, collectors and the wider world of cultural heritage to make evident and contextualise historically the contributions of women artists. As such, the books, each written by a leading specialist in the field of art history, will appeal to audiences from the academic sphere to the general public. Beautifully illustrated, the volumes collectively offer an unprecedented visual contextualisation of the lives and works of their subjects, to whom in some cases a monograph has yet to be dedicated.

Books in the sub-series *Illuminating Women Artists: Renaissance and Baroque* critically reappraise the lives and works of female artists in Europe from the fifteenth to the early eighteenth centuries. Many of the women represented by the volumes were celebrated professional artists in their own eras, yet their names and works have not been passed down continually in the history of art. As the first series dedicated to correcting this omission, the books interweave established conclusions with new discoveries to reframe how women's artistic production is approached and understood.

Artemisia Gentileschi

SHEILA BARKER

GETTY PUBLICATIONS
LOS ANGELES

Third printing

Published in the United States of America by Getty Publications, Los Angeles
1200 Getty Center Drive, Suite 500
Los Angeles, California 90049-1682
getty.edu/publications

Distributed in the United States and Canada by the University of Chicago Press

Printed in China

ISBN 978-1-60606-733-8
Library of Congress Control Number: 2021938579

Published simultaneously in the United Kingdom by Lund Humphries
Huckletree Shoreditch
Alphabeta Building
18 Finsbury Square
London EC2A 1AH
UK
lundhumphries.com

Copy edited by Jacqui Cornish
Designed by Crow Books
Set in Adobe Caslon Pro

Front cover: Artemisia Gentileschi, *Lucretia*, *c.*1635–45, oil on canvas, 92.9 × 72.7 cm (36 5/8 × 28 5/8 in), The J. Paul Getty Museum, Los Angeles

Back cover: Artemisia Gentileschi, *Self Portrait as the Allegory of Painting (La Pittura)*, *c.*1638–9, oil on canvas, 98.6 × 75.2 cm (38 13/16 × 29 5/8 in), The Royal Collection Trust, London

Contents

Series Foreword

The series *Illuminating Women Artists: Renaissance and Baroque* was conceptualized at a pivotal moment in contemporary life, when the call to dismantle structural bias was taking on a new urgency. As social justice movements, such as #MeToo, #BlackLivesMatter, and #TransLivesMatter, exposed assumptions about gender, race, and sexual identity, academic research has been infused with a new energy around these topics. Although approaches to, and even the very applicability of, identity categories as they are defined today vary in regard to the past, early modernity and the contemporary moment share a desire to contend with the power structures that have repressed individuals and groups, albeit in historically distinct ways. Books in *Illuminating Women Artists* advance a specific aspect of this study – the feminist academic enterprise – by making evident various ways that early modern women of the fifteenth through eighteenth centuries negotiated, and sometimes resisted, structural constraints in the sphere of the visual arts.

The series is indebted to feminist art-historical studies produced from the beginning of the 1970s that aimed to disrupt the traditional academic focus on early modern male artists by writing their female counterparts into the discipline of art history. These and other scholarship also began to investigate gender norms in the Renaissance and Baroque, which created different conditions for women and men who sought to practice art as professionals or amateurs. Societal limitations disadvantaged most women (and some men) who aspired to a life in the visual arts. For example, girls were excluded from the formal apprenticeship system through which most male artists were trained, and therefore they sought informal instruction, often from male relatives. Women practitioners who married and became mothers generally experienced a lapse in artistic production while they attended to the responsibilities that came with these roles. On the other hand, fathers sometimes supportively promoted their daughters as artists, which also aggrandized the family and improved its financial standing through patronage and sales.

This series considers early modern women artists within their social, cultural, temporal, and geographic contexts. These female artmakers worked in a period when a literary defense of women's merits began to challenge the patriarchal misogynist ideas that sought to suppress women and their potential. Some women artists may have been aware of this incipient feminism or have visually voiced related issues in their art. But the female artists represented by the series also identified with the social structures of their place and time. These structures, prominent among them gender and class, contributed to shaping their identities and to forming their conceptions about others. While women challenged normative structures in important ways (some more overtly than others), they also were acculturated into dominant cultural attitudes and thus complicit in supporting social hierarchies of class and race. Renaissance and Baroque women artists themselves derived from a spectrum of social classes – artisan, merchant, professional, or patrician. Membership in these classes made it possible for some women artists to have servants or even to enslave persons who contributed to their households. This practice reduced their own domestic obligations and freed time for artmaking, but in turn contributed to reinforcing existing systems of social stratification regarded as the norm.

Some gendered conditions with which female artists contended did not necessarily impede their success, but, even when women's artistic production was critically acclaimed, it was often evaluated according to gender stereotypes. Yet, certain women independently challenged, and circumvented or broke, restrictive gender protocols to enable prolific art production. In the process, they revised those protocols and influenced the history of art. Some established their own professional studios and trained pupils, both female and male, who in turn established themselves as professionals in workshops of their own. Others produced large bodies of work as amateurs, and some rendered porous the boundaries between these two statuses by bridging them. Still others produced works for members of communities to which they belonged, such as professed nuns in enclosed convents, or for personal reasons, such as to have in their possession a portrait of a family member. Some worked under contract for patrons, producing images for prestigious European courts and churches, where their art came under the eyes of the public. These women in the aggregate produced works that varied widely in subject, including both sacred and secular themes, and in artistic media. Represented in the latter category were the familiar forms of sculpture, painting, and printmaking, and also other ways of artmaking that were valued more highly in the past than they are in the present, including papercutting, embroidery, and weaving.

Five decades of sustained research have transformed our understanding of early modern women artists. *Illuminating Women Artists: Renaissance and Baroque* takes stock of this work through books that offer state-of-the-question analyses of their subjects. These peer-reviewed volumes variously interweave established conclusions with new discoveries investigated through emerging modes of analysis to reframe our understanding of the lives, artistic production, and works of art by European women. Together the books reveal the varied ways in which women of the fifteenth through the seventeenth centuries skillfully and often successfully navigated restricting gender norms to stake out productive lives as artmakers and develop innovative approaches to the works they produced. The volumes offer an unprecedented contextualization of the lives and works of their subjects, to whom in some cases a monograph has not previously been dedicated.

Marilyn Dunn, Loyola University Chicago
Andrea Pearson, American University, Washington, D.C.
April 2021

Acknowledgments

In many ways, this book's beginnings can be traced back to 2010, when Jane Fortune made it possible for me to dedicate a part of my time to searching for documentation about Artemisia Gentileschi in the archives of Florence. Without the ability to return to the archive year after year, I could have never made the unexpected discoveries that were the reward for patient, repeated looking. This was quiet philanthropy that Jane did with grace, enthusiasm, appreciation and constancy. Jane would have been 'over the moon' – to borrow her characteristic expression – had she lived to see this book. Notably, it is only because of the outstanding generosity and encouragement of the wonderful Trustees of the Medici Archive Project that I was able to bring the work begun under Jane's tenure to its completion. I thank them all!

The path Jane put me on led to many collegial friendships, and I wish I had space here to thank the numerous scholars of all ages who have helped me along my way. In particular, I owe enormous debts of gratitude to two eximious scholars and extraordinary mentors, Sheila ffolliott and Mary D. Garrard. I count both as guiding lights and guardian angels. The particular history of this book reflects the remarkable contributions of Erika Gaffney, whose inspirational vision and hard work gave rise to this timely series. She has guided me at every pass of the process, carried some of my burden, and delicately intervened to help shape my amoebic research into a readable book. Several others have lent their efforts to that same last, gargantuan task. Alessio Assonitis did so in a timeframe that was hardly convenient for him, yet he brought his unsurpassed erudition, as well as his astonishing kindness to the task, adding to the many reasons I am grateful to him. Nicole Sobolewski and Katie Rabogliatti each helped me unstintingly, contributing notably to the readability of the text. I owe a great deal as well to the two anonymous readers and the series editors, Marilyn Dunn and Andrea Pearson, for their exacting readings and prudent advice. With ideas and corrections, many friends measurably improved this second edition: Eve Straussman-Pflanzer, Keith Christiansen, Richard Spear, Greg Fisher, Maria Cristina Terzaghi, and Alessandra Masu. Finally, I give heartfelt thanks to my dear friend and fellow early modern historian J.M.M., who rejuvenated my enthusiasm for storytelling and who gave me the greatest gift of all: the time needed to transform the dream of this book into a reality.

Preface

More has been written about Artemisia Gentileschi (1593–after 1654) than any other early modern woman artist. I like to think that this is with good reason. Artemisia – and I will use her first name, just as I will use her father's first name, in order to avoid confusion between the two Gentileschis – was one of the most esteemed artists of her time. Moreover, the little we know about her life story is far richer and more enthralling than any fictionalised interpretation yet.

Artemisia's biography has been a work in progress for centuries. Although it has been undertaken from multiple viewpoints, the earliest account of Artemisia's life – written by the prelate and philogynist biographer Cristofano Bronzini while she was in her late twenties – was part of an explicitly feminist enterprise. It was one of thirty-three profiles of women artists in a mammoth manuscript literary project entitled *On the Dignity and Nobility of Women* [*Della dignità et della nobiltà delle donne*] whose aim was to document the achievements of notable women from Classical Antiquity up through Bronzini's day.

By the time Bronzini crossed paths with Artemisia in Florence, perhaps around 1619, he had already written the biographical profiles of several contemporary female artists and was eager to include one on Artemisia. She, however, was not content to leave her portrayal in his hands. Although the five manuscript pages of Artemisia's biography were doubtlessly written down by Bronzini, this account of her youth contains so much decisive input from Artemisia that she should be considered its true author. From this perspective, one could say that the first person to have attempted to recount the life of Artemisia Gentileschi was Artemisia herself.

When informing Bronzini about her childhood and adolescence in Rome, Artemisia ingeniously crafted her life story in the manner she thought would best serve her goals.[1] As a result of her intervention, Artemisia's *vita* stands apart from Bronzini's accounts of other women artists with their predictable litanies of praise. Her account breaks this mold in order to follow Giorgio Vasari's historiographic model, outlining such critical artistic events as the discovery of her artistic talent, her struggle to become a painter against her father's will, her precocious adoption of Caravaggio as a stylistic model and the high prices paid for her earliest artworks – all while avoiding the unsavoury figure of Agostino Tassi, who had raped her in her own home when she was seventeen.

Artemisia's growing fame inspired additional accounts of her professional trajectory even while she was alive. Although too brief to be considered a true biography, the memories set down by the German artist-biographer Joachim von Sandrart, regarding their meeting in her Neapolitan workshop, are precious because they allow us to see Artemisia through the eyes of a roughly contemporary painter. The late-seventeenth-century writer Filippo Baldinucci did not know Artemisia personally, yet he was the first biographer to offer a critical analysis of her style and to record detailed impressions of her canvases, including the female subjects he praised as appearing 'beautiful, very lively, and self-assured'.[2]

Writing about Artemisia at the close of the eighteenth century, both Averardo de' Medici, a Florentine patrician who had acquired a painting of hers in Naples, and Alessandro da Morrona, a cleric who compiled the biographies of illustrious natives of Pisa, touched upon her private dealings with men. The more sympathetic of the two writers was Medici, who placed Artemisia on a pedestal and who deemed her Florentine spouse, Pierantonio Stiattesi, unworthy of her virtue. By contrast, Da Morrona portrayed Artemisia as a siren whose charms had led men to their downfall, essentially reprising Giambattista Passeri's recently published *vita* of Agostino Tassi. Both opinions now appear irredeemably obsolete in light of the subsequent documentary findings. Nonetheless, Medici's and Da Morrona's biographies remain valuable for their shared primary focus on the exaltation of Artemisia's painterly achievements across the long arc of her career, particularly Artemisia's ability to paint complex, large-scale compositions and to convey the inner feelings of their protagonists.

The next important contribution to Artemisia's biography was made in the immediate aftermath of World War I. Bent on identifying and distinguishing followers of the Baroque painter Caravaggio, Roberto Longhi published a ground-breaking study on Artemisia and her father Orazio in 1916. Although Longhi erroneously ascribed many paintings to Artemisia that have since been discarded from her oeuvre, he advanced our understanding of the father and the daughter by placing both firmly in Caravaggio's circle; he also made a derisive innuendo about Artemisia's promiscuity and referred in passing to the trial against Artemisia's rapist, but he clearly did not think the affair to be relevant to a discussion of her art.

The first biographer to take issue with Longhi on that last point was Longhi's wife, Anna Lopresti. Publishing under the pen name of Anna Banti in 1947, Lopresti indelibly marked the perception of the painter with her fictionalised novel, *Artemisia*, by calling explicit attention to Agostino Tassi's rape of Artemisia during her adolescence. She was also the first to draw a connection between that rape and Artemisia's subsequent artistic practice, implying that the act of painting the Uffizi's *Judith Beheading Holofernes* helped Artemisia to process the psychological trauma of the attack that had occurred many years prior. Although that specific causal theory has since been challenged and debunked by many scholars, we are all beneficiaries of Banti's curiosity about the rapport between the artist's life and her art.

The late 1970s ushered in a vigorous period of historiographic research that uncovered much biographical information.[3] Thanks to the investigations carried out by Mary D. Garrard, R. Ward Bissell, Elizabeth Cropper, Judith W. Mann, Patrizia Cavazzini, Alexandra Lapierre, Jessie Locker and others, the artistic personality faintly adumbrated by Longhi took on three-dimensional relief, and the connections between the artist's life and her art came to be redefined on a factual basis. It now became possible to envision Artemisia's domestic situation, her patronage circles and her artistic influences. Moreover, several key exhibitions served as engines for new scholarship on Artemisia's art and life. From the vital early ones – *Women Artists: 1550–1950*, curated by Ann Sutherland Harris and Linda Nochlin in 1976, *Artemisia*, curated by Roberto Contini and Gianni Papi in 1991, and *Artemisia and Orazio Gentileschi*, curated by Keith Christiansen and Judith W. Mann in 2002 – the number of works that could be securely attributed and cross-checked against original inventories grew quickly, while incorrect attributions (including Longhi's) were progressively shed.

In the twenty-first century, Artemisia's growing presence in both entertainment media and university curricula has sparked renewed interest in her life story. A salutary outcome of that interest has been a reinvigoration of the archival quest for additional documentary sources. Each passing year seems to introduce a fresh revelation – a new document or even a whole cache of Artemisia's personal writings, as in the case of the love letters that were found in the Frescobaldi Archive and published by Francesco Solinas in 2011.[4] Artemisia's sonnets are a recent sensation, having been discovered serendipitously in the Vatican archives by music historian Eric Bianchi, with whom I recently co-wrote an article explaining their significance.[5] These new additions enhance the precision with which we can explain Artemisia's professional trajectory and delineate her place in society.

Nevertheless, many gaps remain in the available historical sources. Some of these unfortunate lacunae cast darkness over the most dramatic events in Artemisia's life, including the demise of her husband, the specifics of her stay in England, the fortunes of her one surviving daughter (or perhaps two daughters?), and even the date and circumstances of her own death. As with the case of Rembrandt and his many self-portraits, the abundance of Artemisia's self portraits has fostered a sense of familiarity with the artist, simply because we can recognise her face. The truth is, however, we have only begun to get to know her.

To tell the life story of our artist, this book must occasionally span large voids between islands of known facts. It does so with reasoned hypotheses based on what is known about Artemisia herself, what is known about other painters of her time, and what we can learn from the expanding literature on early modern women's lives. At the same time, the book takes pains to eradicate a few intransigent misconceptions, particularly those that loom prominently in panegyrical writings on the artist. Beyond these immediate goals of extending and correcting Artemisia's biography, it is hoped that the narrative presented here will stimulate continued research on the artist by raising unexpected questions, many of which simply cannot be answered without further historical documentation. In that sense, this book invites other scholars to carry the torch yet further.

Like the expanding documentation, previously unknown paintings have been coming to light of late, with noteworthy frequency. Among the more recent discoveries is the *Caritas Romana* (*Cimon and Pero*), *c.*1644–5, which, after Nicola Spinosa's indication, was introduced to the world by Viviana Farina, with a fascinating historical account of the patron in her 2018 exhibition *Artemisia e i pittori del Conte: La collezione di Giangirolamo II Acquaviva d'Aragona a Conversano*. In addition, two further paintings have been identified by Gregory Buchakjian in a private collection in Beirut, Lebanon, one of which was borrowed for an exhibition in 2021, Le Signore dell'Arte. This same impression of progress does not, unfortunately, characterise the challenge of cataloguing many of the works traditionally associated with her oeuvre. Controversies over dating and attribution continue to divide scholars with respect to all but a small number of Artemisia's paintings.

To determine the chronological ordering of Artemisia's oeuvre in the absence of documentation, I have adhered generally to R. Ward Bissell's 1999 catalogue raisonné and, especially in the case of recent attributions, the catalogue of the exhibition *Artemisia* curated by Letizia Treves and held at London's National Gallery from 3 October 2020 to 24 January 2021. This book's format does not permit me to defend every choice of date, nor would the vast majority of readers find such technical considerations worth their time, especially when it is a matter of five years or less. Nevertheless, because these are only reasoned guesses, the reader should keep in mind that date ranges and the use of the qualifier 'circa' mean that such dates are subject to future revision pending new evidence.

Certain historiographic contributions are indispensable to an understanding of Artemisia

Gentileschi: Garrard's 1989 monograph, Bissell's 1999 catalogue raisonné and the catalogues of the exhibitions dedicated to Artemisia beginning with Gianni Papi and Roberto Contini's 1991 show at Casa Buonarroti. In addition, three recent publications are essential *vade mecums* of the present book. It is hoped that the curious reader, the student and the researcher will make avid use of them, cross-checking accounts and supplementing the material and concepts that are dealt with here. The first of these is the catalogue for the exhibition *Artemisia* that opened in 2020 at the National Gallery, London. It contains Elizabeth Cropper's and Patrizia Cavazzini's important biographical essays, as well as Letizia Treves' informative forewords to each chapter. The next is Sheila ffolliott's annotated bibliography on Artemisia Gentileschi for the Oxford Bibliographies Series. Her scrupulous dedication to the gargantuan task of tracking down, evaluating and summarising the historiography on Artemisia in the major European languages has considerably lightened my own burden. Readers who wish to explore beyond the present book's limited bibliography of directly cited texts will be well served by the valuable resource that ffolliott has created. The third publication is Mary D. Garrard's most recent contribution to Artemisia studies: *Artemisia Gentileschi and Feminism in Early Modern Europe*.[6] It places Artemisia's art in the context of coeval writings that drew attention to women's unjust treatment and undervaluation in society, and it demonstrates that several of her paintings resonated with that discourse. Besides the many works focused specifically on Artemisia, a number of which appear in this book's bibliography, there is also a vast literature on Italian Baroque painting and a growing library of books dedicated to early modern women artists, both individually and collectively.

Once a cue for raised eyebrows, the category of women artists is now a mainstay of twenty-first-century academic historiography. Indeed, it has become reflexive to situate the investigation of any individual female artist within this broader collective framework. The present book on Artemisia Gentileschi, for example, belongs to a series dedicated to the category of women artists, and it also carries a Series Foreword providing a general background on the status of women artists in the early modern period.

Lest we forget, however, some of the most influential historians to have studied women artists have contested the utility of this very category, precisely because it belies the diversity of its component members. This view was articulated by Ann Sutherland Harris and Linda Nochlin in the above-mentioned catalogue of their exhibition, *Women Artists: 1550–1950*, where they declaimed that their exhibition's artworks by women from 1550 to 1800 'do not share any special visual characteristics due to their female authorship'. Yet Harris and Nochlin were also quick to point out that: 'If work by women artists has more in common with that by their male contemporaries than that by other women, nevertheless women shared some experiences that affected the kind of work they produced'.[7]

Although the collective category of women artists was invoked in the historiographic literature of Artemisia's lifetime, it had not been in existence for very long. It was still an inchoate notion in 1546, when Francesco da Sangallo observed in his private correspondence to Benedetto Varchi that, 'you must know how many women there are in Flanders and France, and in Italy as well, who paint so well that in Italy their pictures are much appreciated'.[8] The notion was fully crystallised by the artist-biographer Giorgio Vasari in 1568, in the course of his expansion of *The Lives of the Most Excellent Painters, Sculptors, and Architects*, yet probably without much premeditation, judging from his hasty notes.[9]

Vasari's book had first been published in 1550 containing a sole *vita* dedicated to a woman, namely the Bolognese sculptor Properzia de' Rossi. In the longer edition published in 1568, Vasari added short biographical sketches of three additional women artists, Sofonisba Anguissola, Lucrezia Quistelli and Plautilla Nelli. Notably, he folded all three of their sketches into the *vita* of Properzia de' Rossi, who was still the sole woman artist to have a *vita* in this compendium. It is striking that the only thing that these three new artists had in common with De' Rossi was their gender. None of them belonged to her generation, none of them was Bolognese, none of them was a sculptor, and none of them had practised exclusively in a professional and artisanal context.

Within his *vite* about male artists, Vasari had also frequently inserted additional short biographical profiles, but he always did so in accordance with substantive personal bonds such as familial ties, master–apprentice relationships or a shared geographic origin. In putting four very different female artists into a single *vita*, Vasari's text not only underlined both the variety that existed among these women – and the very disparate situations in which women artists could succeed – but he also tacitly implied that gender itself was of relevance to an artist's biography. Vasari very well may have thus shared Harris and Nochlin's above-cited view that the commonalities of women's experiences did in fact have an impact on their production of art.

Vasari's establishment of the category of women artists for historiography had particularly wide implications because of the enormous commercial success of the book in which it was featured. Before Vasari's 1568 publication, it must have been more difficult for families to imagine their daughters becoming artists. Vasari's revised *Lives* provided young women with a spectrum of valid role models, grouped under the catch-all category of female artists: for wellborn wives, there was Lucrezia Quistelli; for aristocratic ladies-in-waiting, there was Sofonisba Anguissola; for commoners in the secular world, there was Properzia de' Rossi; and for female monastics there was Plautilla Nelli.

One could argue that, as the daughter of an artist, and even more so, as one also gifted with an inborn vocation, Artemisia would have found her way to the easel and picked up paintbrushes even without Vasari's provision of female role models. Yet there were other ways that Vasari's 'women artists' category inevitably shaped Artemisia's outlook. It taught her to expect that even as an accomplished artist she would still be treated as a woman, appraised differently than her male peers, and expected to adhere to society's stricter behavioral codes for females. Vasari's segregation of women into their own category also suggested the improbability of a woman ever being compared to a male artist that she hoped to equal or surpass. Yet, instead of discouraging Artemisia, Vasari's indications of the challenges faced by women in the profession may have kindled Artemisia's feminist sentiment.

How Artemisia stood with respect to her society's views of womanhood is, in fact, one of the main questions driving this book. Her late correspondence, which contains her verbal rebuttals to facile equations of womanhood with inferiority, implies she took a highly critical stance. The treatment of the subjects in her paintings largely corroborates this view – as argued first and best by Garrard. My interpretation of such responses as signs of a feminist outlook might strike some readers as anachronistic. To defend my use of the term 'feminism', I could do no better than to invoke Garrard's compelling arguments in *Artemisia Gentileschi and Feminism in Early Modern Europe* (pp 8–9), which I cite here at length:

> Throughout the book, I use the term 'feminist', rather than 'proto-feminist' or 'pre-feminist', terms used by writers who would distinguish early modern feminist writers and texts from the 'real' feminist movements of the nineteenth and twentieth centuries. It is true that early modern pro-female and anti-misogynist writers were not called 'feminists' in their time. But, to repeat an analogy I have used before, the work of Galileo and Newton was not called science in their day; it was natural philosophy. Today they are regarded as foundational figures in the history of science – that is, scientists. Like science, feminism existed before we

> knew what to call it, and as with science, we must see the larger picture. If we do not recognize feminism as a continuum that has evolved over time, from the fourteenth century to the present, we risk separating women from our history and minimizing feminism's significance in history writ large.
>
> Some say that the early modern writers were not really feminists because they didn't call for political action, that their dialogues about 'the woman question' were essentially upper-class parlour games. Ideas about gender injustice may have been embroidered in courtly settings, but they were no less serious or incisive for that. Arcangela Tarabotti's passion and pain scream out in her words. Christine de Pizan and Veronica Franco spoke out on behalf of women – who were not yet identified as a social category – which surely counts as a political act. Moreover, before the eighteenth century, few if any women or men envisioned collective political action as a viable way of righting social wrongs. We do not fault Leonardo da Vinci because his aeroplane designs would not have worked; we see his vision of human flight as an inspirational starting point that led to the Wright brothers. The first writers to challenge the gender status quo got people thinking and talking; they inspired other writers, and created a conceptual foundation for the political movements that brought change. If a distinction is to be made between stages of feminism, we might distinguish between the early modern theoretical phase and the modern activist phase. But let us position and teach the entire history of feminism as a major, continuous strand in our larger histories.

In alignment with Garrard's position, my use of 'feminist' or 'feminism' refers to the commonalities that link the continually evolving discourses around 'the woman question' over the ages. At the same time, however, I have also sought to avoid easy recourse to such terms whenever the subtleties and ambiguities of the situation are not adequately conveyed by such an embracing concept.

As this is meant to be a small book, I have had to renounce the elusive goal of covering everything that has been brought to light by the many scholars who have worked on Artemisia. Rather, the present book focuses on weaving a credible explanation for the vicissitudes of her progress as an artist and for the timeline that is widely diffused in many excellent publications. Composing this book with the question 'why?' in mind has meant highlighting just a fraction of her paintings – including some that are lost and for which we have no image – and interrogating some of her life events while ignoring others. The well-documented affair with Francesco Maria Maringhi, for instance, occupies somewhat less space here than Artemisia's religious proclivities or her sonnet writing. The reason is that the former, in this writer's opinion, does not inflect her artistic choices as much as the latter two issues. Artemisia the artist – her vocation, her training, her obstacles, her materials, her patrons, her entrepreneurial strategies, her collaborations, and above all the imaginative and poetic vision that animates her extraordinary creations – takes priority here in the accounting of the life of an artist, a woman artist.

Introduction

Finding Female Role Models in Counter-Reformation Rome

To explain how Artemisia got her start as an artist, it is not enough to say that her father was a painter. Her father was a male painter, and in seventeenth-century Italy, this was quite different from being a female painter. Given the times, Artemisia could never comport herself in society as a male painter did, no matter how sublime her canvases. Moreover, to suggest that her father's example sufficed to introduce her to the profession overlooks the degree to which emulation in early modern Italy was a gendered and inveterately homosocial phenomenon, meaning that young women hesitated to pursue art seriously unless they knew of other women who had won admiration for their achievements in this realm. As testimony of this, we might recall Fredrika H. Jacobs' important observation that both Lavinia Fontana (1552–1614), the daughter of a Bolognese painter, and Irene di Spilimbergo (1538–59), a Friulian noblewoman, were inspired to pursue painting when they heard about the success of Sofonisba Anguissola.[1] Without Anguissola's example to encourage them, perhaps Fontana and Spilimbergo would never have dared to become artists.

As a motherless teenager awakening to the conditions of womanhood and to the challenges these conditions presented to her professional ambitions, Artemisia must have begun to seek out appropriate female role models in her immediate surroundings: talented, formidable women who had managed to win the admiration of society. Had Artemisia received a humanist education, we could reasonably speculate that she had perhaps found her female role models in feminist treatises such as Moderata Fonte's *The Worth of Women* (1592/1600) or Lucrezia Marinella's *The Nobility and Excellence of Women* (1601). Instead, because she received only the most basic instruction in reading and writing (as is evident from her atrocious spelling in the earliest letters of her Florentine period), she depended much more on oral histories, sermons, plays and artworks that featured famous women. Living or dead, real or legendary, they became the paradigms for her own boldly unconventional life and the living exemplars of her nascent feminism.

Most visible and admired of all women in late sixteenth-century Roman society was the phalanx of reforming noblewomen at its helm. Driven by Counter-Reformation fervour yet also sympathetic to feminist causes, they helped to lead the city's urbanistic and institutional renewal in directions that addressed the plights of their poorest sisters. One of these illustrious women was Felicia Orsini (1535–96), the widow of Marcantonio II Colonna (1535–84). A keen enthusiast of humanist learning, she hosted salons and promoted music, and she organised some of the earliest all-woman musical concerts in Rome. She, herself, was so highly conversant in music that she was able

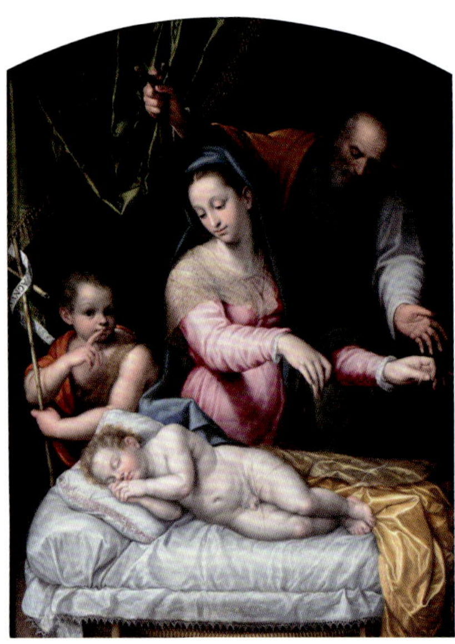

1 Lavinia Fontana, *The Virgin of Silence*, 1589, oil on canvas, 180 × 127 cm (70 ⅞ × 50 in), Real Monasterio de San Lorenzo de El Escorial

to use musical notation as a means of enciphering her most sensitive correspondence, as discovered recently by Valerio Morucci.[2] Her most serious efforts were directed towards social reform. Taking inspiration from Filippo Neri and his revival of early Christian piety, she emulated the concern of early Christian matrons for the less fortunate of their sex by helping to co-found Santa Maria del Rifugio, a convent that served as a sheltering home for undowried girls, repentant prostitutes and indigent widows.

Orsini demonstrated her interest in helping women in the case of a polymathic orphan named Margherita Sarrocchi (*c.*1560–1617), to whom she opened the doors of her own home. Although Sarrocchi lacked the wealth needed to imitate Orsini's philanthropic work, her intellect allowed her to build upon Orsini's legacy through another form of active feminism. With her astonishing accomplishments in Latin, Greek, geometry, philosophy, theology and astronomy, she gained entrée into Rome's academic circles, where she overturned assumptions about the supposed intellectual inferiority of women. Seemingly no realm of humanistic study was beyond Sarrocchi's reach. She produced a commentary on Giovanni della Casa's poetry; she translated Musaeus' *Hero and Leander* from Greek to Latin; she wrote a tractate on the geometrical calculation of volumes and densities; she kept abreast of Galileo's discoveries and corresponded with him; she entered into current theological debates with a treatise on predestination; and in 1606 she wrote the *Scanderbeide* – the first heroic epic authored by a woman – and dedicated it to Felicia Orsini's daughter, Costanza Colonna, also a patron of Caravaggio. The historian Rinaldina Russell has recently suggested that the praise Sarrocchi received in Roman society reinforced 'that great sense of her own value that distinguished her, as well as her determination to outshine all others'.[3] That observation applies just as well to the young Artemisia, who took great encouragement from the praise she received as a child in Rome, as will be explained in the next chapter.

At the same time that Sarrocchi was bringing new lustre to the image of womanhood in Rome with her intellectual prowess, Lavinia Fontana (1552–1614) was doing so with her artistic skill. Born in Bologna where she went on to raise four children, Fontana first built her reputation as a portrait painter. Then, with *The Virgin of Silence* (fig.1), painted for King Philip II of Spain in 1589, she attained an international fame for her devotional imagery. In 1599, she became the first woman to paint an altarpiece for a Roman church when her *Vision of Saint Hyacinth* took its place in the Basilica of Santa Sabina. She repeated that achievement in 1603 with her altarpiece of *The Stoning of Saint Stephen* for Rome's Basilica of San Paolo fuori le Mura. By 1604, Fontana had settled permanently in Rome at the invitation of Clement VIII Aldobrandini (*r.*1592–1605) and later found favour under the successive pope, Paul V Borghese (*r.*1605–21).

With few recent professional female artists to look to as precedents, Fontana had to improvise her handling of the entrepreneurial and social aspects of her commercial enterprise. Perhaps following the example of famous female musicians of her time such as Vittoria Archilei (*c.*1550–*c.*1620), or better yet, the universally celebrated Commedia dell'Arte actress Isabella Andreini (1562–1604), Fontana eventually adopted an approach to the business of art that hinged upon the performative aspects of gender and nobility. A vivid example of this occurred when the Borghese Pope selected Fontana, who was 57 at the time, to serve the portraiture needs of a Persian ambassador, who visited Rome in the fall of 1609. In the course of her work for Ali-Qoli Beg, the artist and her high-profile foreign male client adopted the conventional roles of a noblewoman and a nobleman engaged in a romantic courtship for their interactions, communicating primarily by means of charming and flirtatious witticisms. According to witnesses at the papal court, the ambassador penned a love poem to her in his native Persian and then plied her with amorous gallantries to convince her to transfer to the court of Isfahan. In these highly visible exchanges, Fontana demonstrated how, under the scrutiny of Counter-Reformation Rome, a woman artist could summon her feminine graces to control the pattern of discourse with her artistic patron and exploit her gender to her best advantage. That lesson was not lost on Artemisia, whose strategic self-fashioning as a female courtier will be discussed in Chapter 2.

Relevant to Artemisia's shameless embrace of the nude figure in her artistic oeuvre was Fontana's production of several mythological images featuring erotic female nudes, dating from her years in Rome under the Borghese Pope. With works such as the *Minerva Dressing* that entered the Roman collection of Cardinal-Nephew Scipione Borghese in 1613, Fontana became the first female European artist to take up the risqué genre of erotic nudes. This fact has been understood only recently, in large part because art historians previously sought to reconcile Fontana's carnal subjects with her religious imagery by interpreting her paintings of unclothed Minervas as non-sexual, chaste allegories of peace and Platonic love. However, it is no longer possible to deny that Fontana's female nudes are deliberately sensual with the emergence in recent years of several patently saucy works, including the *Mars and Venus* of *c.*1595 (fig.2) and the *Galatea and Cherubs Riding the Stormy Waves on a Sea Monster* of *c.*1590.

While growing up in Rome, Artemisia surely must have heard of Fontana's profitable commerce in provocative images of the female nude. Indeed, almost from the very beginning of her career, Artemisia made the female nude her strong suit. In embarking down this path, she must have perceived – to some extent – the subversive powerplay behind Fontana's appropriation of the male artist's traditional agency in the production of erotic images of female bodies for the male gaze. After all, Fontana's seductive female nudes were not just a symbolic reminder of women's social struggle to gain more control over their own bodies. They were also verifiable demonstrations of a woman artist's power to arouse the male sexual response, and, in this sense, they were striking instances of a situation in which a woman exercised physical control over the male body. When Artemisia began investing her female nudes with some of her own identifying features (as in the painting of *Inclination* from 1615, to be discussed in Chapter 2), she realised the startling energy she could generate by compounding her painterly prowess with her own sexual allure. Thus, in 1620, she could cheekily warn her lover of the moral dangers of masturbating before her self-portrait; ten years later, she impishly advised her patron at the papal court to give a few lashes to the self-portrait she was sending to him.[4]

Fontana was not the only highly esteemed female artist active in Rome during Artemisia's youth. Sharing that designation was Diana Scultori (1535–1612), a reproductive engraver who moved to the papal court from Mantua in 1575. That same year she shrewdly obtained, from Pope Gregory XIII, a Papal Privilege that safeguarded her business interests by giving her exclusive license over the sale

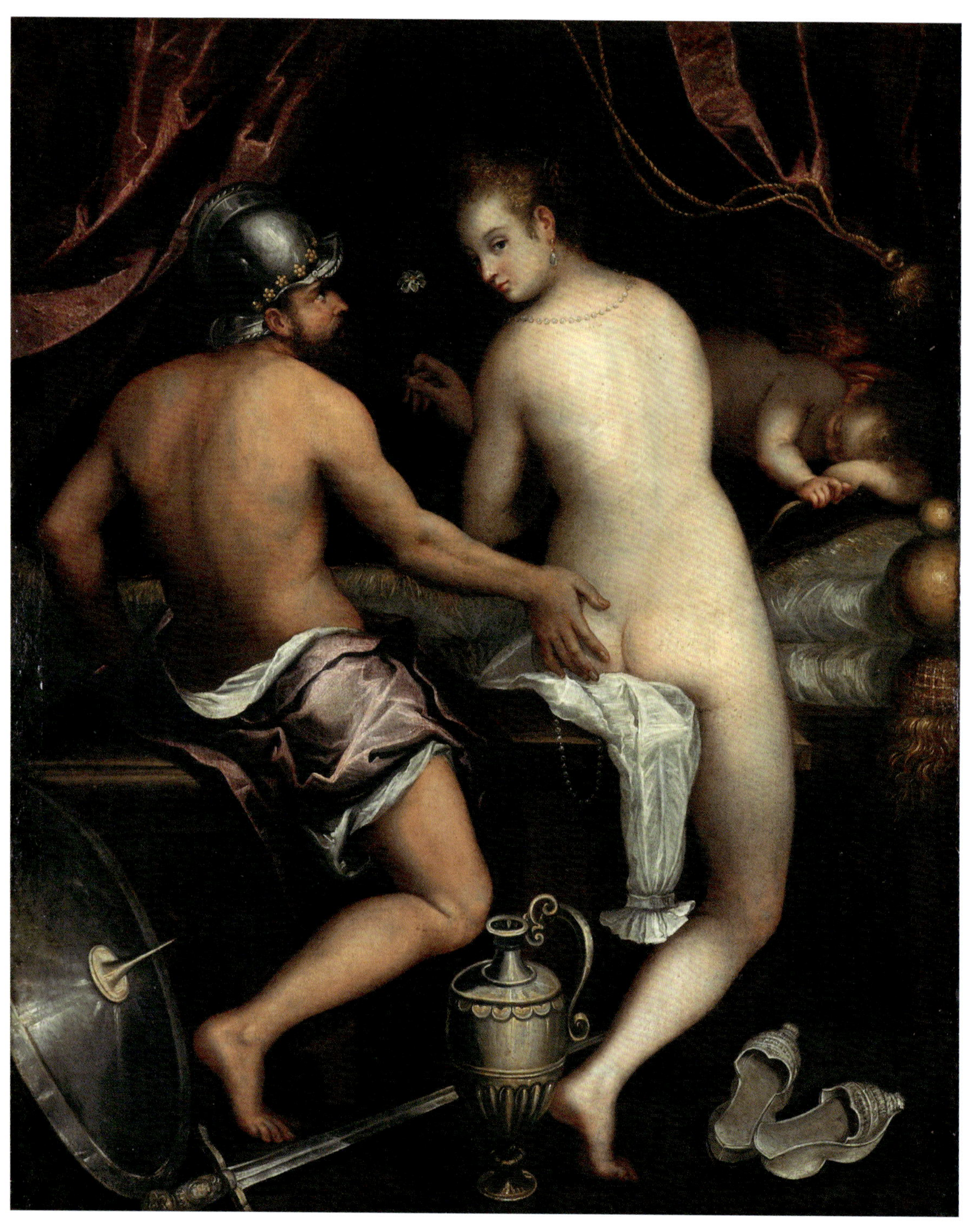

2 Lavinia Fontana, *Mars and Venus*, *c*.1595, oil on canvas, 140 × 116 cm (55 1/8 × 45 11/16 in), Palacio de Liria, Madrid

of her prints throughout the papal territories. The paintings and drawings that Scultori translated into engravings reveal the wide swathe of her connections with professional artists, most of whom she met in Rome: Raffaellino da Reggio, Giulio Campi, Durante Alberti, Daniele da Volterra, Federico Zuccari, Nicolò Martinelli, Giulio Clovio, Giorgio Vasari, Peter de Witte and Paris Nogari. Supplementing the largesse Scultori continued to receive from the Duke of Mantua, she expanded her patronage network in Rome as well. Her patrons at the papal court included Pope Gregory XIII, Duke Pompeo Colonna and Livia de' Massimi, as well as Cardinal Alessandro Farnese, who also helped Scultori by giving her access to the *Farnese Bull*. The engraving that Scultori produced of this exceedingly large and complex Greek sculpture group (fig.3) showcases her mastery of the heroic male nude, seen from both the front and the back. Even more than the female nude, the male nude was a challenge that few women artists before or after Scultori dared to undertake because of the moral danger it implied. Her accomplishments in this special arena would therefore have furnished valuable encouragement to Artemisia.

Thanks to the cultural prominence of these women and others like them, the city in which Artemisia grew up scintillated with positive female role models. Moreover, at least some of Rome's male inhabitants showed support for their causes. In the realm of the arts, for instance, Cristofano Bronzini, the above-mentioned prelate and defender of women, took an interest in female artists while living in Rome between 1591 and 1614, both as a collector of Scultori's prints and as a personal acquaintance of Lavinia Fontana. Thanks to Bronzini, we also know that Rome abounded in writings that lauded women and defended their cause, and that many of these writings were available at the library of the Vatican, including defences of women penned by two cardinals of the Catholic Church: Pompeo Colonna and Girolamo della Rovere.[5]

The mention of ecclesiastical men in association with the defence of women in early modern Rome is not accidental. If anything, the Counter-Reformation reinforced Rome's propitious climate for promoting positive notions of women's nature and their capacities. Although the religious climate of the Counter-Reformation was formerly considered to have been a repressive force in the social history of women, historians have brought to the table new evidence with positive implications. The Tridentine reforms of the late sixteenth century provided Catholic women with the legal option of remaining unmarried in the secular life; they instituted regulations to prevent the forced placement of women into monasteries or marriages against their will; and they addressed the predicaments of women trapped in abusive marriages or desiring to marry without their father's approval.

Part and parcel of the Counter-Reformational Church's influence on Roman women's lives was its concern for girls' education in convents and in their homes, so that in their later lives they might exercise Christian virtue, make informed choices between marriage, spinsterhood, and monasticism, and raise their children with orthodox beliefs. Often included among their didactic readings were devotional books designed for female readers that compiled brief descriptions of the lives of female martyrs to serve as moral exemplars. The two most popular of these all-female hagiographies, namely the *Legends of the Holy Virgins Who Wanted to Die for Our Lord Jesus Christ & to Keep the Holy Faith*, published eighteen times between 1532 and 1731,[6] and Antonio Gallonio's *History of the Roman Holy Virgins* of 1591,[7] were both abundantly illustrated with woodcuts representing the torture and killing of Christian women. The popularity of this didactic subject matter for female audiences is further demonstrated by Antonio Tempesta's series of unbound etchings titled 'Images of Many Roman Virgin Saints Being Put to Death' ['Imagini di molte SS Vergini Rom.e nel martirio'], which was published by Giovanni Antonio de Paoli between 1570 and 1591 (fig.4). Such imagery was designed to help girls construct notions of female

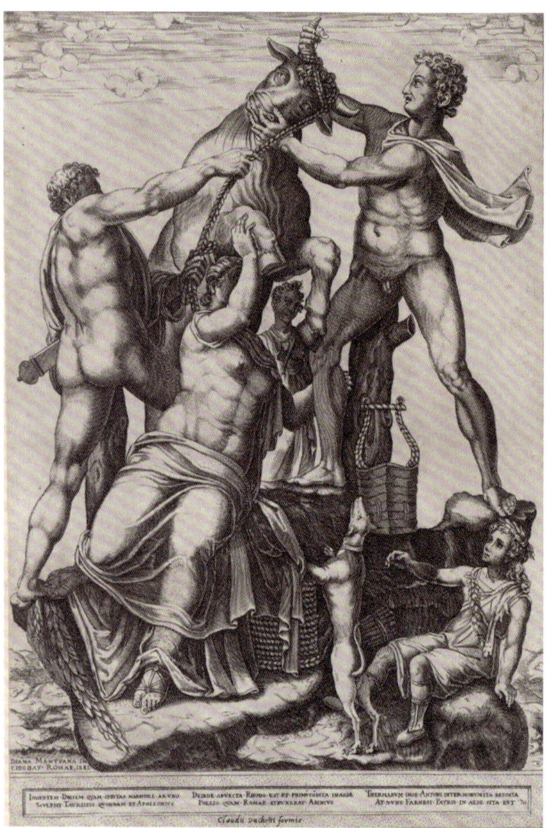

3 Diana Scultori, *Speculum Romanae Magnificentiae: Amphion and Zethus Tying Dirce to a Wild Bull* [*The Farnese Bull*], 1581, engraving, 46 × 34.4 cm (18 ⅛ × 13 9/16 in), The Metropolitan Museum of Art, New York. Rogers Fund, transferred from the Library

subjectivity and Catholic community appropriate to the goals of the Counter-Reformation. Inadvertently, that imagery may have also given them insight into the heroic potential of their own female bodies.

In the case that Artemisia did not have access to such books and prints intended for the instruction of Catholic girls and women, Rome provided a plethora of similar imagery by way of the decoration added to its churches during the Counter-Reformation. Niccolò Circignani's fresco cycle of martyrdoms in the Basilica of Santo Stefano Rotondo from 1582 features harrowing scenes of Saints Agnes, Agatha, Catherine of Alexandria, Felicity, Bibiana and others being tortured and executed for their faith, while his frescoes for the church of San Tommaso di Canterbury included the slaying of Saint Juthwara of Dorset. In 1597 Girolamo Massei decorated the church of Santi Nereo e Achilleo with frescoes depicting three early female Christian martyrs, Flavia Domitilla, Teodora and Eufrosina, as they are cast into the flames of a Roman furnace. Female martyrdom is the focal point of the convent-church of Santa Susanna: here Tommaso Laureti's altarpiece from around 1600 for the high altar shows the beheading of Saint Susanna of Rome; immediately to the left, Paris Nogari's fresco from the same period shows the beheading of Saint Felicity. Along with these painted images of women willingly dying for their faith, there was also Stefano Maderno's widely celebrated white marble statue of Saint Cecilia's nearly life-size partially decapitated body, commissioned in 1600 for the Basilica of Santa Cecilia in Trastevere shortly after the clamorous discovery of the martyr's intact remains beneath the altar.

It is generally accepted that Counter-Reformation Rome's representations of the crucified, cleaved, bludgeoned and asphyxiated male martyrs were intended to anneal young missionaries against the challenges ahead of them in places like England, Japan or Hungary. What scholars have ignored, however, is that the essentially identical imagery of the tortured deaths of female martyrs was equally capable of offering examples of strength and courage. This saintly fortitude of female martyrs had its secular avatar in the heroic fortitude that is referred to as 'womanly virtue' ['virtù donnesca'] in Torquato Tasso's *Discorso della virtù feminile e donnesca* (1582), published just one year after his *Gerusalemme liberata*, an epic poem that abounds in courageous female characters. This secular 'womanly virtue', although usually displayed by Amazonian warrior women in uncivilised contexts such as the battlefields and deserted islands of chivalric literature, was not totally

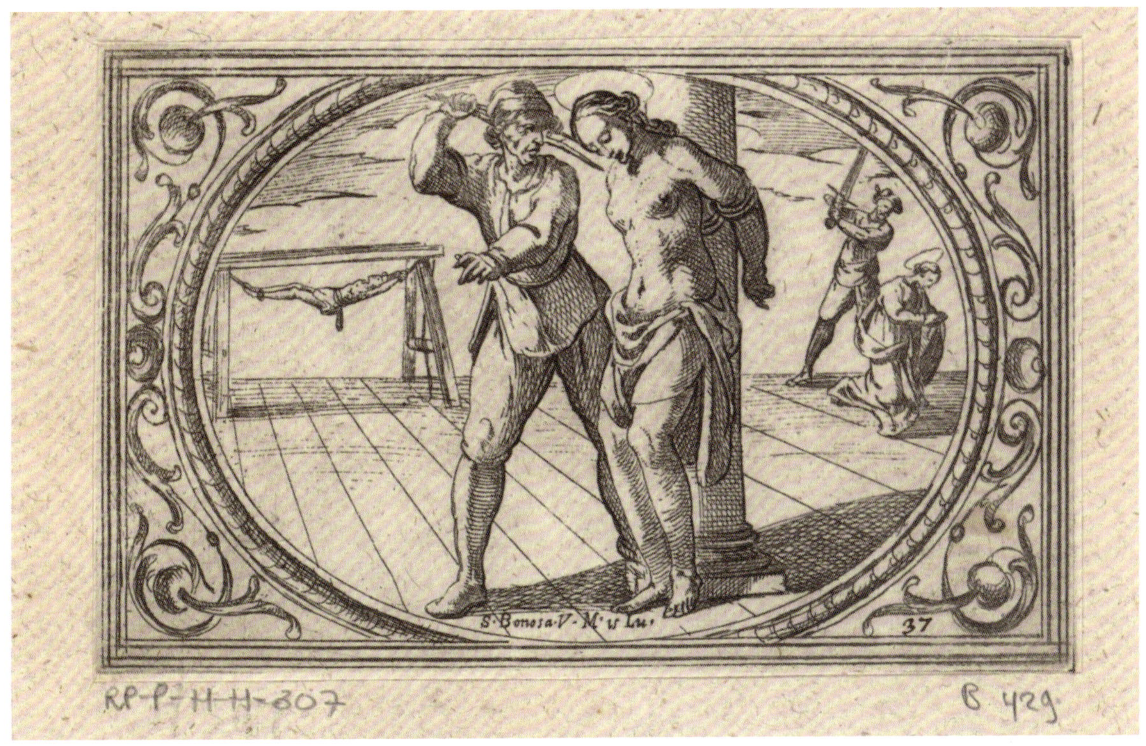

4 Antonio Tempesta, *Saint Bonosa*, *c.*1570–91, engraving, 73 × 114 cm (28 ⅞ × 44 ⅞ in), Rijksmuseum, Amsterdam

out of place in Artemisia's Rome. Despite its many paragons of female entrepreneurship and cultural leadership, the city was still no paradise for women, as proven by the tragic end met by the twenty-two-year-old noblewoman Beatrice Cenci, a victim of incest who was publicly executed in 1599 for having abetted the murder of her wicked and depraved father. Concern for the injustices and suffering to which women in their contemporary society were subject no doubt inflected Roman audiences' reception of the Counter-Reformation imagery of female martyrs. Each new local domestic atrocity would have given those depictions a caustic and urgent poignancy.

Growing up in Rome amidst the proliferation of galvanising images of saintly *femmes fortes*, inspired by the vibrant contributions that women artists and patrons were making to her city, vaguely aware of heroic female characters in modern epics like *Gerusalemme liberata*, and at the same time cognisant of the hardships and obstacles that befell her sex, Artemisia began to lay the foundations both for a career in painting and for overturning cultural biases against women. These intertwining aspects of her legacy are the basis for the present telling of her life story, recounted in the next four chapters.

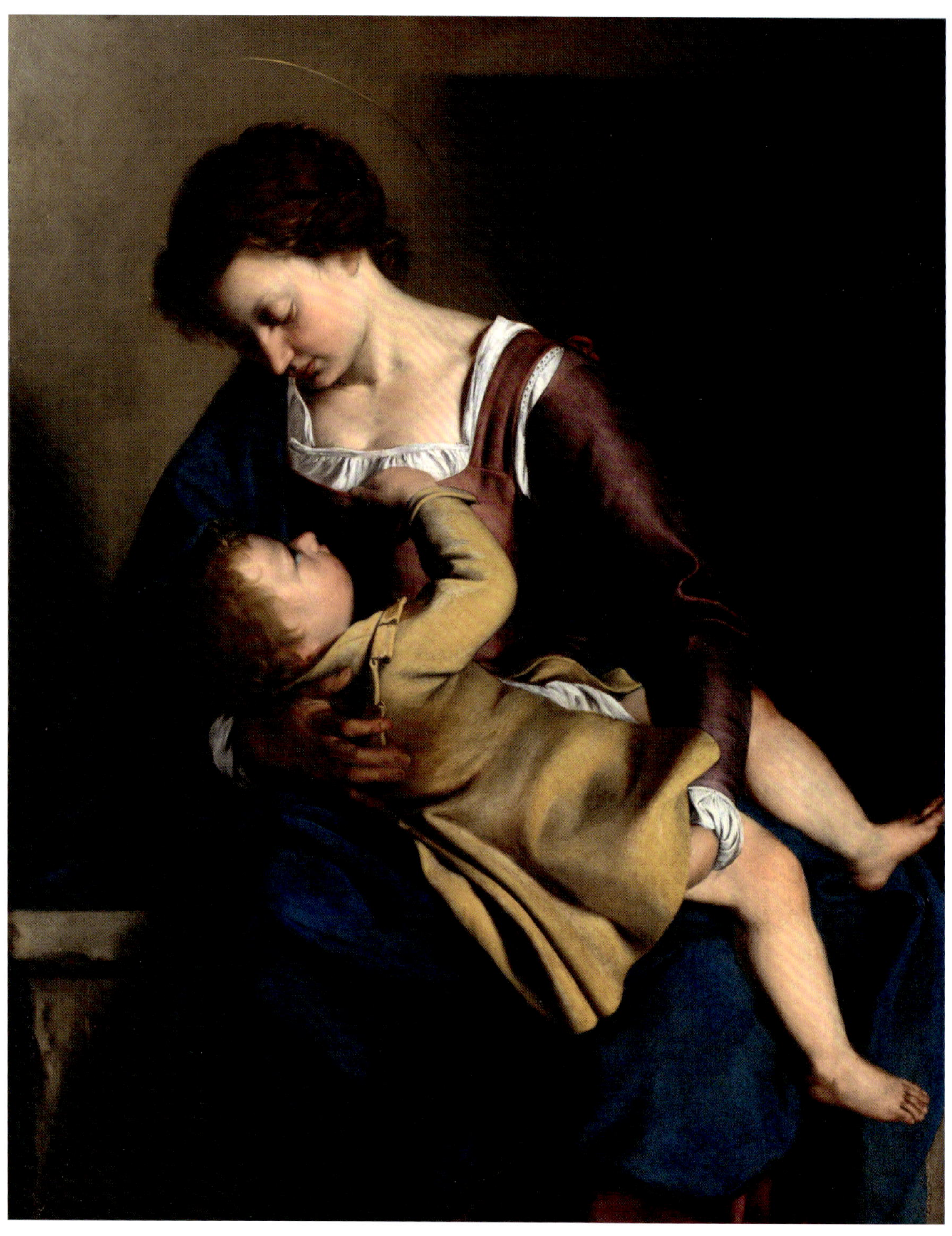

5 Attributed here to Artemisia Gentileschi, *Weaning Virgin*, 1611, oil on canvas, 131 × 91 cm (51 9/16 × 35 13/16 in), Galleria Corsini, Rome

I

'Mizia': The Artist's Youth in Rome

A LONELY GIRLHOOD

On 8 July 1593, Artemisia Gentileschi was born in Rome, but this did not suffice to make her a Roman citizen. Instead, she inherited the Tuscan nationality of her father, Orazio Gentileschi (fig.6), a painter and occasional mosaicist who was born in Pisa thirty years earlier, to a Florentine goldsmith named Giovan Battista Lomi. Artemisia's complex national identity was by no means unusual in a cosmopolitan capital like Rome. Nevertheless, being of 'Florentine ancestry but born in Rome'[1] shaped her sense of identity, conditioned her early ambition to go to the Medici court and offered her distinct advantages when she later moved to Florence.

Whereas much is known about Orazio and his Tuscan family of painters and goldsmiths, almost nothing is known about Prudenzia di Ottaviano Montoni (*c.*1575–1605) (fig.7), the woman who brought Artemisia into the world followed by her three little brothers: Francesco, born in 1597; Giulio, born in 1599; and Marco, born in 1604. It must have been through her mother's side of the family that Artemisia was related to an illustrious prelate of that era, Lanfranco Margotti (1559–1611) (although so far it has not been possible to confirm this genealogical link). Originally from Parma, Margotti received the Cardinal's hat in 1608 from Paul V Borghese and resided at the pope's Quirinal Palace until his death in late 1611. Prudenzia's relationship to Margotti seems to have helped her husband obtain three commissions between late 1610 and 1611: the fresco decorations of the Sala del Concistoro in the Quirinal Palace, the Casino delle Muse built by Scipione Borghese and Margotti's own apartment in the Quirinal Palace. All three commissions were collaborative undertakings involving Agostino Tassi (1578–1644), an expert in landscapes and *quadratura* [illusionistic paintings of architecture] who would soon become Orazio's bitter enemy.

Prudenzia died at the age of thirty due to complications from a stillbirth on the day after Christmas in 1605, when Artemisia was twelve years old. In her adolescent years, Artemisia's father lamented that 'she was always alone and did not have anyone'.[2] It was this solitude, however, that forged the young girl's resilient and self-reliant character, and which created an opportunity for her to discover her interest in art.

Many years later, when she was already a mother herself, Artemisia still had poignant memories of having to take up the tasks formerly done by her mother. This much is confirmed by her earliest biography, one which, as I have argued elsewhere, was written by Cristofano Bronzini but which was clearly supplied, and thoughtfully shaped, by

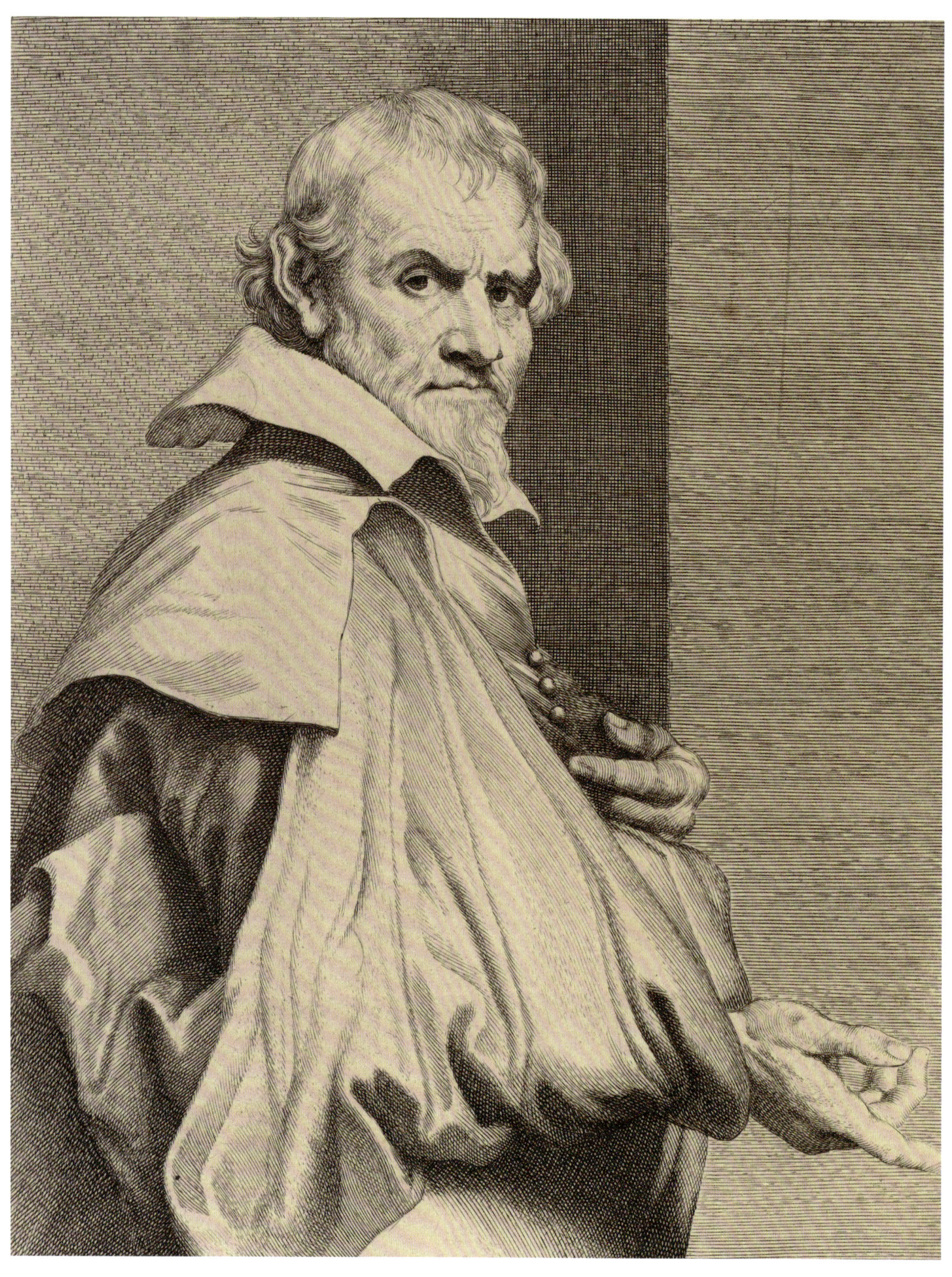

6 Lucas Emil Vorsterman after Sir Anthony van Dyck, *Portrait of Orazio Gentileschi*, *c.*1630, engraving, 24 × 17.6 cm (9 7⁄16 × 6 15⁄16 in), National Gallery of Art, Washington, DC

Artemisia herself – who is referred to in this text by the nickname 'Mizia' that had been given to her in her youth (fig.8).[3] Bronzini's account begins with the vivid recollection of how 'one day, when she was about twelve years old, [she] wanted to wear a skirt that her mother had made for her a few years earlier. Finding the skirt now to be by far too short, she decided to lengthen it by herself.'[4] At this point, something very momentous happened: Artemisia decided to decorate the newly adjoined fabric with 'an embroidery design that she had invented'. So impressive was the child's first artistic creation that the professional artists who saw it lavished praise on the young girl. According to Bronzini's biography of Artemisia, 'experts in the realms of design and painting . . . were convinced by what they saw that the young girl had a potential for great achievement in these arts'.[5]

This story of the serendipitous discovery of Artemisia's design skill derives its charm from the literary commonplaces typical of artists' biographies. The recognition of artistic vocation in spontaneous acts of a humble nature recalls, for example, the legendary story recorded by Vasari about the initial recognition of Giotto's talent, when he drew a sheep on a rock. Nevertheless, the story about Artemisia remains credible in its essence. Since Orazio's house on via Margutta doubled as the location of his workshop, it is entirely plausible that visiting artists, art dealers or patrons could have seen Artemisia's skillfully embroidered skirt. Moreover, in associating the adolescent girl's design skills in embroidery with potential for achievement in the arts in general, including painting, these enthusiastic critics were taking only a short step, not a big leap. At the time, professional embroiderers were sought after at European courts, and the books that circulated their ingenious designs for lace and embroidery enjoyed pan-European success (fig.9). Giovanni Paolo Lomazzo (1538–92), a major academic art theorist of that time, considered embroidery relevant to the triad of the arts of design in his 1590 treatise entitled *Idea del tempio della pittura* [*Idea of the Temple of Painting*], in which he reserved his highest praises for a female practitioner, Caterina Cantoni (fig.10).[6]

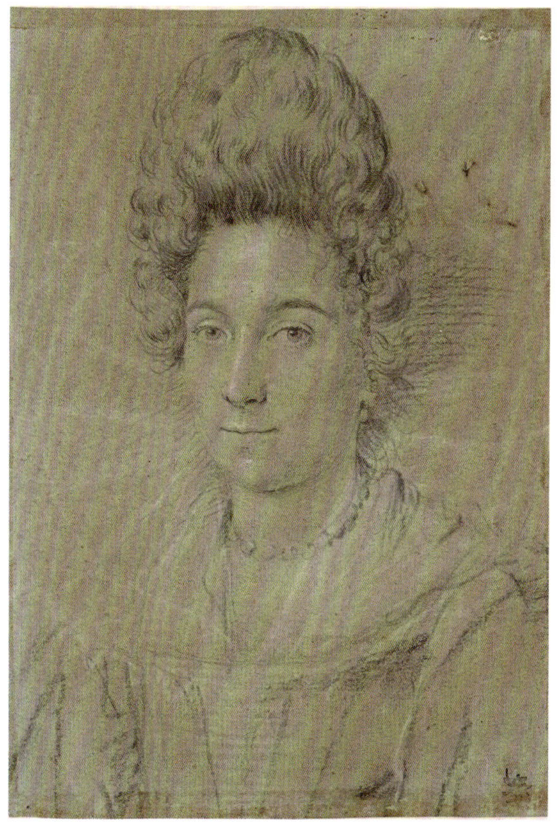

7 Ottavio Leoni, *Portrait of Prudentia di Ottaviano Montoni*, *c.*1600, black chalk, heightened with white chalk on laid paper, 21.4 × 14.9 cm (8 7⁄16 × 5 7⁄8 in), The Morgan Library & Museum, New York. Acc.no.I, 25e. Purchased by J. P. Morgan (1867–1943) in 1909

Artemisia's decision to tell Bronzini that her early textile work put her on the path to painting could be interpreted as a sign of her feminist outlook. By tracing the origin of her vocation to the embroidery skills taught to her by her mother, Artemisia and her biographer effectively associated her artistic gifts with a matrilineal line of descent, rather than a patrilineal one. The exclusion of Artemisia's father from the

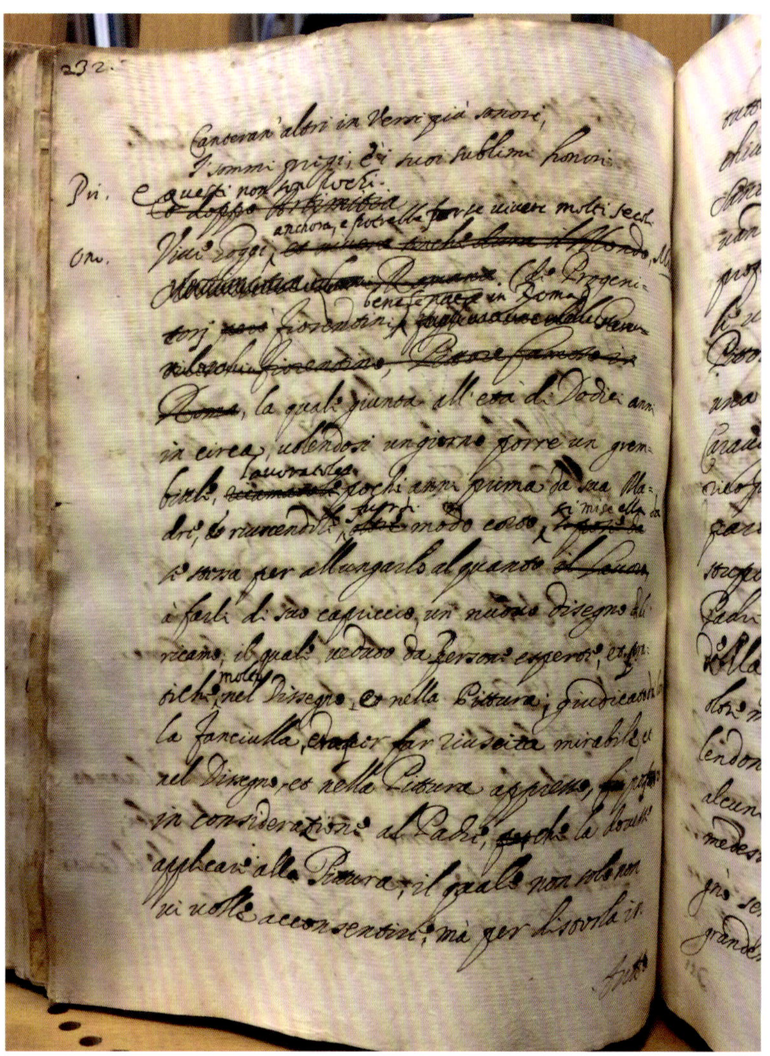

8 Biblioteca Nazionale Centrale di Firenze, Magl. Cl. VIII, cat. no. 1525, vol. II, *c.*1618–20, manuscript, 30.5 cm (12 in) (4to), Biblioteca Nazionale Centrale, Florence

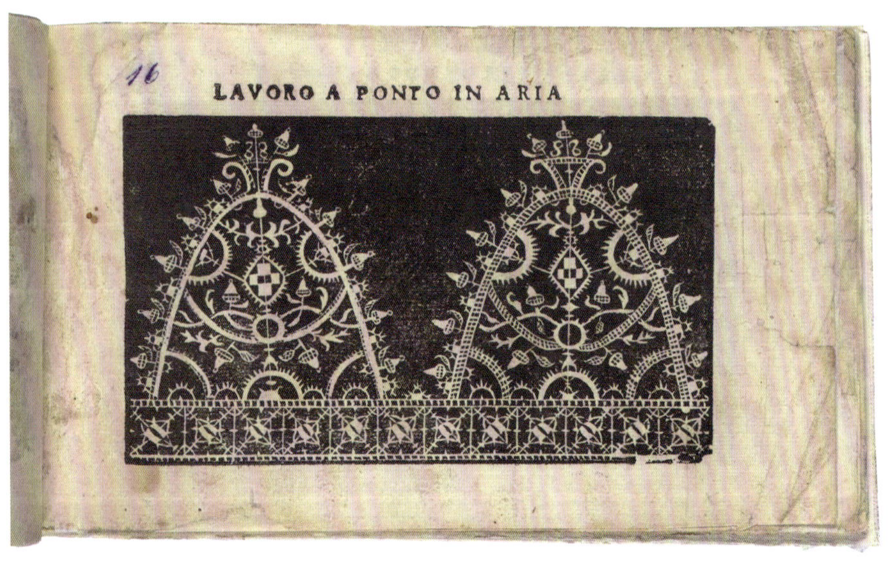

9 Elisabetta Catanea Parasole, *Gemma Pretiosa*, fol.16r, 1600, woodcut (embroidery pattern), 13.5 × 19.5 cm (5 5⁄16 × 7 11⁄16 in), The Metropolitan Museum of Art, New York. Gift of Mary M. Greenwood, in memory of Eliza Rudd Greenwood, 1953

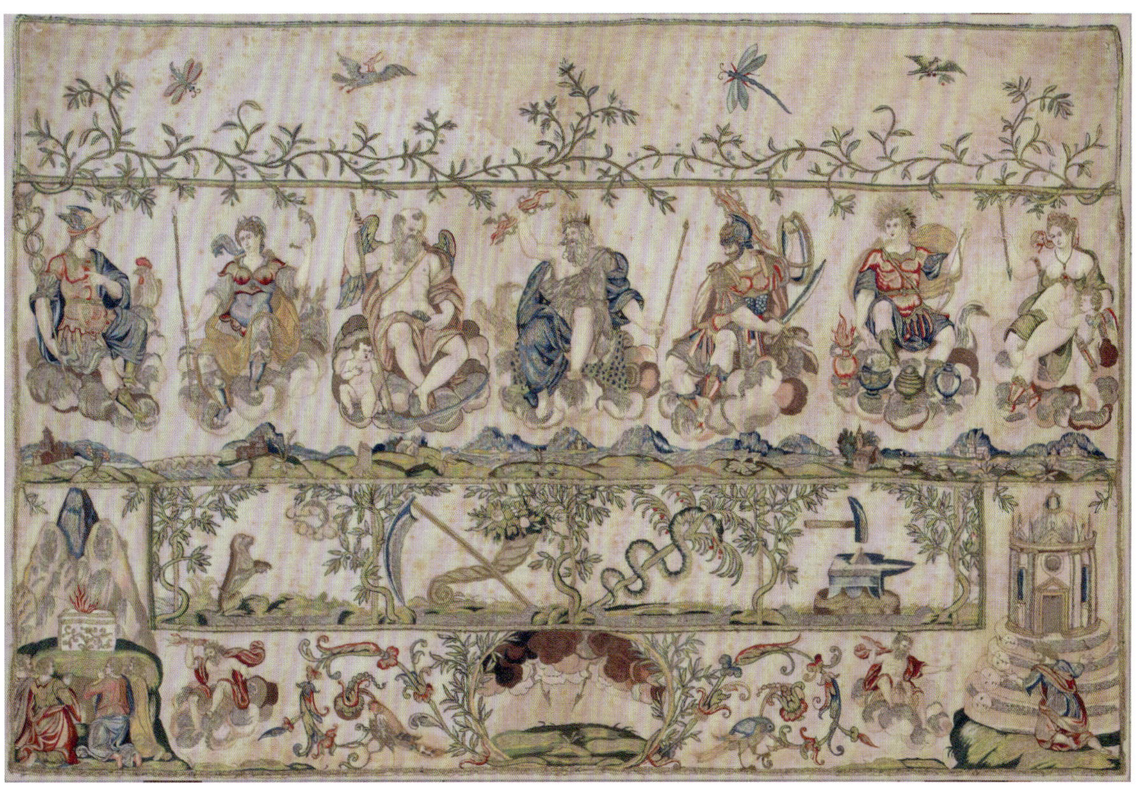

10 Caterina Cantoni, *The Planetary Gods*, *c.*1590, embroidery, 62 × 94 cm (24 ½ × 37 in), Gallery Moshe Tabibnia, Milan

story of her artistic debut carries other implications as well. According to Bronzini's biography, Orazio had scoffed at other artists' suggestions that his daughter should be trained in painting, and then for safekeeping, he placed her at the convent of Sant'Apollonia in Trastevere (a claim which cannot be verified at present and which no one mentioned at all in the 1612 rape trial). This insistence that Orazio had no role in her formation – except as an antagonist – inadvertently sheds light on one of Artemisia's lifelong preoccupations: she wanted to be recognised as an independent professional of the first rank. Orazio did not agree with Artemisia, for when he wrote to the Dowager Grand Duchess of Tuscany in 1612 to implore her to protect his daughter, he boasted of Artemisia's artistic skills and identified himself as her teacher.

ACQUIRING SKILLS AND DEFINING AN ARTISTIC APPROACH

The presentation of Artemisia as an autodidact in Bronzini's biography also flies in the face of a common-sense historiographic tradition going back to Giovanni Baglione, who, writing in the mid-seventeenth century, stated that Artemisia learned to paint from her father. It is undoubtedly true that Artemisia acquired the essential skills for working with oil paints from her father. Beginning at an early age, she must have raptly observed her father at work, gleaning, at a minimum, the trade secrets passed down from shop-master to apprentice, regarding the preparation of supports, the handling of brushes, the way to grind pigments, the rules for mixing paints and the procedure for laying down color.

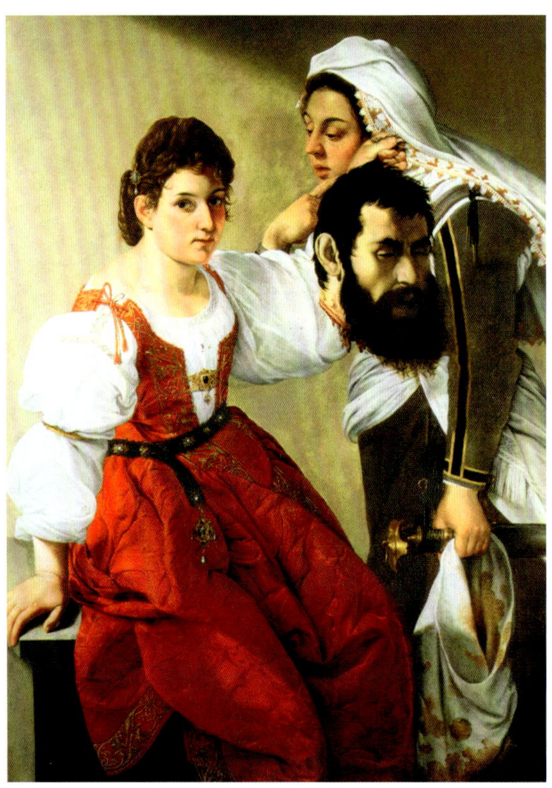

11 Attributed here to Artemisia Gentileschi, *Judith and her Maidservant with the Head of Holofernes*, *c.*1609, oil on canvas, 130 × 99 cm (51 ⅛ × 39 in), Collezione Fabrizio Lemme, Rome

Orazio doubtless imparted many fundaments of painting to Artemisia. Nevertheless, there were also some limits to what she owed to him in this realm. This is because between 1605 and 1609 – the years in which Artemisia must have been studying at her father's knee – Orazio was shedding his original Mannerist tendencies in order to emulate the startling realism introduced to Rome by a Lombard painter who had been Orazio's associate since 1603: Michelangelo Merisi, known as Caravaggio (1571–1610). Because Artemisia was learning to paint from her father at the very same time that he was struggling to unlock the secrets of Caravaggio's method and style, the father and his daughter were simultaneously assimilating the same lessons. Side by side, they reconstructed Caravaggio's revolutionary methods of working up the picture from a dark ground and illuminating the pictorial elements with strongly contrasted directional light; and, side by side, they analysed Caravaggio's use of live models and his recording of the imperfections of the flesh to enhance the impression of lifelike and immediate visuality. The fact that Artemisia came to Caravaggism fresh and uninhibited by any previous artistic indoctrination may even have given her an advantage over her father, who first had to unlearn his old techniques and approaches.

Bronzini's early biography asserts that Artemisia took Caravaggio's artworks – not her father's – as models for her studious copying. That Artemisia emulated Caravaggio in her stylistic development, in addition to her technical practices, is confirmed by her earliest surviving independent paintings. In the *Judith and her Maidservant with the Head of Holofernes* (*c.*1609) in the Lemme Collection (a work also attributed to Orazio, fig.11), in the signed and dated *Susanna and the Elders* (1610) in Pommersfelden (fig.12) and in the *Weaning Virgin* (1611) in the Galleria Corsini (fig.5), Artemisia deployed Caravaggio's avant-garde naturalism to great effect.

At the tender age of seventeen, she had quite fully comprehended Caravaggio's innovative art. With reference to the concurrent works of Orazio such as the *The Vigin with the Sleeping Christ Child* (*c.*1610) in the Fogg Art Museum (fig.13), Gianni Papi has recently argued that she also had attained a better grasp of anatomy and a keener sensitivity to the emotional rapport between figures than her father had at that moment. The extraordinary proficiency she had reached by the year 1611 is attested by four significant milestones. In that year, she was already giving drawing and painting lessons to a young male apprentice named Nicolò Bedino; her younger brother Francesco and Bedino both worked under

12 Artemisia Gentileschi, *Susanna and the Elders*, 1610, oil on canvas, 170 × 119 cm (66 ⅞ × 46 ⅞ in), Schloss Weißenstein, Pommersfelden, Bavaria

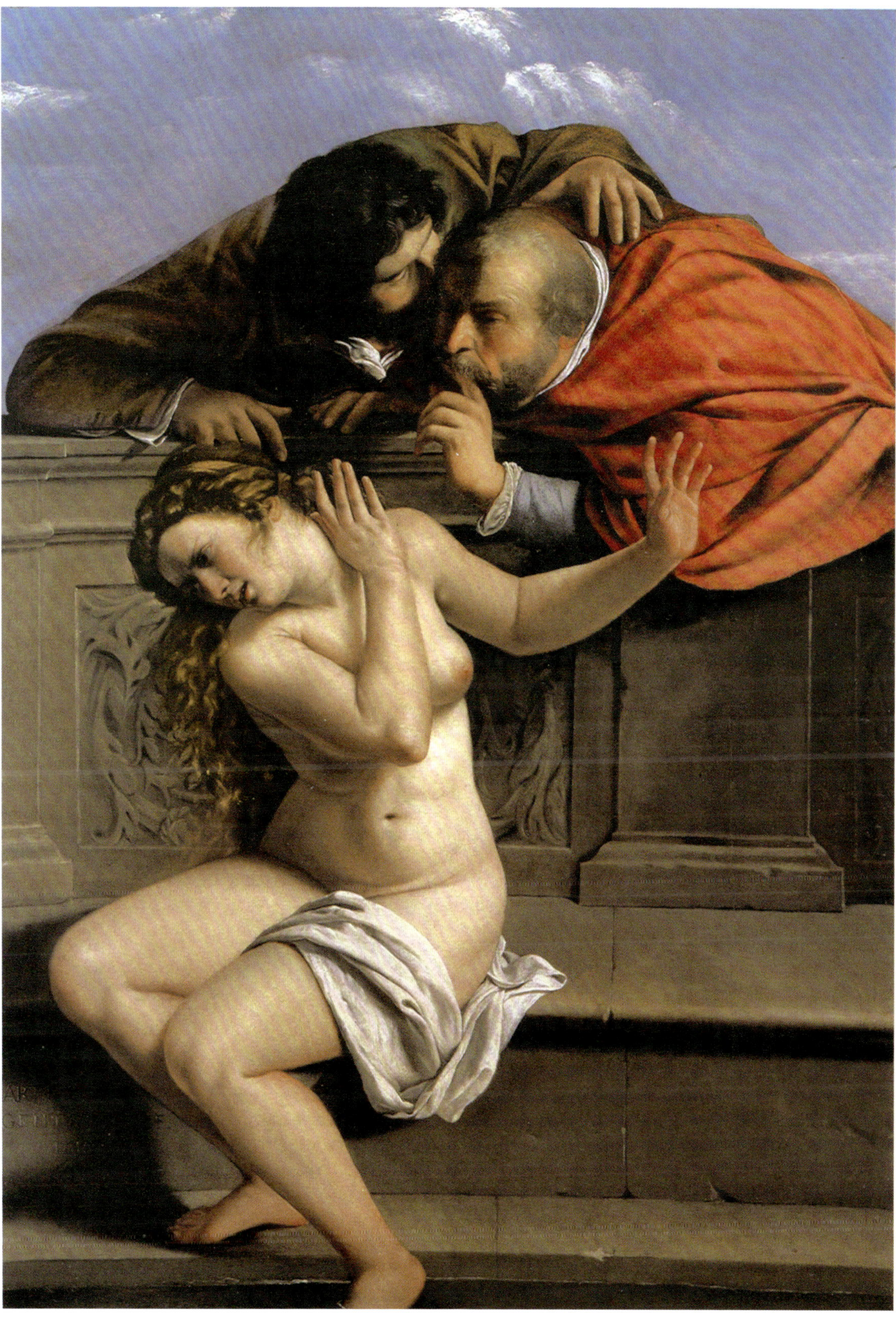

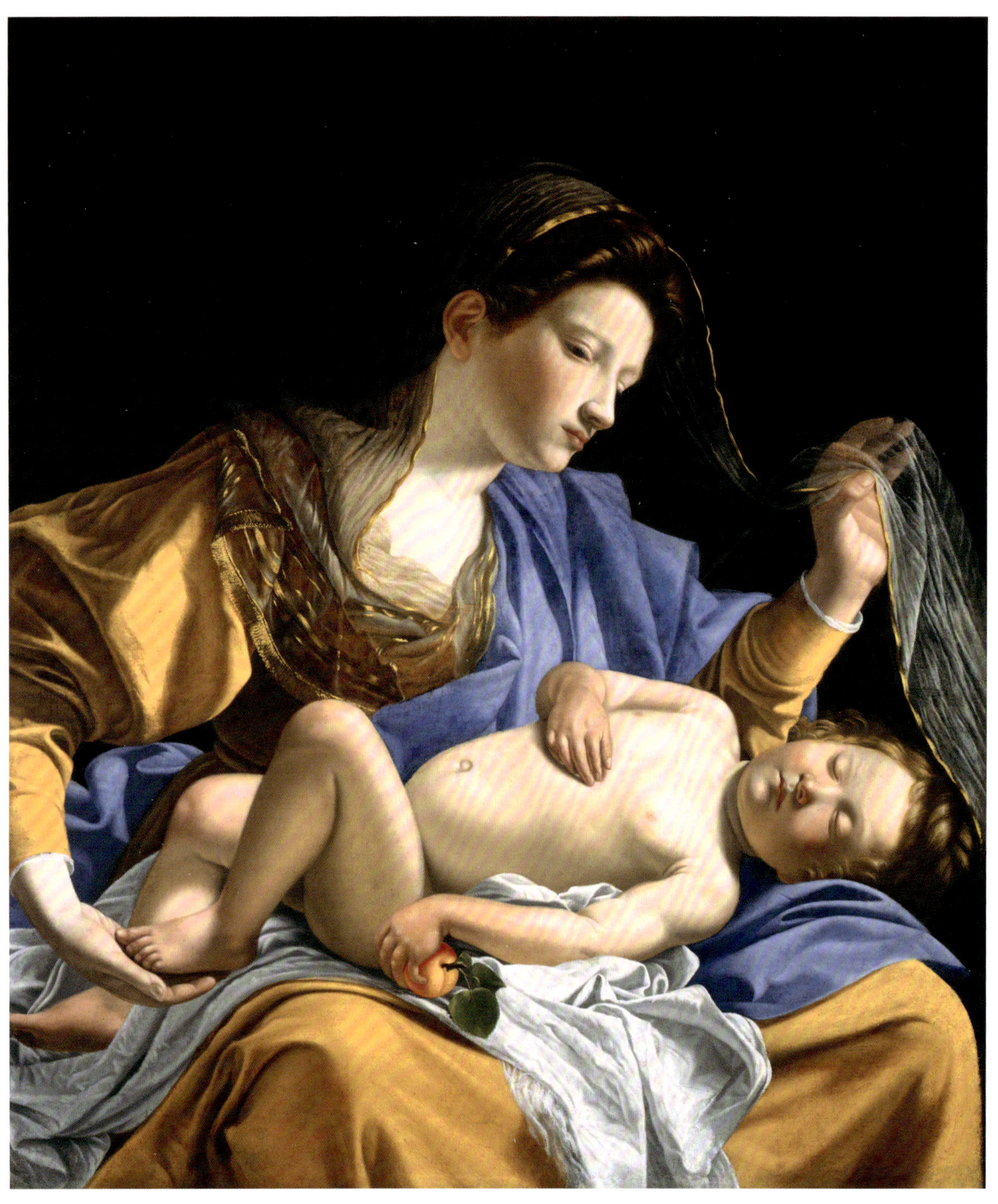

13 Orazio Gentileschi, *The Virgin with the Sleeping Christ Child*, *c.*1610, oil on canvas, 99.8 × 85.3 cm (39 5⁄16 × 33 9⁄16 in), Harvard Art Museums/Fogg Museum, Cambridge, Massachusetts

her, preparing her paints; a male model with black hair had been hired to pose for both father and daughter; and Artemisia had already received a commission – given to her by a woman – for the portrait of a man named Artigenio.

Artemisia's adoption of Caravaggio as an artistic model required leaving the confines of her home in order to see his works. In the company of her father, her chaperone Tuzia, or her friend Costanza Francini, she could have seen several of Caravaggio's religious works in nearby churches: *The Calling of Saint Matthew* (*c.*1600), *The Martydom of Saint Matthew* (*c.*1600) and *The Inspiration of Saint Matthew* (1602) in the Contarelli Chapel of San Luigi dei Francesi; the *Madonna of Loreto* (1604–6) in Sant'Agostino (fig.14); the *Entombment of Christ* in the church of Santa Maria in Vallicella and *The Conversion of Saint Paul* and *The Crucifixion of Saint Peter* (both 1604) in the Cerasi Chapel of Santa Maria del Popolo. Given the debt that Artemisia's paintings of the same subject owed to it, it has been proposed that she also saw Caravaggio's *Judith Beheading Holofernes* (1602) (fig.15), which at that time was in the collection of Ottavio Costa. She may have seen additional such paintings when, under Tuzia's vigilance, she went to the house of the papal steward-cum-art merchant Cosimo Quorli in order to watch a carnival-season play.

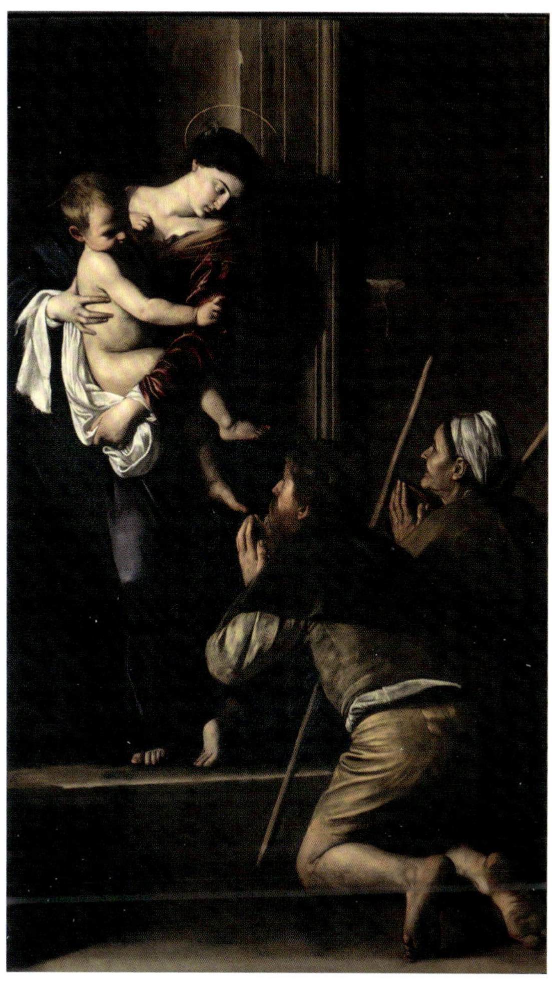

14 Caravaggio, *Madonna of Loreto*, 1604–6, oil on canvas, 260 × 150 cm (102 3/8 × 59 1/16 in), Chiesa di Sant'Agostino, Rome

HER INNOCENCE IN THE PUBLIC EYE

Artemisia's growing curiosity about the world of art around her was not easily reconciled with her society's morality codes for female behavior, particularly its strong disapproval of women's unattended presence in public spaces. Even her habit of looking out of the window of her house was censured as an action done 'very impudently' ['molto sfacciatamente'].[7] In the same manuscript that contains Artemisia's early biography, Cristofano Bronzini articulated a harsh proscription against women's mobility: 'As for going outside on occasion, as we've said, this should only be done very rarely [. . .], and on holy days with good and virtuous companions [. . .]. The virtuous woman flees from all places where her purity and her honor could be put at risk.'[8] Tragically, Artemisia's enthusiasm for her city's artistic and cultural ferment left her dangerously exposed to the sordid and savage side of Roman life. In 1611 she made two excursions in the company of family and friends to tour the principal artistic and religious sites of Rome, including Saint John in the

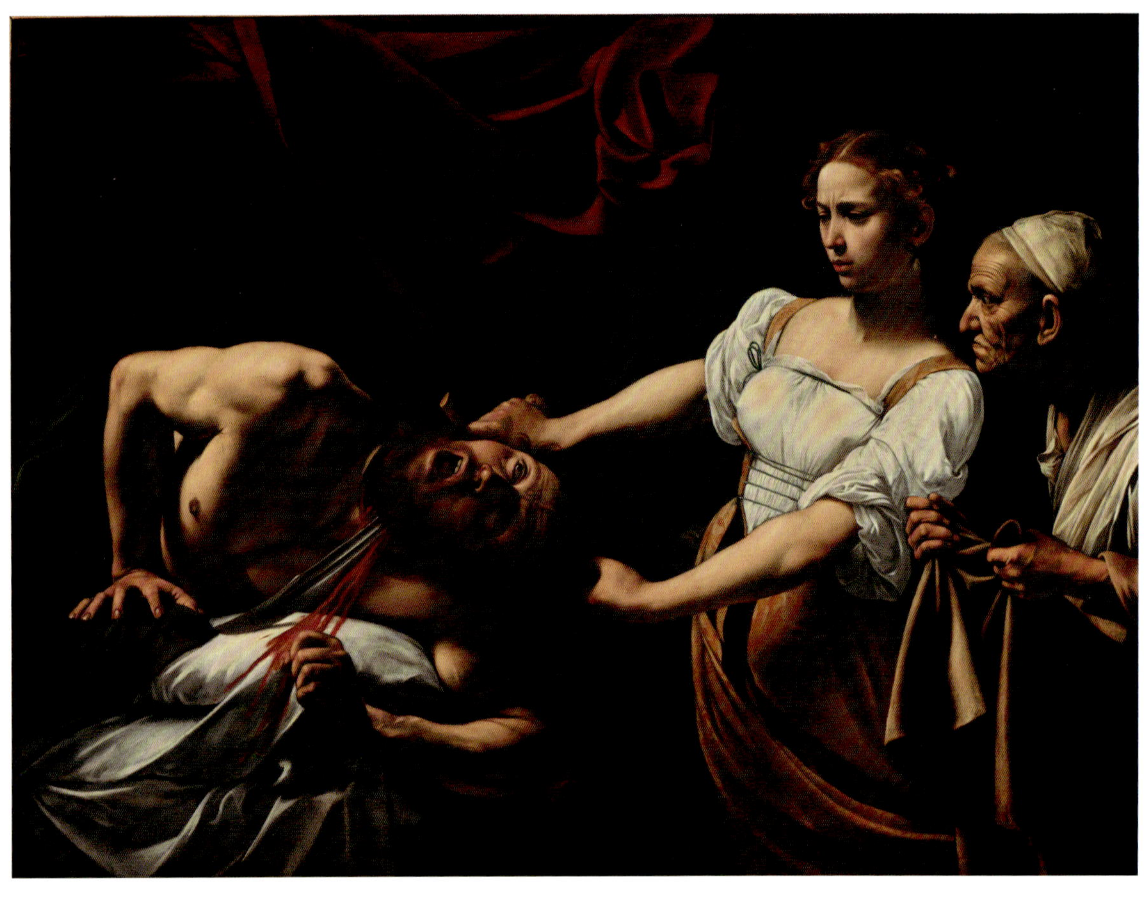

15 Caravaggio, *Judith Beheading Holofernes*, 1602, oil on canvas, 145 × 195 cm (57 1/16 × 77 3/4 in), Palazzo Barberini, Rome. Originally in the collection of Ottavio Costa

Lateran, Saint Paul's Outside the Walls and the Quirinal Palace. During the first of those outings, which was made at dawn 'because her father was jealously protective of this girl and did not want her to be seen',[9] she was aggressively waylaid by her father's colleague, Agostino Tassi. Then, on 6 May 1611, Tassi went to her home and forced himself on her.

The details of the rape, and the complicated relationship that ensued over the following months between the victim and her aggressor, can be reconstructed from the various testimonies gathered in the course of the criminal trial brought by Orazio against Tassi, as well as from the letter that Orazio wrote to the Dowager Grand Duchess Christine de Lorraine on 3 July 1612 to petition her assistance in the trial. From these sources, it is clear that Tassi manipulated his victim into a continued relationship with talk not only of marriage but also of her nascent career, promising to introduce her to the Medici Grand Duke in Florence and – if Tassi is to be believed – instructing Artemisia in perspective. By appearing to support Artemisia's ardent aspirations to become a professional painter, he was able to buy her silence and keep her under his power.

In February of 1612, some nine months after the initial assault, Orazio brought charges against Tassi that resulted in a formal inquest the following month. This belligerent move set off a chain of events that would polarise the Gentileschi's neighbours and associates according to their allegiances. Moreover, it obliged Artemisia to endure a rape trial that, in accordance with the legal codes of her society, factored her reputation into the judgment. Specifically, if it had been possible to show that Artemisia, as the victim, already had a reputation about town for impudicity or easy virtue, this circumstance would have mitigated the severity of Tassi's crime in the eyes of the law. This legal technicality effectively incentivised Tassi and his allies to besmirch Artemisia's name with malicious slander, which they needed only to present as hearsay rather than as eye-witness testimony.

Artemisia was no soft target for Tassi's character assassination. Although quite young, she already possessed a sophisticated understanding of the potent malleability of reputation in both its positive and negative dimensions. She had learned the power of praise as a very young girl, when her embroidery had incited the adulation of strangers. During her adolescence in 1611, she had learned how to handle slander: when a former servant named Francesco began spreading malicious gossip about Artemisia, she confronted her attacker directly and discredited him. Life had prepared Artemisia to defend her reputation.

As the court magistrates took the depositions of dozens of Orazio's and Tassi's associates and servants – in order to ascertain whether Artemisia's account was credible and whether the neighbours held her in disrepute – the trial drew unwelcome attention to her. Regardless of her innocence, the questioning of her honor must have made it difficult for the young woman to foresee herself attracting artistic commissions from Rome's nobility, especially from the women of that wellborn class. At this point, Orazio intervened to salvage Artemisia's hopes for a prominent career. Fulfilling the promises Tassi had made in bad faith, the father improvised various strategies to help his daughter to obtain the patronage of the Medici Grand Dukes. One of the first things he did in this regard was to write the above-mentioned letter of 3 July 1612, to Christine de Lorraine, the Dowager Grand Duchess of Tuscany and the mother of the reigning Grand Duke Cosimo II, in which he petitioned for help in the trial and encouraged her to engage Artemisia as a painter. Nevertheless, the letter fell on deaf ears, not only because of Orazio's uncouth, direct manner, but also because of the impropriety of the request.

Orazio's next strategy was to arrange a marriage between his daughter and Pierantonio Stiattesi, a Florentine man eight years her senior who professed himself to be an apothecary. Pierantonio was also the brother of Orazio's informal legal counselor, the

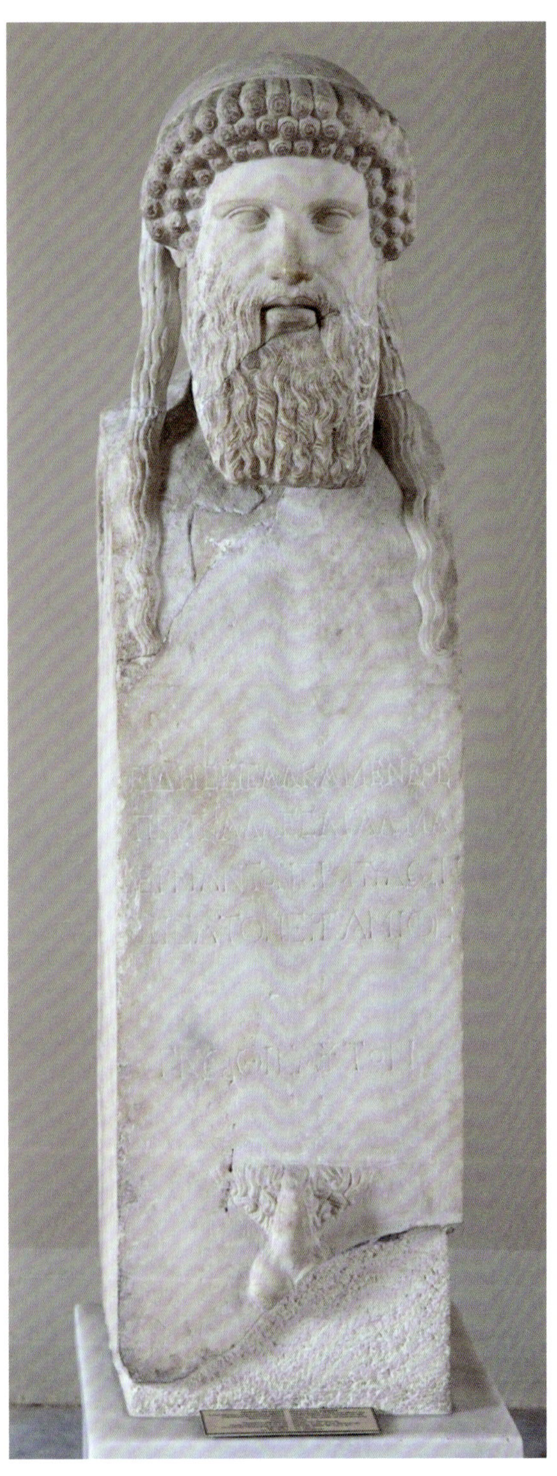

notary Giovanbattista Stiattesi. The latter, together with Orazio, drew up the wedding contract in Rome on 11 August 1612, while Tassi's rape trial was still underway. Six days later, this contract was signed in Florence by the groom, who cannot be said for certain to have previously met the bride.

The dowry Orazio provided to his daughter was a relatively rich purse of 1,000 gold *scudi* – far larger than the average artisan-class dowry of roughly 200 *scudi*. Orazio's dowry should not be misconstrued as a pay-out to the groom, since the contract specified that Artemisia would retain control over any expenditure made with her dowry. Moreover, it seems that Orazio planned to keep a close eye on his new son-in-law, because at the same time that the marriage was being negotiated, Orazio Gentileschi and his brother Aurelio Lomi, also a painter, co-signed a rental contract for an apartment in Florence. It was a clear signal that, for a moment at least, there was a plan to settle the extended Lomi-Gentileschi family in the same city as the newlyweds.

Mentioned above, the notary Giovanbattista Stiattesi who counseled Orazio Gentileschi during the trial may have also helped prepare his future sister-in-law for her depositions. Particularly with regard to substantiating the charge of forcible defloration, he could have explained that it was essential to convince the judges of both her prior virginity and her attempt to resist the assailant. Artemisia fulfilled this task impeccably, providing a testimony that painted a vivid picture of her innocence through reference to material evidence: a bloodstained bedsheet, a gag that Tassi used to stifle her screams and the knife with which she threatened him afterwards. Moreover, she emphasised details with direct bearing on legalistic interpretations of the criminal codes and she consistently presented herself as a perspicacious and conscientious young woman. Ultimately the judges determined that she was a credible and sympathetic victim, and so on 28 November 1612, they condemned Tassi to five years' exile from Rome.

16 *Herm*, copied after the *Hermes Propylaios* by Alcamenes, second-century CE copy of fifth-century BCE original, sculpture, marble, height: 119 cm (46 ¾ in), Istanbul Archaeology Museums, Inv. 1433

17 Agostino Carracci, *Susanna and the Elders*, *c.*1594–7, engraving, 15.6 × 10.9 cm (5 ½ × 4 ⅛ in), Rijksmuseum, Amsterdam

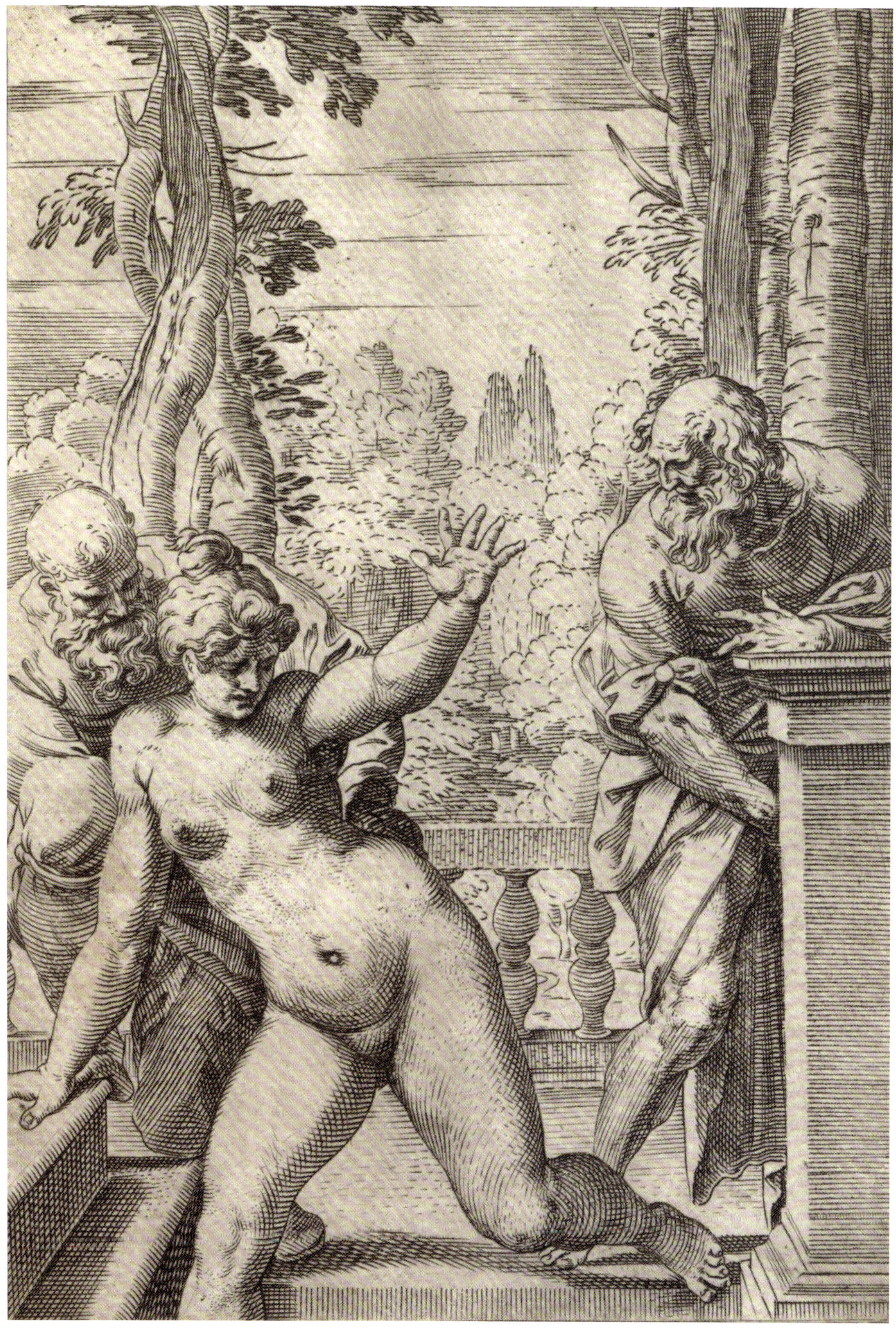

ARTEMISIA AS A DEFENDER OF WOMEN

Whatever help Giovanbattista may have offered, it is also the case that Artemisia had already reflected upon the legal and Biblical definitions of rape a couple of years earlier, while designing her 1610 *Susanna and the Elders* (fig.12), as Patricia Simons had recently argued.[10] The Bible's most explicit legal definitions of the crimes of adultery and rape are found in Deuteronomy 22:24, where it is explained that a woman subjected to unwanted sexual advances must cry out for help in order to be recognised as a blameless victim. If she did not cry out, she would be considered a willing adulteress. Artemisia depicted Susanna in line with this legal definition of innocence. By showing Susanna's mouth open, she indicated that Susanna cried out in self-defence. Adding to this effect, Susanna's flushing cheeks point to her discomposure and shame, while her ungainly, spastic posture demonstrates sheer surprise and terror. To give further evidence of Susanna's cries, Artemisia showed the white-haired elder nervously beckoning Susanna to be silent by pressing his finger to his lips, a gesture also seen in Annibale Carracci's painting of *Susanna and the Elders* from *c.*1603, now in the Galleria Doria Pamphilj.

Aspects of Artemisia's *Susanna and the Elders* indicate that the seventeen-year-old's drawing and painting skills were still in development. Even so, the painting treats its Biblical story with originality, sophistication and conviction, confirming Artemisia's capacity for masterful storytelling. Despite the complete nudity of its youthful heroine, some scholars have recently downplayed the painting's erotic potential, insisting that the subject is anything but a mere pretence for exhibiting a female body for male delectation. In accordance with the tenets of the Counter-Reformation Church, the image instead induces male and female viewers alike to empathise with the beleaguered woman, and to repudiate the lust of the sinful elders.

In seeking to pinpoint the source of the image's originality, we should not fail to take into account one of its most dominant compositional elements: the monolithic wall that establishes the boundaries of the private garden in which Susanna went to take her bath. Unlike the settings for this scene in other representations of this subject, the wall as imagined by Artemisia is solid and unperforated. Moreover, we see no buildings or trees beyond it, indicating that it is taller (or higher) than its surroundings, such that Susanna's nude body can only be seen by a person who crosses over the wall onto her husband's property. The perfect closure of this wall – as opposed to the semi-open balustrade in Carracci's painting – demonstrates to the viewer that Susanna has in no way tempted the elders, whose crime is now magnified to include trespassing. As Susanna recoils from their threatening presence, she compresses her body under the wall's profile, instinctively seeking its shelter.

The wall in Artemisia's painting functions as a character witness, communicating through symbols its judgments regarding the humans in its vicinity. Behind Susanna's swivelling torso is an inset panel carved in bas-relief with encircling vegetative motifs. Evoking laurel wreaths, they crown the young woman's wisdom and glory. By contrast, the wall holds sinister implications when it takes the shape of a short pilaster directly underneath the cloaked bulk of the leering, white-haired elder. This configuration of the wall makes the elder appear like a living herm, that is, an ancient statue-type in which a male head and male genitals are carved atop a rectangular base and associated with the phallic deity Hermes (fig.16). It is an obscene analogy that would have reminded historical audiences of Agostino Carracci's popular engraving of *Susanna and the Elders* from *c.*1594–7 (fig.17), in which one of the lecherous elders has gone behind a pilaster to masturbate while his companion gropes the naked victim.

More deliberately still, Artemisia's wall communicates with words. In the lower left corner beneath the overhanging edge, the face of the stone is carved with Artemisia's signature 'ARTEMITIA / GENTILESCHI F[ECIT]. / 1610'. In contrast to the danger represented by the intruding men, Artemisia's name on the wall does no harm or dishonor to the bare body pushed right up against it; indeed, Susanna bends in the direction of the signature as she recoils from danger represented by the men. The placement of Artemisia's signature on a wall poetically identifies the female painter with a shielding barricade that gives a woman privacy and defines a space in which she is not subject to the directives of male desire. Whether or not Artemisia made this association consciously, that protective wall would become an almost a prophetic symbol of the path that her art would take, because more than any artist before her, she would endeavor to defend her female protagonists, treating their stories with empathy, admiration and unprecedented intimacy.

At the same time that the prominent signature asserts Artemisia's authorship of this impressive achievement, it also implies her ability, as a woman, to utilise nude female models without the slightest taint or suspicion of impropriety. This was not true for the vast majority of painters, particularly Caravaggio, who had unleashed a scandal by using recognisable female models of questionable moral status in his depictions of holy saints. Even Artemisia's father had been targeted by defamatory gossip about his supposed use of Artemisia as a model. From this point of view, Artemisia's ability to study the nude female body without moral compromise was a tremendous advantage for an artist in the era of Counter-Reformation piety. Moreover, the chaste status of Artemisia's painted female nudes could have also inflected the audience's reception of the work. Viewers perhaps were comforted by the knowledge that they were looking at Susanna's nude body through the eyes of a woman rather than through the eyes of a man, and perhaps they were also guided by the artist's example of how to imagine Susanna's beauty with honest admiration, which in turn facilitated their ability to benefit spiritually from contemplating the virtuous woman's story. In a metaphorical sense, one could say that viewers of Artemisia's painting are encouraged to join with the artist and her nude model on the internal side of the wall, in a special female precinct that serves as a protected sanctuary for the contemplation of Susanna's virtue.

With the *Susanna and the Elders*, Artemisia proved that history painting was her métier. She had also discovered that by injecting her own persona into her images, if by no other means than a visible signature, she could catalyse time-worn stories with fresh and irresistible intrigue. Although there was no assurance that she would be able to continue on her artistic path, she was already learning that her gender could be wielded to her advantage.

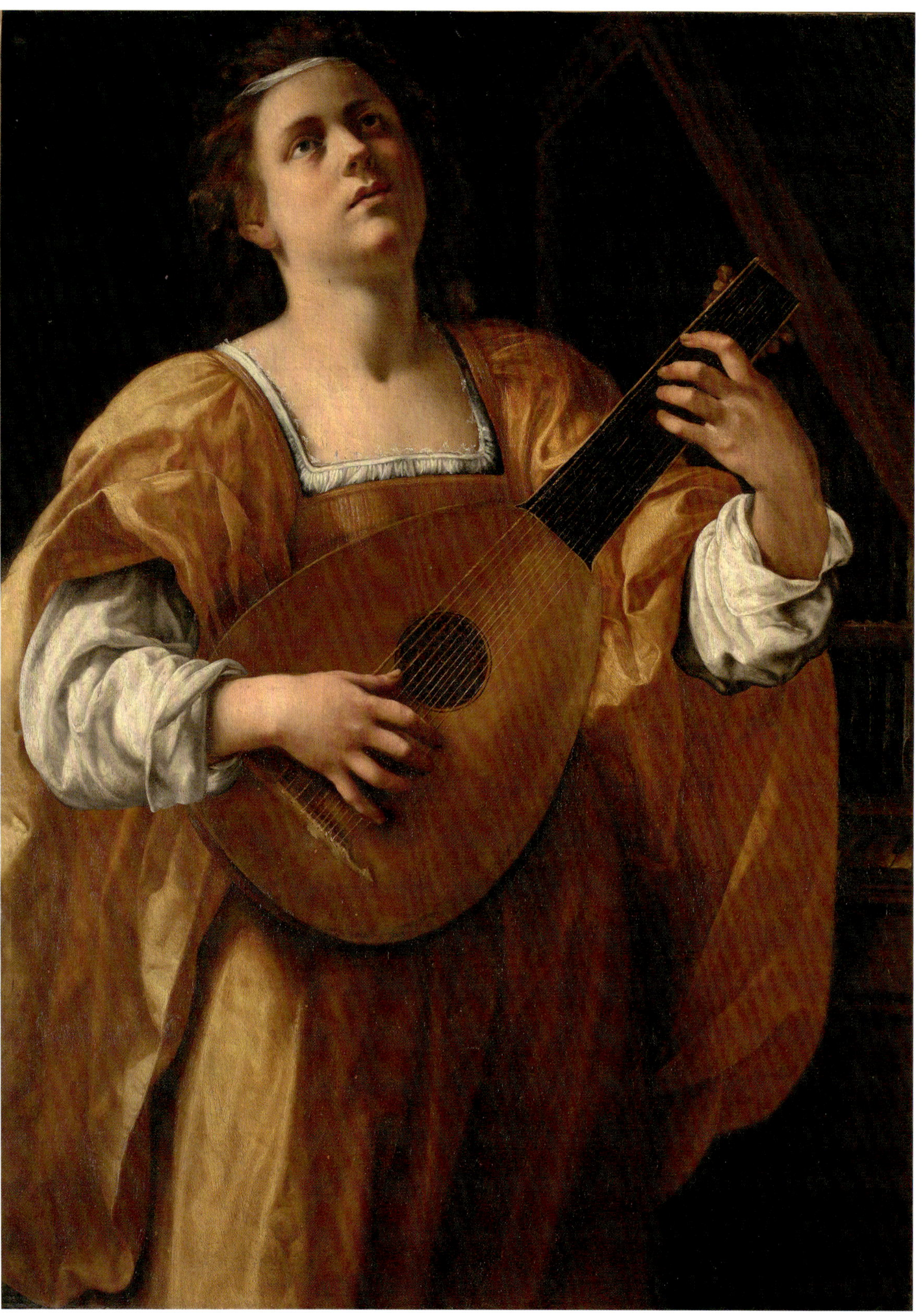

2

The Excellence of Women at the Medici Court

THE DREAM OF FLORENCE

Artemisia's move to Florence in January of 1613 fulfilled a long-held dream to reach the Medici court, where her grandfather, the Florentine goldsmith Giovan Battista Lomi (1520–75), had been paid to embellish Cosimo I de' Medici's ducal crown with mounted jewels in 1552. That same dream of becoming a court painter to the Medici also belonged to her father, Orazio, who still occasionally used the designation 'florentinus' when signing his paintings.

In 1610, Orazio made the mistake of revealing these aspirations to Agostino Tassi shortly after meeting him. Ever the operator, Tassi responded with false promises to introduce Orazio to the Medici court minister Lorenzo Usimbardi. Tassi manipulated Artemisia in the same way, declaring that he would take her to meet the Medici Grand Dukes. Ironically, it was only when Tassi betrayed the Gentileschis that the disillusioned father and daughter finally took action on their ambitious plans. As noted above, in July of 1612, Orazio wrote to the Medici Dowager Grand Duchess Christine de Lorraine to promote his daughter's talent, and he and his brother Aurelio Lomi began renting a house that same month near the Medici palace in Florence's San Jacopo neighbourhood. In the following month of August, Orazio drew up a contract giving the hand of his nineteen-year-old daughter to a Florentine apothecary, Pierantonio Stiattesi.

The marriage contract indicates that Orazio counted on Artemisia benefitting from the marriage mainly in two ways: first, through Pierantonio's Florentine citizenship, which provided an initial foothold for setting up a business in the Tuscan capital. Second, through Pierantonio's willingness to cede to Artemisia the oversight of her large dowry of 1,000 gold *scudi*, including use of it for business expenditures. Perhaps Orazio had also believed that his daughter's husband would supply her with the pigments typically prepared in apothecary shops.

Several early documents identify Pierantonio as an apothecary. These include the marriage contract of 1612, the death certificate for his and Artemisia's infant son Giovanni Battista in 1613, as well as the merchant court's 1614 record of the seizure of his and Artemisia's clothing items as pledges against Artemisia's debts. Nevertheless, no records have yet been found of Pierantonio's matriculation in the Florentine apothecaries' guild of the Arte dei Medici e Speziali, or in any other guild, for that matter. It may very well be that Pierantonio chose to abandon his apothecary career in order to assist his brothers, his father, and, above all, Artemisia, in more profitable enterprises.

18 Artemisia Gentileschi, *Saint Cecilia Playing the Lute*, *c.*1614, oil on canvas, 108 × 78.5 cm (42 ½ × 30 15⁄16 in), Galleria Spada, Rome

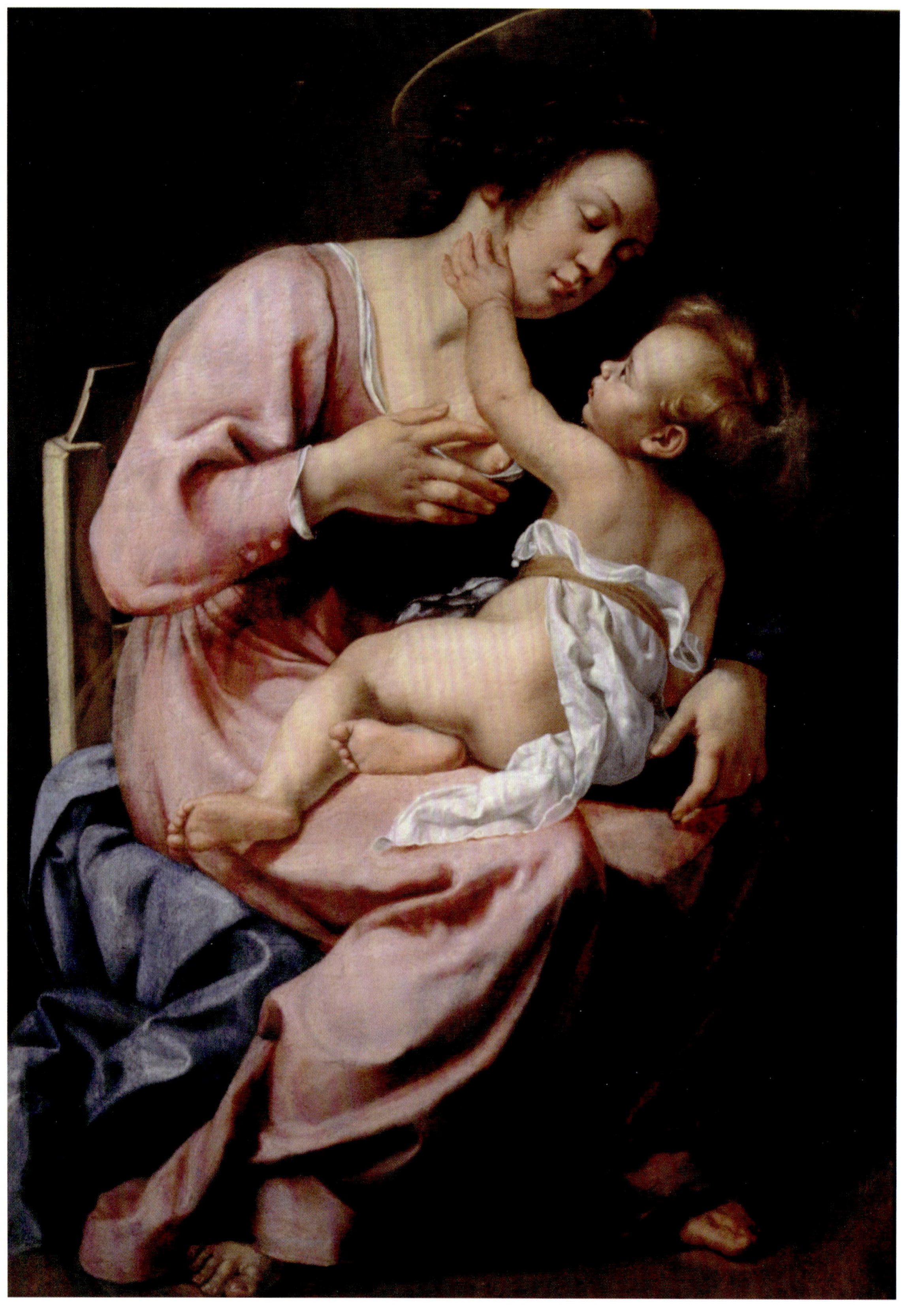

19 Artemisia Gentileschi, *Madonna and Child*, *c.*1614, oil on canvas, 116 × 87 cm (45 ⅝ × 34 ¼ in), Galleria Spada, Rome

PAINTING AS A FAMILY BUSINESS

Artemisia commenced painting shortly after settling into her father-in-law Vincenzo Stiattesi's multi-level house situated on Florence's via Campaccio near the Basilica of San Lorenzo. Her first obligation was to finish commissions that had been given to her by her former Roman clients, such as the *Madonna and Child* at the Galleria Spada (fig.19) for a Roman wool merchant named Alessandro Biffi (also a patron of Orazio's), and the *Saint Cecilia Playing the Lute*, also at the Galleria Spada (fig.18). Once completed, the paintings were delivered to Rome by her husband, who travelled there in 1614 and 1616. As an artist trying to initiate her independent career, she faced difficulties on several fronts. To begin with, she was pregnant with her first child, Giovanni Battista, who died just a week after his birth on 29 September 1613. Also, she lacked the proper studio equipment throughout her first two years in Florence. Complicating things even more, upon reaching Florence, Artemisia dispensed with the traditional, white-ground procedure of her early works and began painting directly on a dark ground, building up to the light tones – presumably in response to the Grand Duke's admiration of Caravaggio's style.

In these first Florentine years, Artemisia turned to various family members for help. Her uncle Aurelio Lomi, for instance, provided her with paints that were formulated according to the family secrets and whose jewel-like palette appealed to Tuscan tastes (fig.20). This cooperative arrangement soon soured, however. In March of 1614, Aurelio resorted to summoning Artemisia's husband Pierantonio to the court of the artists' guild – known as the Accademia e Compagnia delle Arti del Disegno (or Accademia del Disegno for short) – over the unpaid cost of the paints he had put at Artemisia's disposal. To meet Artemisia's other professional needs, Pierantonio's family pitched in whatever resources they had and allowed her to use their family home for her business. There may have been genuine mutual endearment between the artist and her in-laws, but the Stiattesis also recognised that Artemisia's talent promised them prosperity.

The Stiattesis were a middling and undistinguished family. Two of Pierantonio's four older brothers had attained a trifling professional standing. One of them was Giovanbattista, the previously mentioned *notaio* who had composed Artemisia's marriage contract in Rome. He ran a modest notarial practice between Livorno and Florence while raising a small family. The other was Luca, a priest in the distant village of Calcinaia. Their widowed father, Vincenzo, born the son of a wool carder, had done well as the tailor to the once-powerful Carnesecchi clan, but he hoped to see his children do even better. To this end, Vincenzo had spent 'many hundreds of scudi' to obtain a benefice for his son the priest.[1]

In the same spirit that had animated Vincenzo's efforts to place his sons in respectable careers, and despite having other pressing concerns such as an unwed daughter in need of a dowry, the elderly tailor offered a hand in advancing Artemisia's career. He gave Artemisia a room in his house – probably his former sartorial workshop – for her painting activities; he gave her access to his credit lines with local silk merchants so that she could buy fabric; and with his dressmaking skills he transformed that fabric into elegant, custom-made clothing for her. That last advantage was of no small account in light of Artemisia's larger professional strategy. The stately wardrobe that Vincenzo fashioned enhanced the artist's physical beauty and drew attention to her person when she was in courtly circles. It also gave her the appearance of one of her own painted heroines, since Artemisia's silk and satin dresses simultaneously served as studio props when rigged up on her father-in-law's sartorial mannequins or worn by her models. Most importantly, these dresses were indispensable to Artemisia's painting process because one of the defining hallmarks of her opulent brand of Caravaggesque realism consisted in the painstaking depiction of luxury fabrics and jewels.

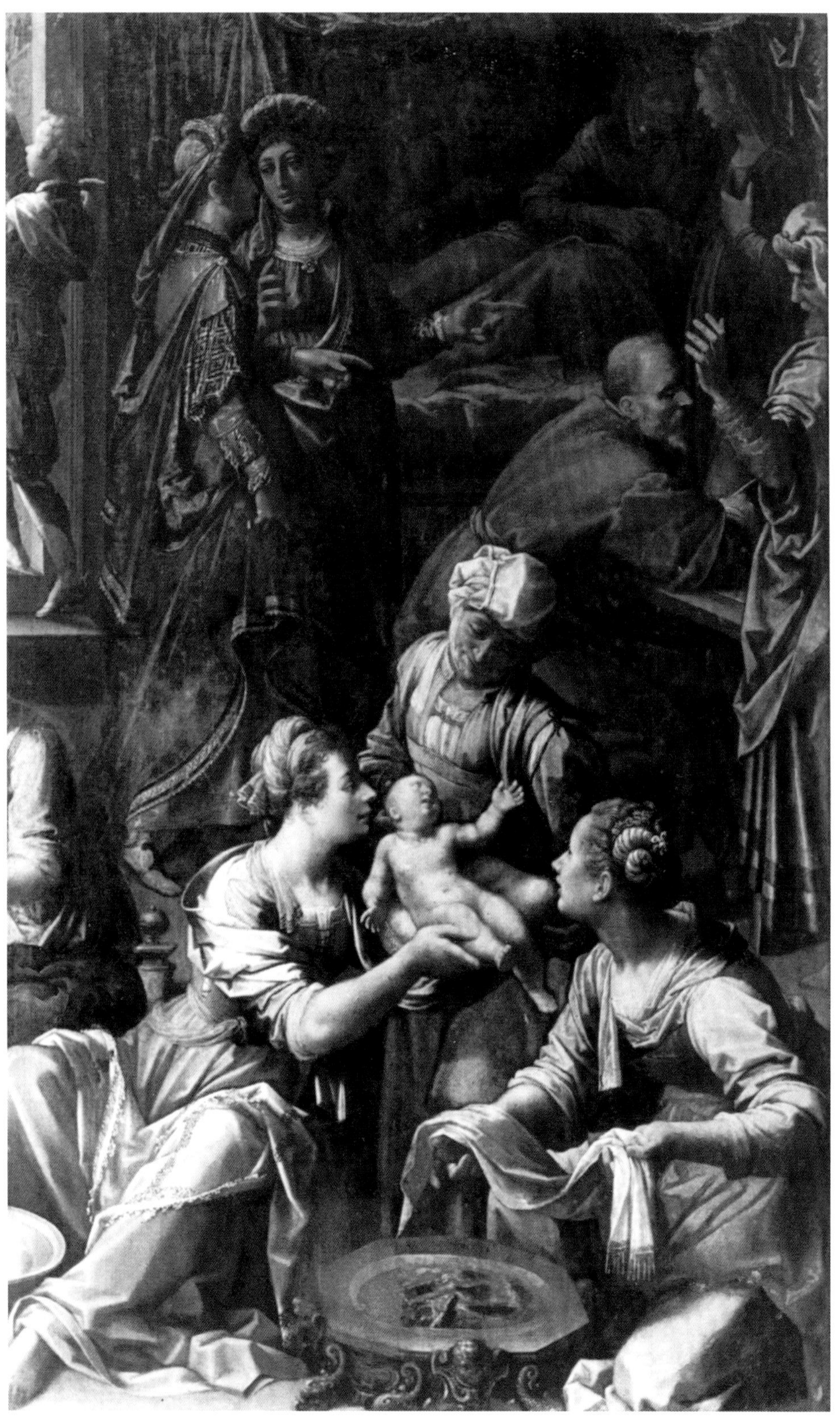

20 Aurelio Lomi, *Birth of the Baptist*, signed and dated 1601, oil on canvas, 234 × 132 cm (92 ⅛ × 52 in), Basilica di San Siro, Genoa

Besides serving as Artemisia's dressmaker and as her advisor on courtly fashions, Vincenzo also introduced Artemisia to the city's artisanal community, thanks to his membership since 1589 in the Scalzo, a lay confraternity that served artists and craftsmen and that was headquartered near the Stiattesi home. Vincenzo's sponsorship of a minor painter named Andrea di Domenico Paolini who joined the Scalzo in 1615 suggests that Artemisia's father-in-law may have known many more painters as well.[2]

Not to be overlooked as an ally among Artemisia's in-laws is Vincenzo's daughter Maddalena, who was close to Artemisia's age. Maddalena surely served as Artemisia's model (much as Tuzia had done for Artemisia in Rome). Available at all hours and charging little or nothing, a model in the family offered an invaluable advantage to an artist like Artemisia who followed Caravaggio's method of painting while looking at a live model. After sharing long hours in the privacy of a room that was probably off-limits to men, Artemisia developed a friendship with Maddalena, and even purchased clothing for her several years after Vincenzo – the patriarch of the Stiattesi household – had passed away and her marriage with Pierantonio had disintegrated.

DRUMMING UP HER FIRST PATRONS

Talent alone did not suffice to bring Artemisia profits. In order to establish her painting business in Florence, she had to think entrepreneurially and even devise clever schemes in order to bring herself to the attention of wealthy art collectors. One of her earliest efforts to find a patron focused on Alessandro Covoni (1599–1619), a young silk merchant who held an appointment as one of the Grand Duke's aristocratic 'pages of the black livery' [*paggi di livrea nera*]. The latter were young knights who had first been sent to the Medici court as pre-pubescent 'pages of the red livery' [*paggi di livrea rossa*] and who received their promotion to black livery upon their induction into the Medici Grand Duke's military order of Saint Stephen, with its requirement of service on the Grand Duke's galleys. Just a few months after arriving in Florence, and more than a year before she invested in furnishings for her painting studio, Artemisia made a very large credit purchase with Covoni for 206 *lire* worth of luxury fabrics. As explained previously, the clothing made from this expensive fabric had utility for her art as well as for gaining entrée to the court. Nevertheless, it was a bold financial decision to spend so much money on credit at this moment, especially since her marriage contract of 17 August 1612 had specified that Orazio's payment of the first half of the dowry was not due to Pierantonio until August of 1615, with the second half coming due in 1620.[3]

Predictably, by September of 1613 Artemisia and Pierantonio had fallen into arrears on this debt with Covoni, as shown by court documents. Their willingness to incur a debt with Covoni indicates two points of their entrepreneurial design: on the one hand it was an urgent priority for Artemisia to dress above her station, and on the other hand, they must have recognised that debt could be used as a negotiation tactic for convincing this rich merchant to take one of her paintings in lieu of cash – or at least to help her find a buyer. Several years later, Artemisia used a similar tactic with the Florentine silk merchant Simone Carducci, offering to make a painting of the Madonna to cover her debt with him. In a lawsuit he filed in 1620, Carducci's complaints were that Artemisia, in his opinion, had involved some of her studio assistants in the commission, and that she was late with the painting.

In Artemisia's patronage strategy, her tactical interest in Covoni extended well beyond the sale of any single painting: he represented an avenue for reaching her ultimate target, the Medici Grand Duke. Although Covoni boasted many important noble appointments, it was his activities as a composer and musical impresario that furnished him with a privileged standing at the court. This fact had much to do with the Grand Duke's chronic bad health, since

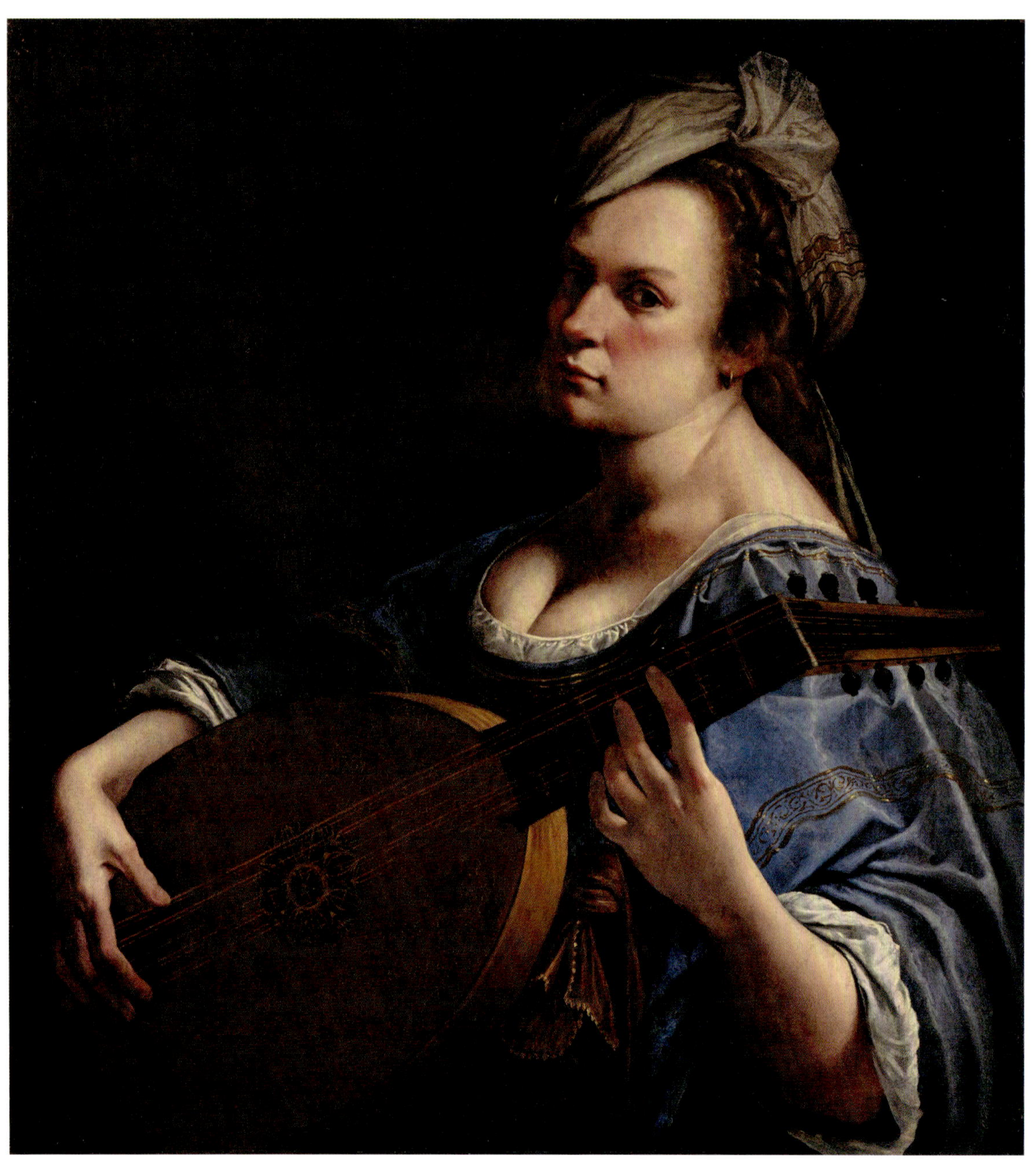

21 Artemisia Gentileschi, *Lute Player*, 1614, oil on canvas, 77.5 × 71.8 cm (30 ½ × 28 ¼ in), Wadsworth Atheneum, Hartford, Connecticut. Charles H. Schwartz Endowment Fund 2014.4.1

the feeble ruler particularly doted on the musicians and actors whose performances were like therapeutic medicine for him. Artemisia must have recognised that Covoni's practice of introducing musicians to the Grand Duke's chambers could be adapted to bring her own talent to Cosimo's attention. This consequential introduction did, in fact, occur quite soon after she met Covoni, and with marvellous results since – as discovered only recently – Artemisia was already working on three canvases for the Grand Duke in October of 1614.

One of the three paintings that Cosimo II had commissioned from Artemisia in 1614 was probably the Hartford *Lute Player* (fig.21), a bust-length, costumed self-portrait showing her in a dark interior, where she is lit from the side after Caravaggio's manner. Artemisia has portrayed herself dressed in a foreign costume, one which has unfairly been called a gypsy's costume in publications of the last decade. Female gypsies in art of this period (including canvases by Caravaggio, Georges de la Tour, Valentin de Boulogne, and Simon Vouet) invariably wear a long cape – often striped – that is clasped asymmetrically atop one shoulder, as well as colorful but common fabrics and sometimes outdoor headgear fastened under the chin. By contrast, Artemisia's lute player wears a dress made of opulent blue brocade silk, with gold embroidery that a gypsy could not afford, a turban-like head covering, and, most unusually, a red silk sash tied around her waist. The last detail in particular marks her costume as roughly similar to that of women at the Ottoman court, as pictured, for example, in Nicolas de Nicolay's *Les quatres premiers livres des navigations et peregrinations orientales* (1568), which was published in an Italian edition in 1577[4] (fig.22). Not only would the Grand Duke have appreciated this allusion to the women of the Levant, but so would his eminent Lebanese guest, Prince Fakhr-al-Din of Mount Lebanon (1572–1635). The latter – a Druze Emir who outwardly conformed with Islamic practices and paid tribute to the Ottoman Sultan but who secretly negotiated with Christians – had fled his palace following an Ottoman invasion of his territories in November of 1613. Accompanied by one of his wives, a son and a retinue of some fifty to seventy Levantine courtiers in Turkish dress, Prince Fakhr-al-Din found a safe refuge at the Medici court as Cosimo II's guest.

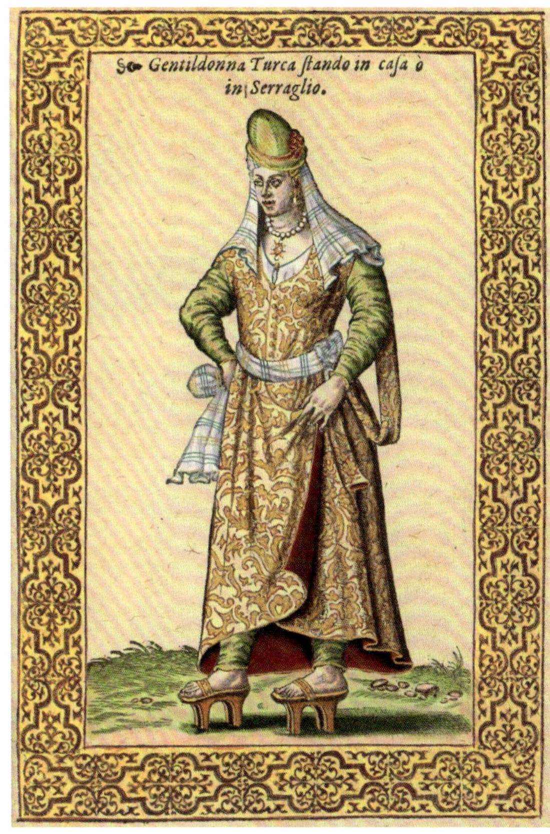

22 'Turkish Gentlewoman in Her Home or Seraglio', Nicolas de Nicolay, *Le navigationi et viaggi nella Turchia* [Lyon, 1567], Antwerp, 1577, p. 65, woodcut with body color, 21.5 cm (8 ½ in) (8vo), Typ 530.77.606, Houghton Library, Harvard University

During the exiled Emir's two years in Florence, coinciding with Artemisia's first two years in the city, he was the recipient of court entertainments designed to promote the alliance between the Medici and the Levantine dynasty of the Ma'n. In February of 1614, the Emir was feted with a choreographed dance of six interfaith couples – each combining a Christian and a Syrian – in the Dance of Courtesy [*Ballo della cortesia*]. In February of the following year, 1615, the Dance of the Turkish Women [*Ballo di donne turche*] was staged featuring sixteen Florentine male courtiers luxuriously dressed, and cross-dressed, in Turkish costumes representing both male and female Ottomans captured in war. According to the Medici court diarist Cesare Tinghi, the male courtiers who were dressed as Turkish women approached the Grand Duke, one at a time. Gesticulating piteously, each sang to him a lachrymose madrigal solo, describing the misfortune that had befallen her as a result of the victory of the Tuscan fleet, and pleading for the Grand Duke's mercy for herself and her husband. The plaintive tone of these performers' appeals and their costumes – consisting of a silk head cloth and a blue silk dress with silver and gold embroidery that was belted with a Turkish sash – would have closely resembled the appearance and effect of Artemisia's nearly contemporary image of a melancholic female lutenist in Ottoman costume. Given these similarities, Artemisia's Hartford *Lute Player* would have struck just the right chord at the Medici court.

The lutenist's dress in Artemisia's painting has been rendered with abundant quantities of ultramarine blue, a very expensive pigment that, according to documents, was supplied to Artemisia by the Grand Duke's pharmacy. Her access to the court's most precious pigment shows that Cosimo II and his advisors had great confidence in Artemisia's knowledge of her craft, since ultramarine blue required very specialised handling to exalt its coloristic properties. In depicting the theme of her *Lute Player*, Artemisia gave proof of a second kind of know-how that the Grand Duke would have appreciated, namely musicianship. Looking directly at the viewer with a brazenly soulful and penetrating gaze, she plays an exquisitely carved lute that occupies as much of the image as she does. The plausibility of this representation of lute playing from a musical standpoint indicates she had consulted with an experienced lutenist, such as Covoni. Possibly made by Artemisia in preparation for her *Lute Player*, an unsigned drawing from this period shows several life studies of a female lutenist's hands from a variety of angles (fig.23). Not only could Covoni have advised Artemisia on the representation of correct chordal fingering, but also, as the owner of several lutes, he could have supplied her with the instruments so carefully rendered both here and in the above-mentioned *Saint Cecilia Playing the Lute* (fig.18).

Artemisia herself may have had some musical talent, perhaps acquired informally by singing with her family as a child in Rome, as recently proposed by Jesse Locker.[5] During the same carnival season in which the Dance of the Turkish Women was performed by an all-male cast, an all-female cast performed the Dance of the Gypsies [*Ballo delle zingare*] in the Medici palace's Salone delle Commedie to celebrate the marriage of Archduchess Maria Magdalena's lady-in-waiting Sofia Binestan. The music was composed by Francesca Caccini (1587–1640), a rising female talent at the Medici court who also sang the role of the principal gypsy. As first pointed out by Mary D. Garrard, it is a tantalising fact that a certain 'Signora Artemisia' performed in this musical spectacle.[6] This 'Artemisia' may very well have been our painter, although it is also true that this could refer to another prominent woman at the Florentine court: Artemisia Tozzi (*c.*1590–1643), the common-born consort of Don Antonio de' Medici, himself a patron of Caccini since 1611. Other women with the same name in Florence in this period include Artemisia di Giulio Sangalli of Cortona who was paid by the Medici court in 1610 for 'service to the Most Serene Princesses' and a certain Artemisia di Filippo Bigazzi.[7]

There is no incontrovertible evidence that Artemisia Gentileschi had musical talents.

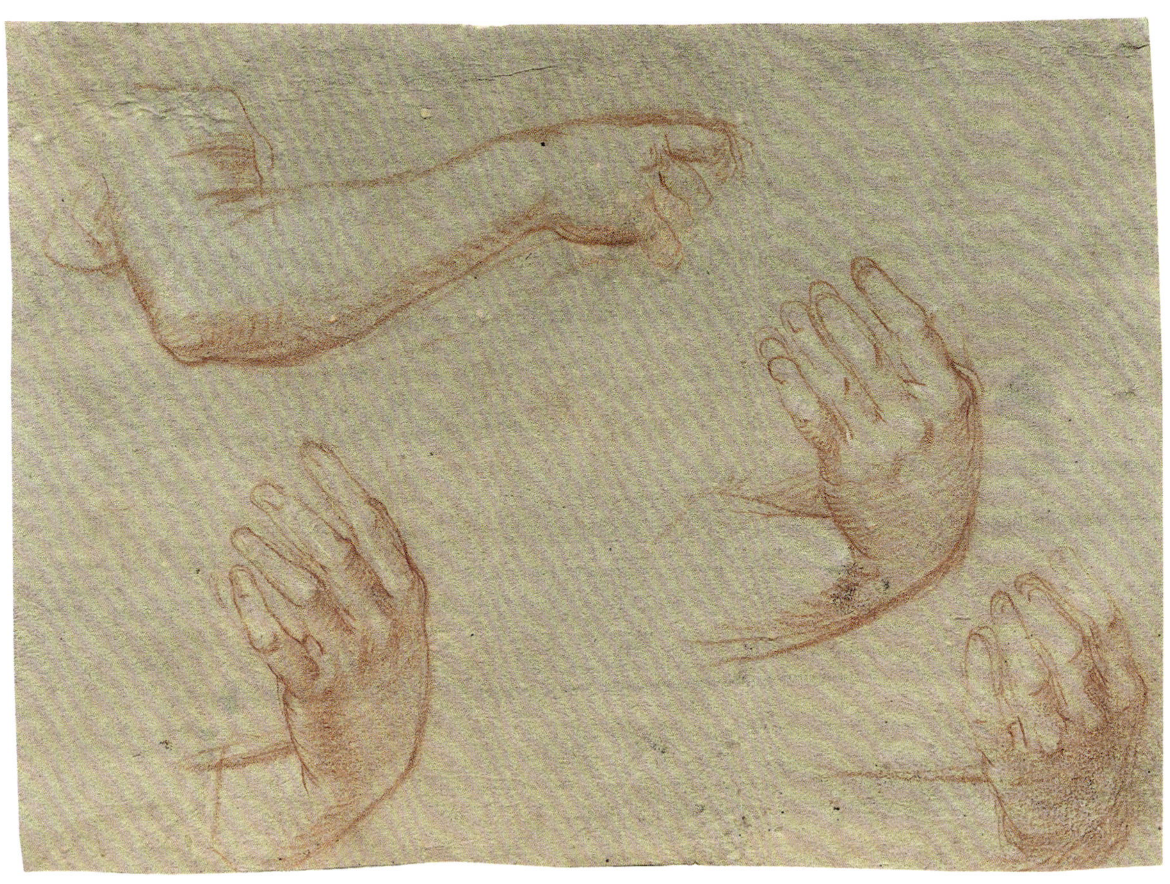

23 Attributed here to Artemisia Gentileschi, *Hands of a Female Musician (Studies for the Self-Portrait as a Lute Player)*, *c.*1614, white and red chalk on light-blue tinted paper, 14.8 × 20.5 cm (5 ⅞ × 8 1⁄16 in), private collection

Nevertheless, her flickering, chiaroscuro illumination, her pairing of earthy pigments with jewel-like ones, and her creation of heroines that are formidable yet sensual, all reveal a striking sympathy with Caccini's popular 'new music' ['le nuove musiche']. At the focus of this innovative style of singing was the female singer's quivering and unpredictable body, whose irregular breathing and unusual motions made possible highly variegated sounds and dramatic contrasts. Never before had women's singing been such a synesthetic spectacle. Artemisia's paintings offered Caccini's fans at the Medici court a visual equivalent to the contradictory, yet captivating aural sensations described so well by the Sienese poet Gismondo Santi:

> [Now] she bends her flexible voice like a bow
> [. . .] Now makes it grave and low
> Now draws it in, now turns it harsh, now sweetens it
> [. . .] Sometimes she hastens its flight with false notes
> And deliberately tunes dissonances
> But while she seems to offend, [she is] opening
> A more delightful path to harmonic sweetness;
> As a beloved woman kindles still more love
> In her lover with disdainful harshness,
> A physician mixes artfully the bitter
> With the sweet, [or] a painter [mixes] darkness with light[8]

Moreover, just as Caccini embodied her art by going on stage in costume to sing the very music she had written, Artemisia, too, embodied her own art. In fact, not only did Artemisia dress in the opulent Florentine fashions and showy jewellery of the very sort seen in her paintings, but also – as indicated by her use of Florentine dialectal spellings and vocabulary ('costi', 'fo', 'outo', 'aniolo') and her citations of Petrarch, Ariosto, Ovid and Tasso in her correspondence – she apparently affected an elevated manner of speech worthy of her painted Biblical heroines. With the dramatic protagonists of her high-keyed images and her own extravagantly fashioned public persona, Artemisia brought to life a visual embodiment of Caccini's dynamic and emotionally expressive female voice. Together, Caccini's music and Artemisia's paintings helped forge a captivating new ideal of womanhood at the Florentine court.

NUDITY AND ARTISTIC BRAVADO

Assisted by Covoni, Artemisia found yet another artistic patron in Florence. He was Michelangelo Buonarroti the Younger, a poet, playwright and theatrical producer named after his famous great-uncle. Strong bonds linked the Buonarroti and Covoni families. In the previous century Antonio Covoni had been Michelangelo Buonarroti's banker; in 1619 Michelangelo the Younger's brother would design Alessandro Covoni's tomb after the latter died during a campaign in Malta.

Long before Michelangelo the Younger gave Artemisia a commission, he proved himself a valuable friend and accepted the role of godfather to Artemisia's second child, Agnola, a stillborn infant who was buried on 16 December 1614. Around the same time, he introduced Artemisia to the luminaries of the Florentine court, at least one of whom would go on to commission a painting from our artist. Those introductions included the astronomer Galileo Galilei, who, in later decades, served as Artemisia's intermediary with the successive Grand Duke Ferdinando II; Niccolò Arrighetti, the Grand Duke's instructor in neo-Platonic philosophy (and whose son Luigi acquired Artemisia's painting of *Aurora* [fig.72 below]); the painter Cristofano Allori, godfather to her third child, Cristofano, born in the autumn of 1615; the poet Jacopo Soldani, godfather to her fifth child, Lisabella, born in 1618; and a close, almost avuncular, companion of the Grand Duke named Enea Piccolomini d'Aragona, who would serve as godfather to Artemisia's fourth child, Prudenzia, born in the summer of 1617 (also her only child born in Florence to survive into adulthood). Piccolomini was remembered by the *letterato* Carlo

Roberto Dati as a 'beloved' friend of Arrighetti, but he is now better remembered for having helped broker Galileo's rise at the Medici court. Indeed, many of the cultured Florentines that Artemisia met through Michelangelo the Younger were connected to each other through a dense, parallel circuitry of shared interests.

The urbane conversation and literary erudition of Michelangelo the Younger and his circle evidently inspired Artemisia to emulate the language of Florence's educated élite, whose mode of expression was at that time considered throughout Europe to be the epitome of refined courtly discourse. From Michelangelo the Younger, she very well may have borrowed a copy of Giovanni Francesco Fortunio's *Regole grammaticali della volgar lingua*. This handbook, written in 1516 and expanded in 1545, was used by many non-Tuscan speakers, especially women, to learn both the rules of Tuscan speech as well as aphoristic phrases from authorities such as Petrarch, Boccaccio and Dante. Reflecting her familiarity with this kind of handbook, Artemisia's correspondence began during her Florentine years to incorporate quotations from these authors and their classical forebears. Moreover, taking her cue from Giovanni Francesco Fortunio's name, she would invent a jocular pen name, Fortunio Fortuni. This was how she signed – and sometimes also addressed – her secret love letters to Francesco Maria Maringhi, beginning in March of 1620.

Artemisia must have felt self-assured among Michelangelo the Younger's circle, because her single canvas for the prosperous playwright was one of the raciest of her career: *The Allegory of Inclination* (fig.24). Initiated in August 1615, this canvas was to be one of many inset components of the ceiling that crowned an elaborately decorated gallery in the stately home of Michelangelo the Younger. He had planned it in every last iconographic detail, intending it as a vivid tribute to his famous great-uncle, Michelangelo Buonarroti. What made this commission particularly audacious was that it called for female nudity in a canvas meant for semi-public display, for Michelangelo used his home almost as a private museum and as a center for socialisation. Had it been painted by a man, the female nudity would have been perceived as an allegorical attribute; however, because it was painted by an attractive young woman, the nude body could be taken as a literal reference to the artist's own body.

Rather than trying to forestall that inevitable association, Artemisia embraced it by giving her own idealised facial features to the nude figure. In reality, that nude figure, which is seen from below and, therefore, required difficult foreshortening, was necessarily made with the assistance of a female model – probably either her devoted sister-in-law, Maddalena Stiattesi, or her disgruntled maidservant Maria Stecchi. Yet, regardless of the fact that Artemisia had based the figure in *Inclination* upon another woman's nude body (which was then enhanced through her own embellishing artistry), there was, nonetheless, an undeniable piquancy to this work that presented itself to the local viewership, not as an allegory, but as a shamelessly intimate quasi-self-portrait made by a woman whom they recognised.

At the time, it was practically unheard of for a female artist to paint erotic female nudes. The only other woman of those times to have undertaken such imagery was the recently deceased Lavinia Fontana. In Florence, where most all of the women artists on record had been nuns, the phenomenon was entirely unprecedented. Yet, as long as women artists refrained from depicting female nudes, they were excluding themselves from one of the primary arenas in which Renaissance painters and sculptors vaunted their knowledge of anatomy, their understanding of beauty and their ability to imitate the appearance of flesh. Both Artemisia and her patron Michelangelo the Younger were well aware that a painting of a nude woman – if it managed to provoke feelings of lust in its viewers – was regarded as an accomplishment that marked the greatest practitioners of the art. As summarised by Elizabeth Cropper, 'the image

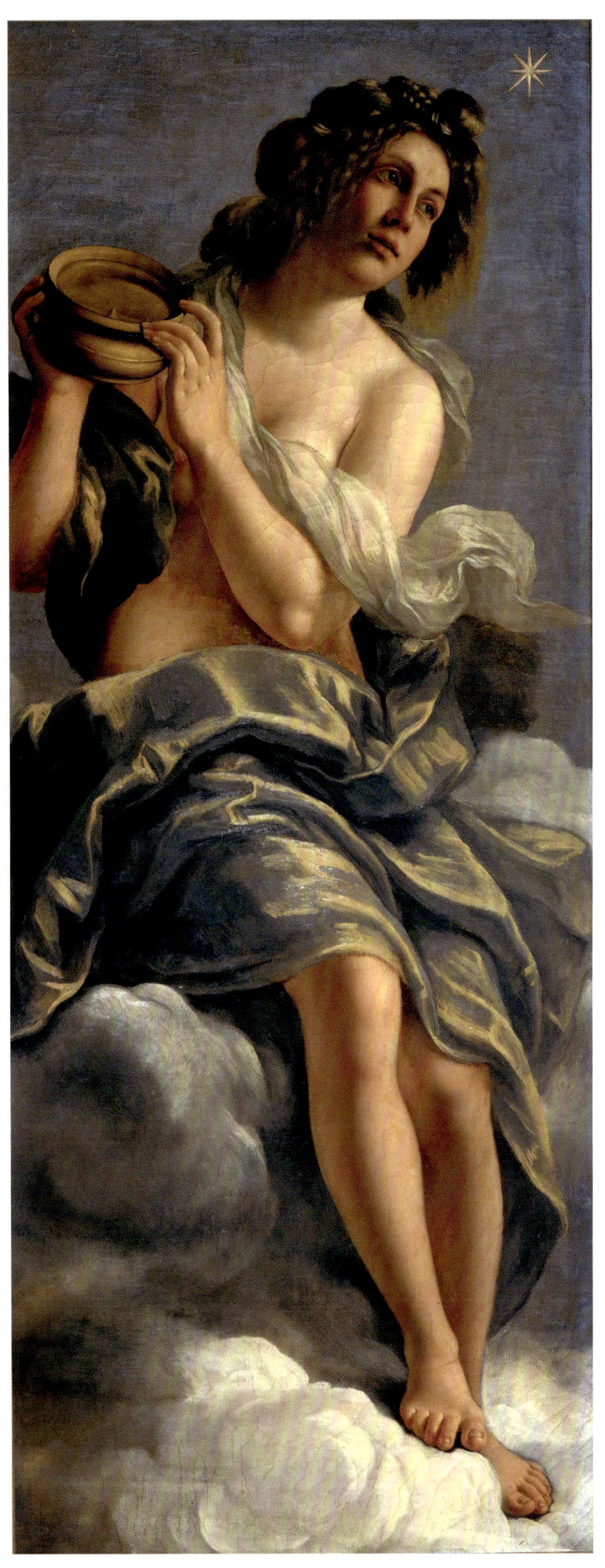

24 Artemisia Gentileschi, *Allegory of Inclination*, 1615–6, oil on canvas, 152 × 61 cm (59 ⅞ × 24 in), Casa Buonarotti, Florence

of the woman was [. . .] an epitome of painting itself'.[9] Given the importance that Renaissance artists attached to nudes, when Artemisia undertook the challenge of painting an alluring female body – portrayed as if seen from below – and then gave it her own likeness, she had truly thrown down the gauntlet to Florence's artistic community.

When Michelangelo the Younger assigned this subject to Artemisia, he may have already seen evidence of her capacity for the female nude. In 1610, he had travelled to Rome along with the painter Cigoli (1559–1613); this was the same year that Artemisia signed her *Susanna and the Elders*, and perhaps also the year she began working on the nude *Danäe* in the Saint Louis Art Museum. Thus, it is a distinct possibility that Michelangelo the Younger picked Artemisia for the subject of Inclination so that she could prove her worth to the Florentine art world with a nude female figure. Notably, around the very same time, Michelangelo the Younger was fostering the career of another bold female talent intent on making her mark in a man's field: the aforementioned composer Francesca Caccini.

While female nudity is undeniably central to the commission, Michelangelo the Younger's decision to reserve this subject for Artemisia must have also stemmed from the special meaning of 'inclination' [*inclinazione*] among Florentine *literati*, that is, an inborn vocation preordained by the heavens.[10] As a member of Florence's art academy, as well as a contributor to the Accademia della Crusca's dictionary project, Michelangelo the Younger was well versed in the centrality of the concept to Giorgio Vasari's notion of artistic genius, and particularly to Vasari's characterisation of his great uncle Michelangelo Buonarroti. By meting out the subject of Inclination to Artemisia, Michelangelo the Younger subtly invited viewers to associate this component of artistic genius not only with his great uncle, but also with Artemisia who – along with the successful mid-career painter Matteo Rosselli (1578–1650) – was hired and paid long before any other artists were involved in the project. Artemisia cemented this association when she incorporated her own facial features into the allegorical representation referring to the divinely innate gifts of the greatest artists. In doing so, she implied that heaven, rather than her father, had fostered her talent.

As for the critical success of the female nude that Artemisia completed for Michelangelo the Younger in August of 1616, there can be no doubt. The excellence of this demonstration carried Artemisia's reputation as a painter of nudes all the way to the Medici themselves, for in 1617 Cosimo II de' Medici commissioned her to make a bathing scene of multiple nude life-size women ['un Bagno di pru [più] donne']. This last work can probably be identified with her now-lost painting of *Diana at her Bath*, commissioned in 1617 and completed on 28 February 1619 for the Grand Duke, who compensated her richly with 150 gold *scudi*. Indeed, the voluptuous figure Artemisia created to embody Inclination was so lifelike and seductive that a later generation of decidedly more bourgeois Buonarrotis felt morally compelled to have the artist Volteranno cover the figure's torso and hips with swags of opaque drapery.

LEAVE THE HUSBAND, JOIN THE ACADEMY

While Artemisia worked on Michelangelo the Younger's *Allegory of Inclination*, her personal and professional circumstances underwent a dramatic transformation. The changes began when her father-in-law died in the fall of 1615, resulting in the annulment of the lease on the house where Artemisia and her husband lived, and where she had her workshop. After leaving via Campaccio, Artemisia never settled anywhere in Florence for very long. She did, however, find a permanent workshop on the street called Borgo Ognissanti beginning in 1615, when the Accademia's tribunal registers begin referring to her as 'Artemisia Lomi pittora in Borgo Ognissanti'.[11] It was far from the parish of Sant'Ambrogio where her domestic life was centred,

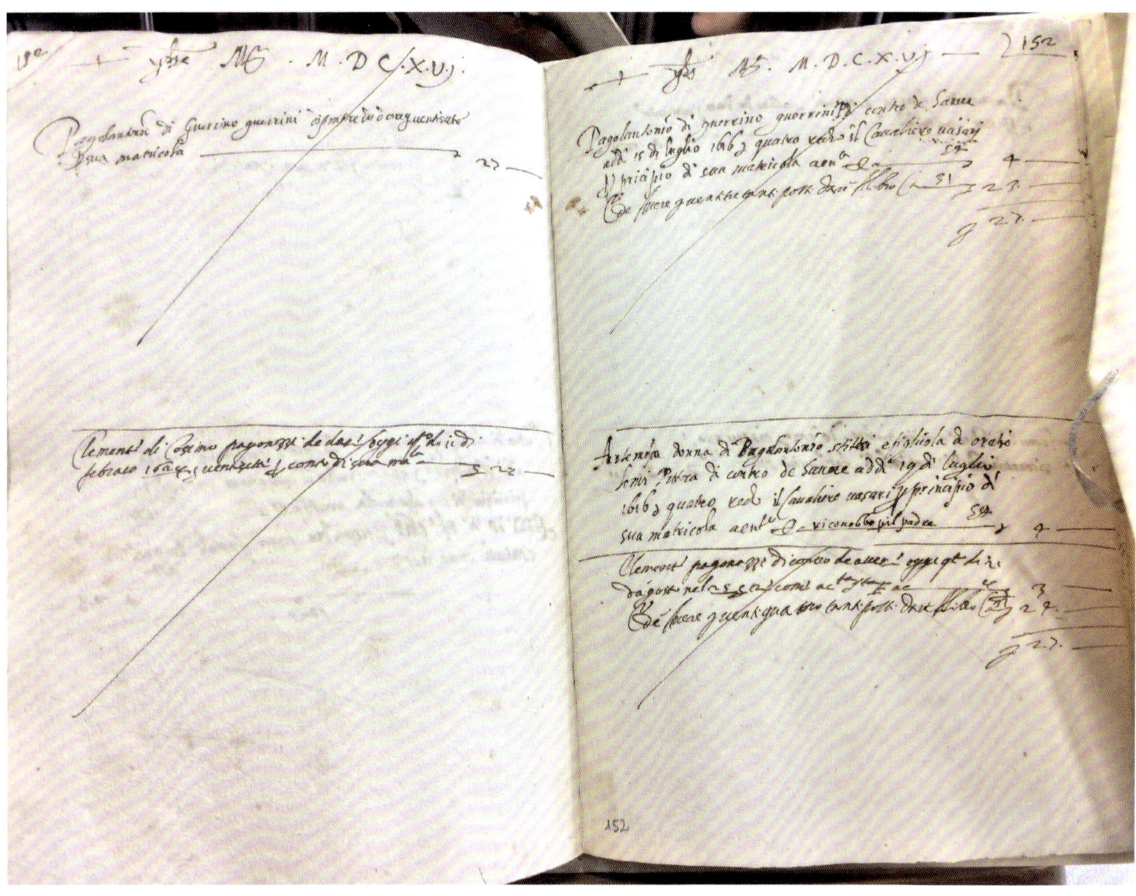

25 Accademia del Disegno 57, fol.152, Artemisia Gentileschi's matriculation record of 19 July 1616, manuscript, 30.5 cm (12 in) (4to), Archivio di Stato di Firenze

but it was close to the Medicis' palace, and a number of Medici artists and musicians such as Cigoli, Cristofano Allori, Giovanni Bilivert and Giulio Caccini lived here. No document, as of yet, furnishes a precise address for her workshop, but it may very well have been the house near the intersection of Borgo Ognissanti and via Santa Lucia sul Prato, which had been owned since 1611 by another branch of the Stiattesi family: the cloth weavers Francesco and Dieciaiuti Stiattesi. Within a few short years, her Borgo Ognissanti workshop would be populated with assistants, just as her home – referred to by her employees as the 'casa di Monna Artemizia Pittora' – would bustle with servants.[12]

At this time, she began to employ servants and assistants directly. Calling her 'lady boss' ['padrona'], these male and female employees looked not to her husband but to her for payment. Similarly, bill collectors and court summons were now addressed directly to Artemisia, especially in the period of late 1616 through early 1617, when Artemisia – now pregnant for the fourth time – fell sick for several months, and ran up a large bill with an apothecary for medications commonly prescribed for infections of the eye. Further evidence comes from a legal proceeding of 28 November 1619, in which it is noted that Artemisia and Pierantonio came to court representing their individual interests, rather than as a married couple ['ciascuno per ogni sua ragione et interesse']. It is also stated here that she entered into a contract on her own account without so much as a woman's legal representative ['mondualdo'], and that her husband had no part in the negotiation. By 1619 it can be surmised that Artemisia lived apart from her husband, on the basis of her solicitor's declaration to the tribunal of the Accademia del Disegno that Pierantonio failed to give her a court summons which had been mistakenly delivered to his house, even though it was in her name. Just as significantly, the solicitor also pointed out that Artemisia – at that moment – had full control of her dowry ['havendo il pieno della sua dota'].[13]

Artemisia's *de facto* fiscal and legal autonomy – something very few women of her era experienced – was confirmed time and time again in her frequent interactions with the tribunal of the Accademia del Disegno. Under the name 'Artemisia donna di Pagolantonio Stitesi e figliuola di Oratio Lomi Pittora', she had matriculated as a guild member of this organisation on 19 July 1616, having been charged the minimal 'legacy' entrance fee of 4 *lire* that was reserved for the children of older members. For Artemisia to be charged the minimal fee, a bit of subterfuge was required, since membership in the Accademia had been held only by her uncle Aurelio Lomi and never by her father, even though this is what her matriculation payment record asserts. Notably, even the visual configuration of her payment record in the account book is highly irregular, and its lack of a cancellation mark suggests, perhaps, she never paid the minimal fee (fig.25).

Despite what is often written, Artemisia never attained the status of academician [*professore accademico*] in this organisation. As first recognised by Robert Contini, her membership should not be construed as a privilege or honor.[14] In truth, she was only ever a fee-paying guild member – and she was a reluctant one at that. This is apparent not only because of what has just been noted about the possible non-payment of the 1616 fee, but also because she had declined an invitation to join a year earlier on 1 June 1615 at the standard entrance rate of 33 *lire* and 3 *soldi*. If membership was not a priority for her, it is probably because she had already been painting professionally in Florence for three years and she had gained the patronage of the Grand Duke.

Rather than providing credentials, membership in the Accademia expanded her opportunities for socialising with artists like Cristofano Allori and dilettante members such as Galileo Galilei and Michelangelo Buonarroti the Younger. If she opportunistically befriended the dilettante members because she saw them as little fish with the potential to lead her to big-fish patrons, she was not alone. She also was not alone in her mixed feelings about the organisation: late medieval and early modern women frequently avoided joining guilds in order to save the cost of membership and the time, and to skirt requirements that could cut into their profit margins, productivity, employment opportunities and market shares. Male artists hesitated to join art guilds for the same reasons. Elena Fumagalli has shown that in the year 1632, only half of Florence's male artists were matriculated in the Accademia del Disegno.[15]

Another mistaken belief about Artemisia's admission to the Accademia del Disegno is that someone of importance – such as the Grand Duke of Florence – must have intervened on her behalf to press for her acceptance. In actuality, her admission did not require a *force majeur*. If she received any help at all with her first admission to the Accademia in 1615 – and there is no certain evidence she did – it may have been merely a customary introduction from someone such as Giulio Portigiani. Prosperous and well-connected, Portigiani was a long-time friend of Vincenzo Stiattesi, as confirmed when Portigiani's daughter served as godmother to the child of Vincenzo Stiattesi's daughter Lisabetta Valgimigli

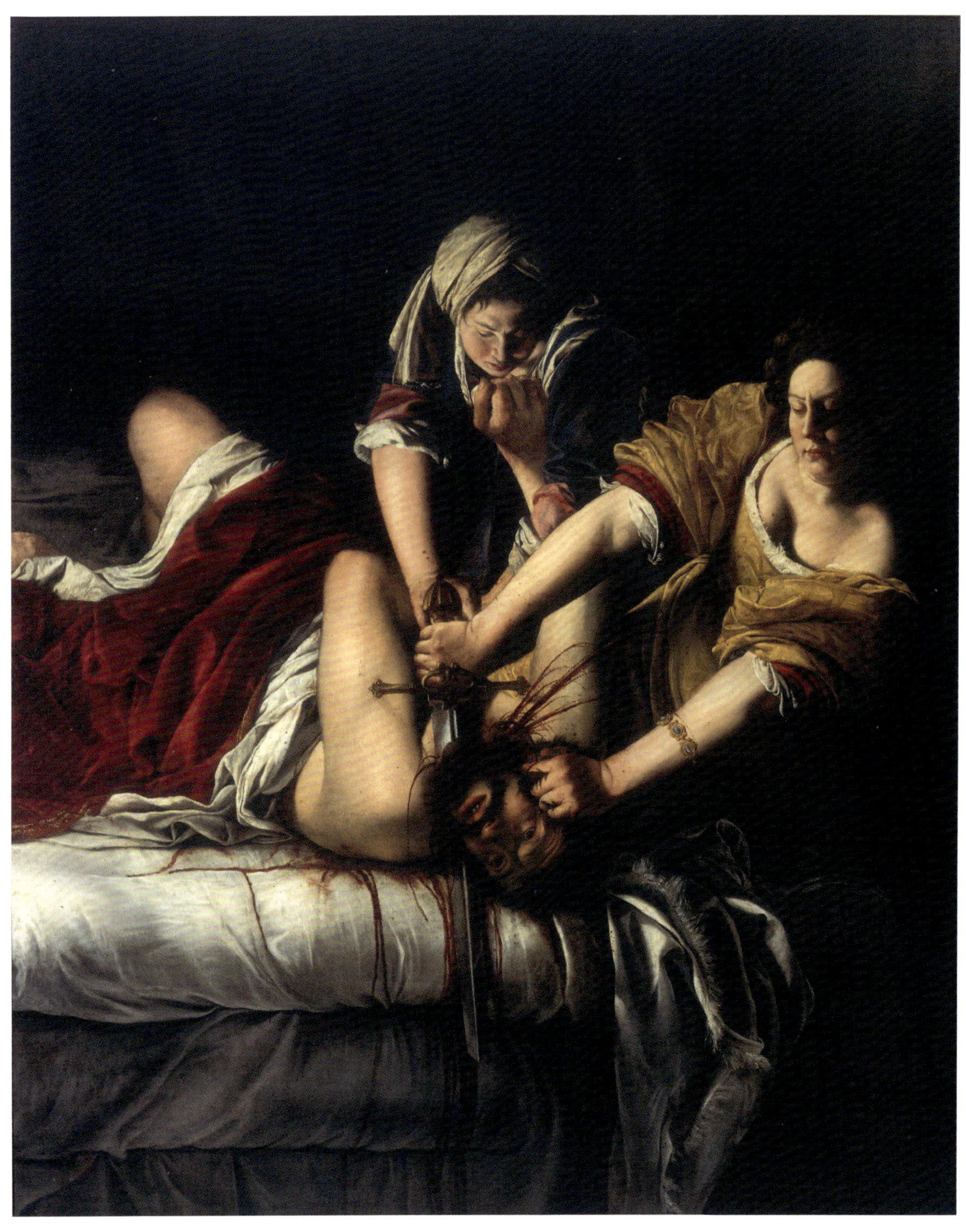

26 Artemisia Gentileschi, *Judith Beheading Holofernes*, *c.*1619–20, oil on canvas, 198 × 160 cm (78 × 63 in), Galleria degli Uffizi, Florence

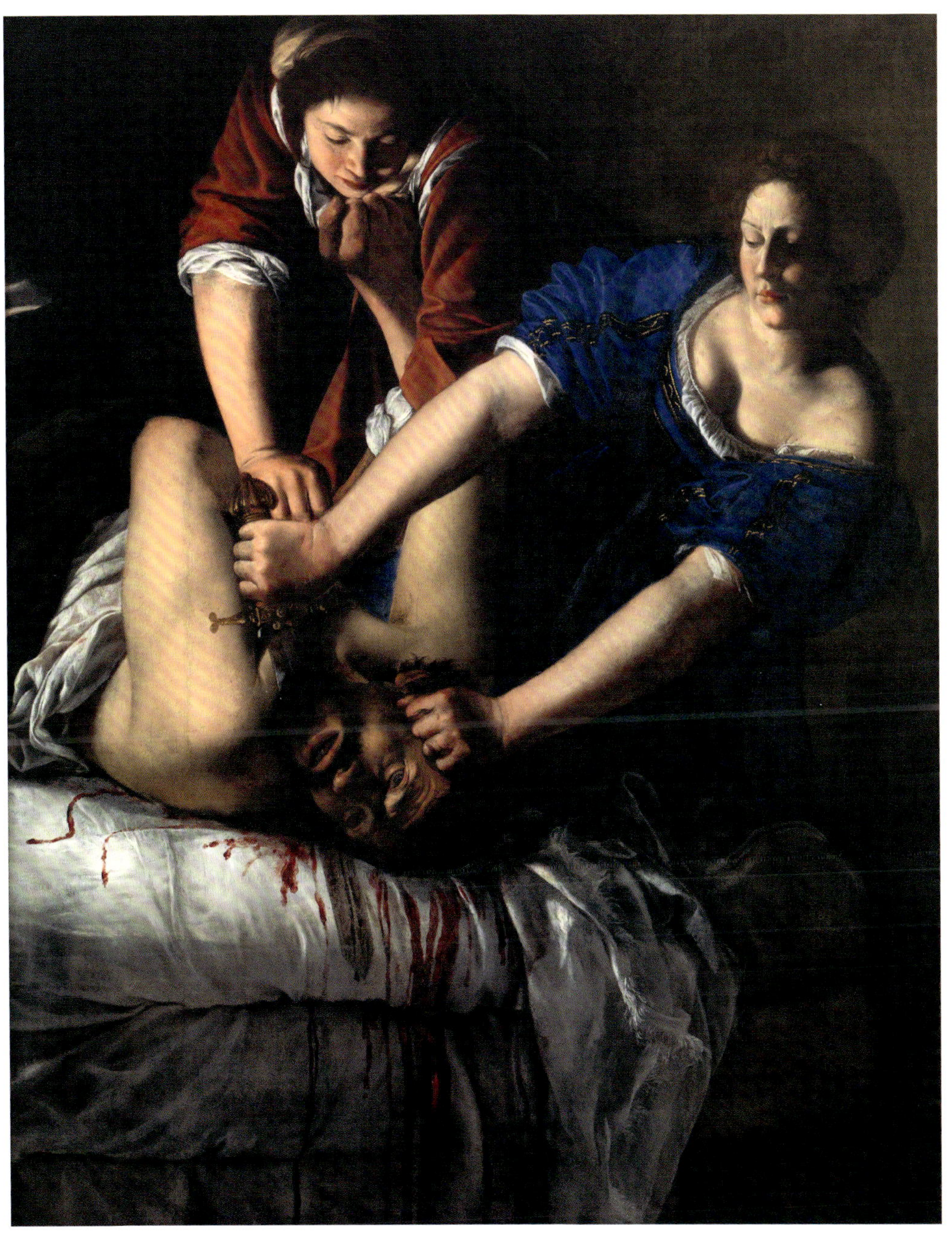

27 Artemisia Gentileschi, *Judith Beheading Holofernes*, *c*.1617, oil on canvas, 158.8 × 125.5 cm (62 ½ × 49 ⅜ in), Capodimonte Museum, Naples

in 1613. Portigiani probably met Vincenzo Stiattesi through his role as the Scalzo's official physician; at the same time, he was a dilettante member ['cavaliere medico'] of the Accademia del Disegno, to which he was connected though his father, the bronze caster and engineer Girolamo Portigiani.

A third fallacy identifies Artemisia as the first woman to join the Accademia del Disegno. Disproving this claim, the Accademia's archival records clearly show that monna Lisabetta di Michele *fantucciaia* [meaning 'doll maker'] preceded her on 13 February 1605. Several women's names appear in accounting records around this time showing donations by women in the same amount as a matriculation fee, yet the cause for these payments is undefined. For example, Isabella Soldani in 1603, and Maria di Giorgio in 1604, each paid the Accademia exactly the same amount that Artemisia and the other male matriculants had paid for their memberships, but we can only guess why they did so. It is perhaps relevant to this argument that there had occasionally been female matriculants in the Florentine painters' society known as the Compagnia dei Pittori di San Luca, including a woman named Albertuccia in 1543, and that women's enrolment in the Compagnia was foreseen by its foundational charter, in which the entrance fee for women is lower than the one for men (presumably because women were recognised to suffer greater financial hardship than their male peers).

JUDITH BEHEADING HOLOFERNES: WOMEN RULE!

After Artemisia attained financial independence from her husband and began to live apart from him (even while continuing to bear his children), she carried out the painting that has come to be seen by today's public as the most defining work of her career: the *Judith Beheading Holofernes* for Cosimo II de' Medici (fig.26). The painting's subject, drawn from the Biblical Book of Judith, recounts how a Jewish widow managed to single-handedly save Israel from defeat by the Assyrian army. Called to the tent of the army's general because he had taken a fancy to her, Judith charmed him until he fell asleep and then beheaded her people's most formidable enemy with his own sword. Presumably it was the work for which the Grand Duke rewarded the artist with 50 gold *scudi* on 4 May 1619 – a work which pleased the Grand Duke so much that he immediately asked her for another painting and gave her an advance of an additional 50 gold *scudi*. She sent a certain Guglielmo di Lorenzo (one of the many men who helped her in these later years) to collect the payment from the court bursar just two days later.

With this commission, the sickly Grand Duke – who was destined to succumb to his mysterious chronic illnesses in February of 1621 at the age of thirty – must have stunned his courtiers and attendants, for they were accustomed to his obsessive need for the merriment of singers and comics, musical jousts, and dances performed by cross-dressing noblemen. His brother-in-law, the Duke of Mantua, remarked as much on 29 June 1620, 'to my Lord [Cosimo II de' Medici], almost always in the throes of convalescence or some illness for which there is no other remedy except staying cheerful [. . .] I offer music, and all the male musicians, female musicians, and instruments at my disposal'.[16]

Amidst this frivolity, Artemisia's painting had the impact of a sudden thunderbolt. The Biblical heroine regarded to be a prefiguration of the Virgin Mary appears here blood-splattered and legs akimbo atop a man's bed. Her arms surge with strength as she severs Holofernes' neck. An agent of God's will, she remains concentrated and steely even as her victim convulses and blood splatters on the dress that is slipping off her shoulder.

Artemisia had tried her hand at nearly the exact same composition before making the Grand Duke's version. This earlier prototype, the *Judith Beheading Holofernes* at the Capodimonte Museum in Naples (fig.27), seduces the viewer's eye with the glint of the sword's brass pommel, the tangle of crumpled bedsheets, the suppleness of female skin, and the sharply corrugated folds of silken blue sleeves. These astonishing imitations of surface effects convince us of the image's material reality despite some problems with the spatial configuration. The painting may perhaps correspond to 'una Juditt[a]' for which the Florentine nobleman, the Marchese Giovanni Corsi, paid 20 *scudi* on 31 July 1617. In that year, Artemisia's Caravaggesque tendencies were reinvigorated by the presence in Florence of Battistello Caracciolo, a Neapolitan painter who alighted at court between 1617 and 1618 to make tenebrist devotional imagery for the private chapel of the Grand Duke's wife. Smaller than the Uffizi version only because it has been cut down on two sides, the Capodimonte canvas is undoubtedly the earlier of Artemisia's two surviving instances of this execution scene, as Mary D. Garrard has shown with her analysis of x-radiographs.[17] The same conclusion is supported by the following reasoning: once the Grand Duke's painting was complete, it would have been improper for Artemisia to repeat the composition except at his request; thus, any other existing version surely preceded the Grand Duke's commission.

Although she admired Caravaggio's art, borrowing the parallel alignment of Judith's arms from his *Judith Beheading Holofernes* of 1602 (fig.15) – Artemisia utterly rejected his portrayal of Judith as a dainty young woman who winces at her task. Artemisia's preference for Rubens' formidable females had already emerged in her *Conversion of the Magdalene* (fig.28), a slightly earlier work of about 1617 that the Grand Duke had likely ordered for his wife Maria Magdalena von Habsburg, as Mary D. Garrard has suggested.[18] For this devotional image, Artemisia conjured up a towering, impassioned Amazon who dwarfs a chair of the sort used by the Grand Duke (fig.30), and who evokes Rubens' ponderously fleshy divas wrapped in oceans of shimmering satin, such as the Saint Domitilla in his 1606 painting for the Roman Oratorians. As first pointed out by Frima Fox Hofrichter, Artemisia's Judith aligns closely with Rubens' corpulent and fearless heroine shown in an engraving (fig.29) based on this Flemish master's lost 'Great Judith', made either during his second Rome period (1605–8) or his first years back in Antwerp (1609–10).[19] Several specific borrowings confirm the importance of Rubens' precedent to Artemisia's *Judith Beheading Holofernes*, from Judith's stolid demeanour, to the sleeve that slips off her shoulder, to the detail of Holofernes' impotent clenched fist.

In repainting *Judith Beheading Holofernes*, Artemisia reinforced Judith's appearance of bodily strength as well as her prominence in the composition. Subtle modifications to Judith's pose allow the Biblical heroine to use the heft of her hips to maximise her force. Her head is low and close to her shoulder, her neck twists rigidly towards her victim, and, with respect to the Capodimonte version, her left leg is positioned farther out in a linebacker's powerful stance. Artemisia's new version also improves upon the color scheme of the earlier picture, bringing it into line with the practice of color perspective that was already established when Matteo Zaccolini penned his treatise between 1618–22, showing that blue implies distance, and yellow proximity. Accordingly, the Uffizi version has Judith wearing a resplendent gold dress that suits her role as a protagonist in the foreground, whereas Judith's servant Abra wears a sooty blue dress that relegates her somewhat to the shadows and enhances the illusion of pictorial depth. Incidentally, the change of Judith's dress to gold also conveniently accommodated comparisons between this painting and *Il Giuditta*, a poem Gabriello Chiabrera dedicated to the Grand Duke in 1610, in which Judith is said to have donned a golden dress to seduce the general.

Borrowing from Rubens, Artemisia added to her Uffizi version jets of blood that squirt out of Holofernes' open artery and fleck across Judith's breast. The horrifying impact of this detail shows us that she is far braver than we are. To further amplify the gory effect, Artemisia changed the color of Holofernes' coverlet from black (in the first version) to blood red, and she traced with obscene fascination

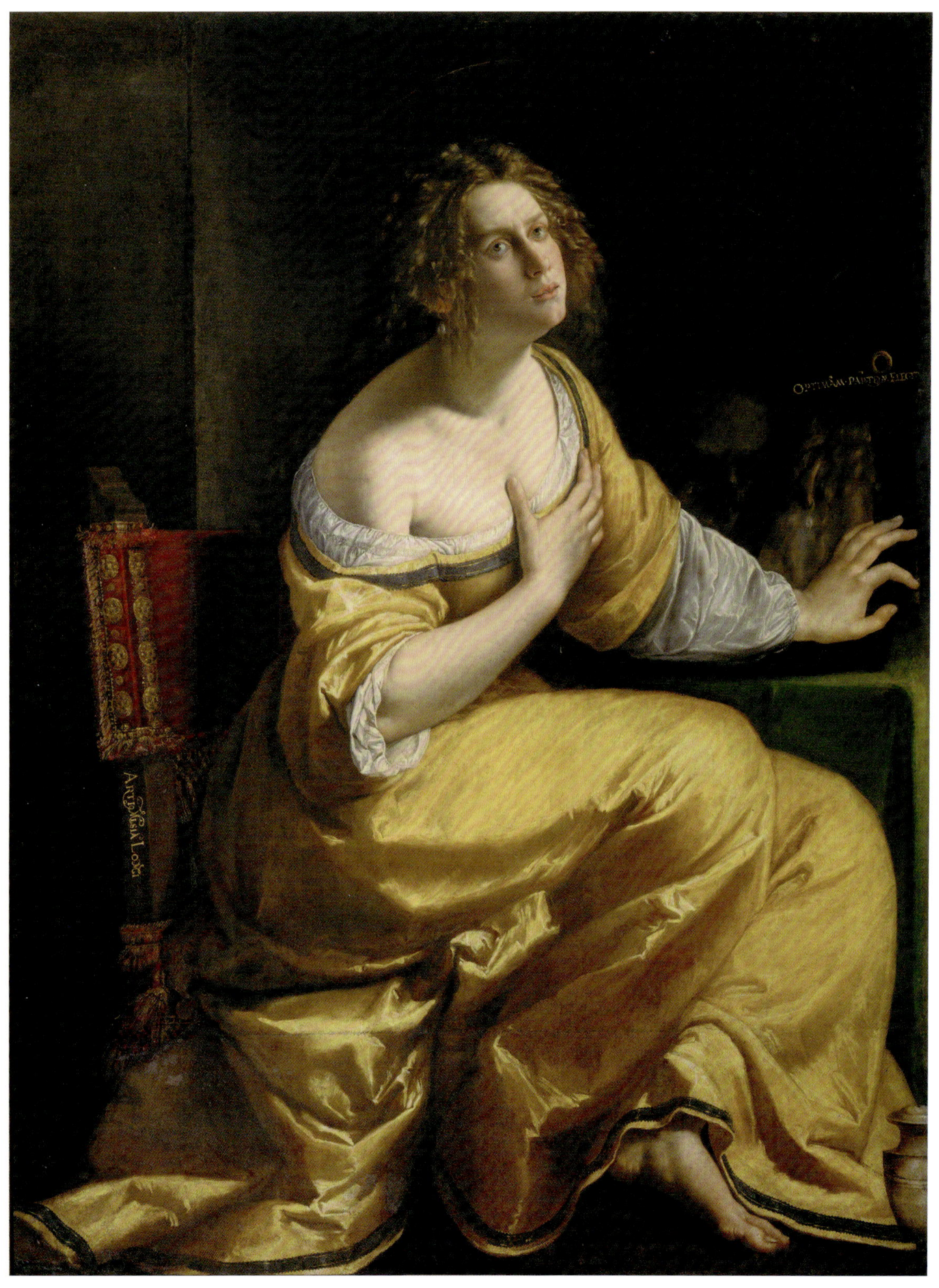

28 Artemisia Gentileschi, *Conversion of the Magdalene*, *c.*1617, oil on canvas, 146.5 × 108 cm (57 ⁹⁄₁₆ × 42 ½ in), Palazzo Pitti, Uffizi, Florence

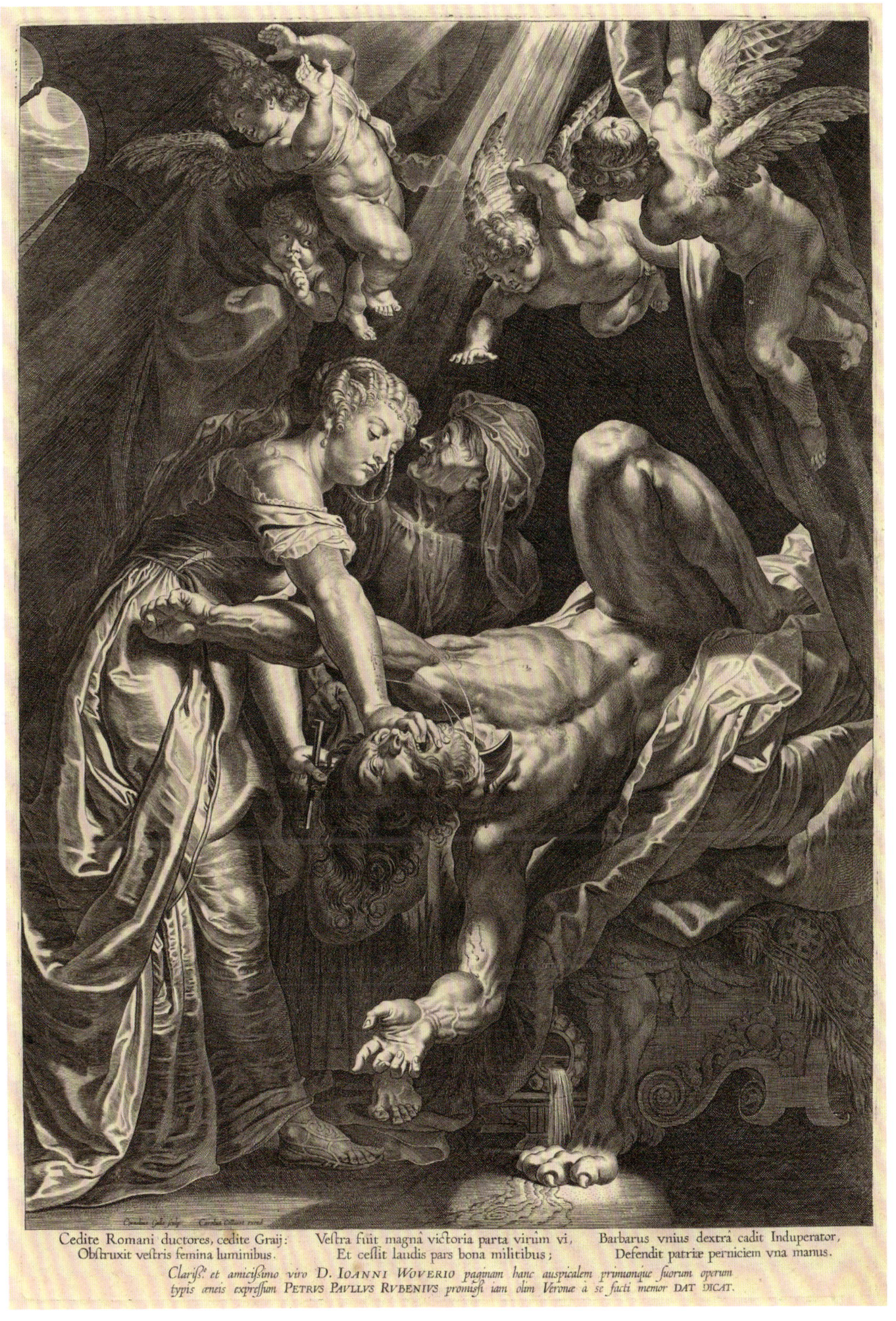

29 Cornelius Galle after Peter Paul Rubens, *Judith Beheading Holofernes*, 1605–01 or 1609–1610, engraving, 55 × 38 cm (21 5⁄8 × 14 15⁄16 in) (platemark), The Metropolitan Museum of Art, New York. The Elisha Whittelsey Collection, The Elisha Whittelsey Fund, 1951

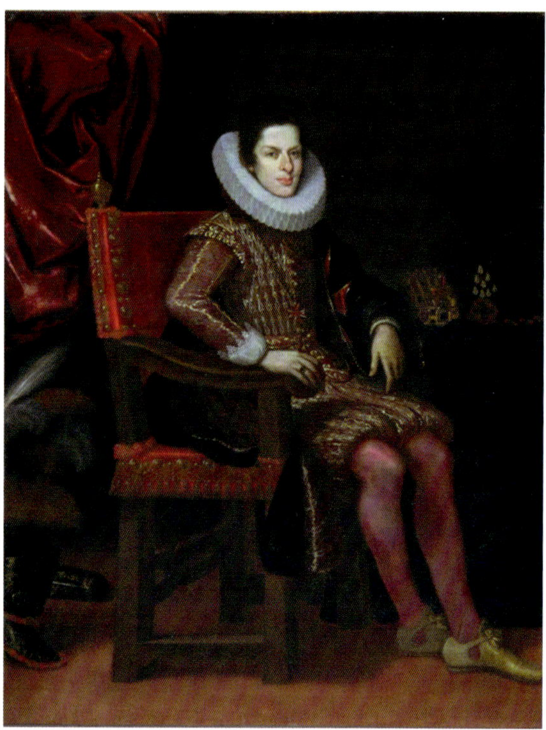

30 Jacopo da Empoli, *Portrait of Cosimo II de' Medici*, *c.*1617, oil on canvas, 172 × 127.5 cm (67 ¾ × 50 ⅛ in), Salone Consiliare, Museo di Palazzo Pretorio, Prato

the pattern made by the blood as it streams out along the mattress. Perhaps Artemisia's most original contribution to the story was to arm Judith with a very special kind of weapon that no previous artist had thought to give her: an executioner's sword, with its wide blade and blunt tip (fig.31). In Florence, this was the instrument used to carry out capital punishment on foreigners who were subject to imperial law (by contrast, the noose was the instrument used to execute the locals). Wielding such a weapon, Judith thus comes to stand for justice, particularly the brand of justice wielded against foreign enemies like Holofernes.

Sculpted images of brutish or foreign enemies being killed by heroes abounded in the streets of Florence, all promulgating the same terrifying message about the Grand Duke's power to crush his opponents. Guarding the entrance to the government offices at Palazzo Vecchio were the giant marble statues of Michelangelo's *David* and Baccio Bandinelli's *Hercules*, each about to slay his foe. In the nearby Loggia de' Lanzi, the post of the Grand Duke's German guards, Cellini's *Perseus* brandished the severed head of Medusa. Near it in the Loggia was Donatello's bronze statue of *Judith Beheading Holofernes,* which had been commissioned by Cosimo de' Medici the Elder a century and a half earlier to herald the Medicis' rise to pre-eminence. The newest addition to this category of indomitable Medici champions was Giambologna's monumental sculptural group of *Hercules Defeating the Centaur Nessus* (fig.32) that Cosimo II's father Ferdinando I de' Medici had erected in the Canto dei Carnesecchi (fig.33), a spot which was quite far from the Medicis' palace and government headquarters. In this location, Giambologna's depiction of a violent killing surely was meant to remind the local families of the execution of their former neighbour, Pietro Carnesecchi (1508–67). That punishment had been carried out in Rome by Pope Pius V, thanks to the assistance of Grand Duke Cosimo I de' Medici.

Giambologna's conceit of Hercules' and the centaur's arms tangled in violent combat must have impressed Artemisia, who could not have failed to pass through the square dominated by the palace of the very same Carnesecchi for whom her father-in-law, Vincenzo Stiattesi, had worked. Looking at the sculpture surely impressed Artemisia's artistic imagination with its illusion of anatomies strained to their limit and forces locked in diametric opposition. In particular, it helped her to think through the arrangement of bodies in Rubens' 'Great Judith' in fully three-dimensional terms, and to meditate on the kinetics of actions that she had probably never seen in life, such as neck-breaking, face-pushing and the intense gridlock of battling limbs. Having studied the representation of violent combat taught by this and

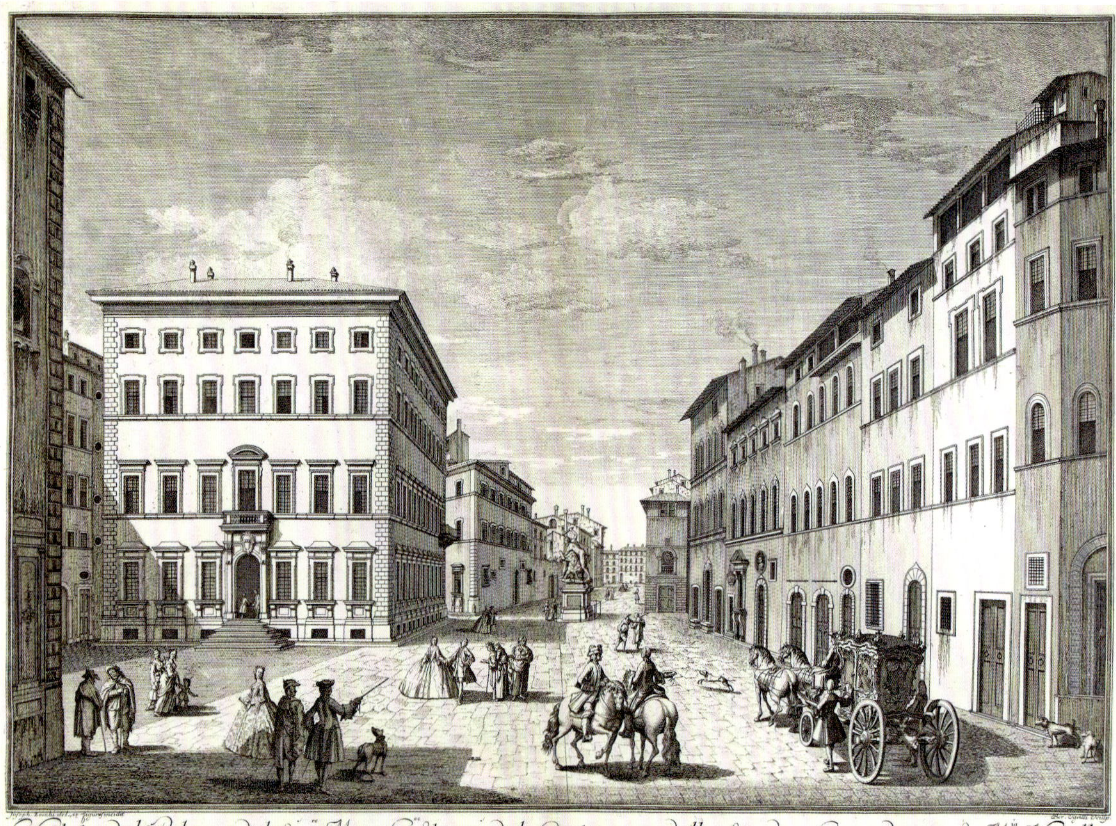

33 Giuseppe Zocchi, *Canto dei Carnescchi*, *c.*1744, etching with engraving, 50.2 × 68.1 cm (19 ¾ × 26 13⁄16 in) (platemark), The Metropolitan Museum of Art, New York

other statues in Florence's public squares, she gave her Medici patron the bloodiest iteration to date of the dynasty's truculent message for their enemies. Soon after this, in the winter of 1619–20, Artemisia received a commission from the Grand Duke to paint a 'Hercules', which, although never carried out for reasons to be explained below, was possibly a scene of combat alluding to the might of the Medici state.

While this symbolic muscle-flexing by means of warrior imagery was hardly unique to the Medici court, the Medicis were gravely in need of it. Already in 1614, it was widely known that behind Cosimo II de Medici's chronic malaise lay a terminal illness. In that year, the Grand Duke's mother, the Dowager Grand Duchess Christine de Lorraine, lost confidence in the ability of the Medici court's physicians to cure her son and so she decided to convoke an international congress of prominent physicians from Louvain, Leiden, Lorraine, Montpellier, Paris, Toulouse, Rome, Urbino, Padua, Bologna, Bari, Siena, Genoa, Brussels, Lecce, Madrid, the court of the archduke of Austria and the Imperial court to review his case. Yet, neither this extraordinary measure, nor the novenas and religious processions that Christine organised, had any positive benefit for her son's failing health. Given the situation, the Grand Duke began to make provisions for the continuation of the dynasty after his death, much as King Henry IV of France (1553–1610) had done in anticipation of Maria de' Medici's regency (1610–14). This meant preparing his government and his subjects for a period of regency, since his eldest son Ferdinand (1610–70) was not even ten years old. At first the Grand Duke considered making his brother Giovanni the regent, but he was soon convinced instead that his son's future would be much safer if he were to put his wife and his mother in charge. Thus, plans were laid for the Tuscan Grand Duchy's female regency shared by the two foreign-born co-regents.

Besides the testament penned by Cosimo laying out the terms of the female regency that would hold the reins of government until his son turned eighteen, softer forms of political strategising were used to enhance support for the co-regents. Some of this groundwork took literary form with a thirty-two-tome manuscript in defence of women's status titled *On the Dignity and Nobility of Women* [*Della dignità et della nobiltà delle donne*], composed by Cristofano Bronzini for the Medicis, largely between 1615 and 1620. The treatise had a grand purpose befitting its colossal size. It was meant to bulwark the political authority of the two female co-regents of Tuscany's Medici grand duchy by demonstrating that women are better suited for rulership than men according to God's design – a claim so contentious that, as discovered by Xenia von Tippelskirch, it drew fire from Rome's Sacred Congregation of the Index.[20]

Bronzini's work not only heaps praise upon both Dowager Grand Duchess Christine de Lorraine and Archduchess Maria Magdalena, whom he calls 'a new Amazon in Tuscany', but it also argues, quite controversially, that women have a natural aptitude for rulership and that they are morally superior to men. Then, following the pattern of the *querelle des femmes* treatises, it musters the biographies of hundreds of valiant, talented and virtuous women from ancient and modern times as exemplars of the worthiness of their sex, proclaiming the universal and transhistorical excellence of women by means of an encyclopedic account of their achievements in every realm of moral and intellectual endeavor.

As a testament to her standing at the Medici court at this moment, Artemisia Gentileschi's biography is one of the longer ones in this treatise. It passes over her entanglement with Tassi in complete silence (presumably out of decorum), and instead focuses on Artemisia's self-directed path to artistic greatness. In claiming that Artemisia attained success on her own and that she overcame the impediments that men, such as her father, had supposedly placed in her way, it debunked the same denigrating views of women that the co-regents wished to eradicate. In effect, the artist had seized upon early modern feminism – with its emphasis on women's boundless potentiality – as a meeting ground between her own experiences as a struggling young painter from an artisan-class family and the very different political challenges facing Dowager Grand Duchess Christine de Lorraine and Archduchess Maria Magdalena as foreign-born widows sharing rule over the Grand Duchy of Tuscany.

As a visual parallel to the political groundwork laid by Bronzini's text, Artemisia's painting of *Judith Beheading Holofernes* furnished the Grand Duke with warrior imagery for the regency that would ensure his son's succession. The painting conveniently depicts not one but two heroic women carrying out their righteous mission with bravery and disinterest. It would not be out of line to identify the Judith in the Uffizi painting as a possible portrait of Archduchess Maria Magdalena (fig.34). Not only is this Judith's face longer and her hair more brunette in color than the Judith in the Capodimonte version, but also the red, gold and white colors of her dress correspond to those of the coat-of-arms of the House of Habsburg.

An even more compelling indication of the canvas's relevance to the political concerns of Cosimo II and the co-regents is the perfect coherence of

Artemisia's *Judith Beheading Holofernes* to the themes of the theatrical spectacles and artworks that Maria Magdalena would commission throughout her future regency, almost as if the painting had set the course for the Florentine court's cultural strategies. As shown by Kelley Ann Harness, most of the spectacles presented during Maria Magdalena's seven-year regency were political allegories involving heroic female protagonists – either Biblical women or saints – and they were staged on the occasion of visits by prestigious foreign dignitaries.[21] One of these spectacles was *La Giuditta*, staged in 1626, which culminated in Judith's act of decapitating Holofernes with his own sword. At the same time, the walls of Maria Magdalena's Villa Poggio Imperiale, which she had purchased upon the inauguration of her regency, were being decorated with the stories of four wives and widows of antiquity who were celebrated for their valour and wise rule: Semiramis, Lucrezia, Matilda, and, of course, Judith. There can thus be no question about the deep affinity between the imagery of Artemisia's *Judith Beheading Holofernes* and the political agenda of the House of Medici.

That affinity is confirmed by the painting's early history of display in the grand ducal residence of Palazzo Pitti. As reported in the 1638 inventory, the painting originally hung in a large room, now known as the Room of Venus, that served as a gateway to two different ceremonial trajectories of dynastic power in Palazzo Pitti, one masculine and one feminine. Through one doorway, this room gave access to the north–south enfilade of Ferdinand II's apartments (which had previously been Grand Duke Cosimo II's apartments). Through a second doorway, this room initiated the east–west enfilade of Archduchess Maria Magdalena von Habsburg's apartments and, continuing past her rooms, the apartments of the Dowager Grand Duchess Christine de Lorraine. By locating Artemisia's painting at the intersection of these two gendered trajectories, its image of womanly heroism underscored Maria Magdalena's and Christine's dedication to protecting the grand duchy during the minority of Ferdinando II de' Medici.

A subsequent inventory indicates that by 1687 the painting had been re-located to the immediately adjacent room in the direction of the Grand Duchess' apartments, a room that was described in documents as the 'camera buia' [the dark room] because of its lack of windows. In this dusky room traversed by all those on their way to an audience with Vittoria della Rovere – who was the Grand Duchess in that later era – the sight of Artemisia's *Judith Beheading Holofernes* by candlelight or gas lamp must have enhanced the terrifying effect of being in Holofernes' tent on that fateful night. That impression served to put Judith's mettle in stark contrast to the viewer's own pusillanimity, and it prepared the visitor to meet with a Grand Duchess who modelled herself after Judith and other such courageous women. There can be no doubt about it: the Medicis had deeply understood the potency and originality of Artemisia's art. With her virtuous, dynamic heroines clad in bold colors (or nothing at all), Artemisia shared the Medici family's determination to convince their contemporaries that women were not only fit to paint the world, but also to rule it.

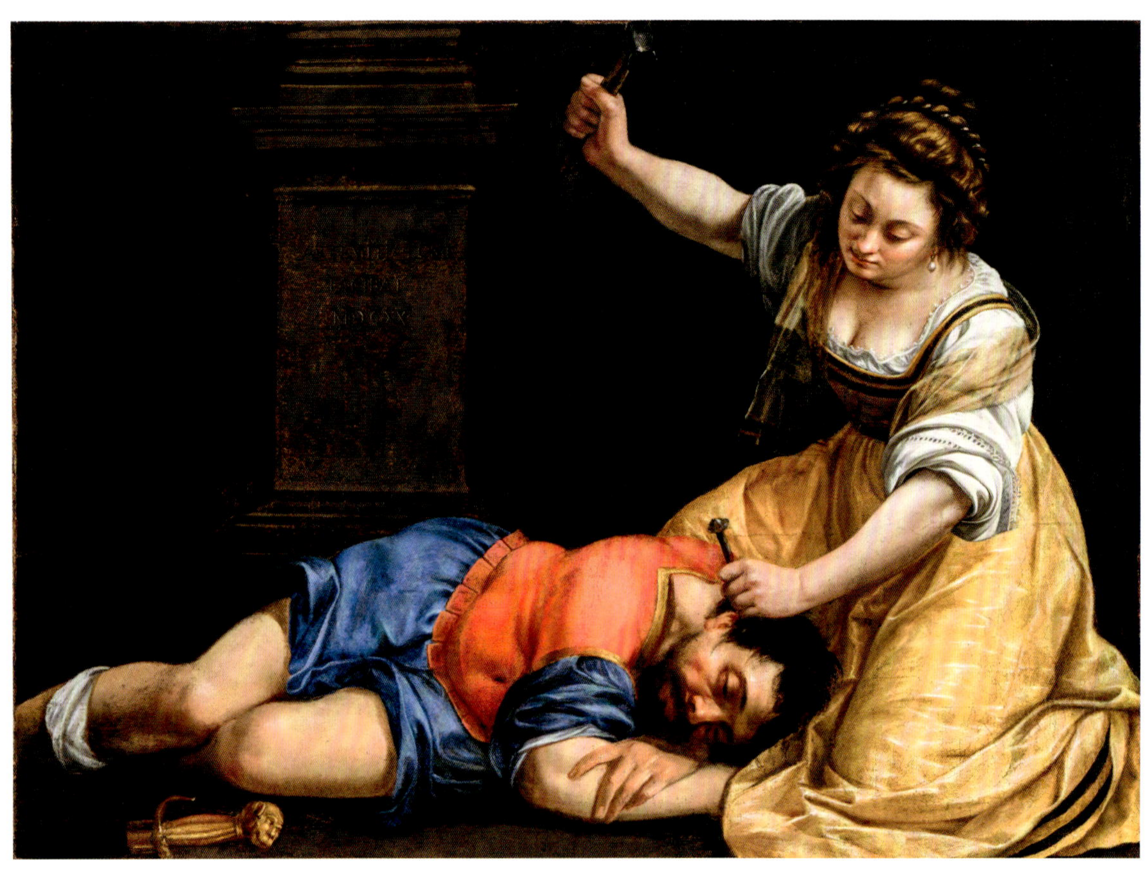

35 Artemisia Gentileschi, *Jaël and Sisera*, 1620, oil on canvas, 86 × 125 cm (33 ⅞ × 49 ¼ in), Szépművészeti Múzeum/Museum of Fine Arts, Budapest

3

A Loquacious and Beautiful Art

A TURBULENT EXIT FROM FLORENCE

In reconstructing Artemisia's professional trajectory, it is occasionally necessary to look at the vicissitudes of her domestic life and her intimate relationships to explain certain decisions of hers that otherwise would be incomprehensible coming from such a shrewd and driven artist. The year 1620 is a case in point. When it opened, Artemisia, now twenty-six years old, had all the outer trappings of a successful and brilliant career at the Medici court, where she was the darling of the Grand Duke of Tuscany. On 10 February, having been granted a very large advance on a new painting, she sent a terse and rather peremptory letter to Cosimo II to inform him of her plans to take an extended absence from the Florentine court:

> So that it will not be hidden from Your Most Serene Highness, I wish with this letter to inform Your Most Serene Highness that I have decided to make a little journey to Rome, my travel being required by the many illnesses that I have suffered in the past as well as the many tribulations that have afflicted my home and my family, and thus to resolve both my problems I will spend a few months down there with my family. In that period, which will not extend beyond two months, I assure Your Most Serene Highness that I am mindful of my debt for the advance I received of 50 *scudi* on your commission. And I shall continue praying to God for the perfect happiness and health of Your Most Serene Highness, I bow before you most humbly, and put myself completely in the hands of Your good graces, from home, in Florence.[1]

Without waiting to receive the Grand Duke's approval, Artemisia fled Florence on horseback, without her paintings, and without her children. Two days later, she had reached Prato, where she alighted briefly with her husband Pierantonio Stiattesi. Even before they could organise a transfer of clothes and paintings, along with their four-year-old Cristofano and their two-year-old Prudenzia, they first had to resolve a humiliating and shameful crisis: the Grand Duke had impounded Artemisia's workshop due to her unauthorised departure from Florence. Artemisia's insubordination had roused Cosimo II to vindictive anger, and time would confirm that her ungrateful letter, followed by her brusque departure, had irreparably damaged her standing at the Florentine court. After struggling so long to gain and keep the favour of Cosimo II, what could have possibly compelled her to act in this way?

Artemisia herself gave different explanations to different people. As we have seen, she told the Grand Duke that she was going to Rome to resolve health issues and family troubles. While this was certainly true, it does not explain the extreme haste of her flight. To Gino Ginori, a Medici court official in Prato, she mentioned her plans to go to Rome in conjunction with complaints about the difficulty of making a living in Florence.[2] She was far more evasive with Francesco Maria Maringhi (1593–1653), a Florentine man of her own age with whom she had been having an affair of late. In a letter written from Prato and dated 14 February 1620, she despairingly noted that 'it seems that I have no luck in this city [of Florence]', yet she indicated no particular destination – only a readiness to go 'even to Bologna'.[3]

There was one pressing issue that would have sufficed to precipitate her flight, yet which she at first kept to herself: her father owed some 500 Florentine *scudi* to Pierantonio Stiattesi for Artemisia's dowry. This was an exceedingly large sum of money, roughly equivalent to what Artemisia might have hoped to earn in two or even three years of working for the Grand Duke. As noted in the previous chapter, Artemisia's marriage contract stipulated that Orazio Gentileschi would pay the first half of his daughter's dowry, amounting to 500 Florentine *scudi*, in 1615, and that he would make the final payment of 500 Florentine *scudi* (plus interest) five years later in 1620. Artemisia must have been deeply worried in early 1620 that Orazio would hear rumours about her financial separation from her husband and that this would lead him to repudiate his obligation to pay out the rest of the dowry. This fear did in fact come to pass. In early 1620 the Medici court functionary Bernardo Migliorati wrote a calumniating letter to Orazio about the scandalous comportment of Artemisia and her husband. As if that were not enough, Migliorati included a mordantly satirical sonnet with his letter.

DIVERGING FEMINISMS: ARTEMISIA AND THE EMERGENT TUSCAN REGENCY

Soon after her arrival in Rome on 2 March 1620, the tensions over the dowry issue drew Artemisia, and Pierantonio as well, into heated, almost violent altercations with her brother. By May of 1620, Pierantonio (who now tried to appear more like a husband) resorted to filing a lawsuit against Orazio to compel his full payment of the promised gift. Amidst all of this brawling over money came a devastating loss: Artemisia's four-year-old son Cristofano died on 6 April from stomach worms ['morto de' bachi'] after eleven days of agonising pain and his parents' helpless bafflement as to the cause.[4] This first spring in Rome must have been a terribly bitter homecoming.

Throughout this turmoil, Artemisia continued painting. Her husband asserted that it was her intention to carry out her previous Florentine commissions before accepting any new ones in Rome: 'She will finish the paintings and give satisfaction to everyone [back in Florence] and afterwards she will do whatever God wills.'[5] To remedy the lingering opprobrium of having displeased the Grand Duke, Artemisia made it her first priority to complete a painting she had begun for Cosimo II while in Florence. For reasons to be explained shortly, this unfinished canvas in question can be identified with the painting of *Jaël and Sisera* (fig.35), now in the Budapest Museum of Fine Arts, which is clearly dated 1620 ('M.D.CXX.') near the signature. The scene's protagonist, Jaël, a typological precedent for the Virgin Mary, is shown in the act of fulfilling the prophecy that a woman would defeat the Israelites' enemies in Cana. According to the Biblical story in Judges 4–5, the Canaanite general Sisera escaped the Battle of Mount Tabor after a devastating loss. During his flight he sought shelter from a Canaanite ally named Heber. Heber's wife Jaël pretended to give Sisera hospitality, but when Sisera fell asleep in her care, she drove a tent peg through the skull of the Israelites' greatest enemy. Like Artemisia's previous paintings of virtuous women for the Medici court, this depiction of a woman calmly assassinating a warlord was designed to lay the cultural groundwork for Tuscany's female regency.

Artemisia signed the *Jaël and Sisera* on a pilaster in the background, where the words 'ARTEMITIA LOMI' appear to be inscribed into the stone. This signature points to the Florentine genesis of work, since 'Lomi' is the surname used by the artist employed while living in Florence, but rarely afterwards. (Presumably she had chosen this surname to remind locals of her uncle the painter.) Also suggesting a Florentine origin are the composition's Florentine artistic models: Jaël's kneeling position recalls the painting of the same subject by Ludovico Cigoli (as first shown by R. Ward Bissell), whereas Jaël's highly anomalous straight-armed blow with a mallet pays homage to the straight-armed wallop in Giambologna's *Hercules Defeating the Centaur Nessus* (see fig.32), the sculpture cited above in relation to Artemisia's *Judith Beheading Holofernes*. An additional possible Florentine element in the painting's imagery is the simian-headed pommel of *Sisera*'s sword, which bears a strong resemblance to the canine-headed pommel on a sword housed in the Medici hunting lodge of Cerreto Guidi (fig.36).

This canvas may have been one of several that Artemisia had to leave behind in her studio when she fled to Prato. Indeed, the *Jaël and Sisera* may have been the painting that Pierantonio Stiattesi referred to when he wrote from Rome in March of 1620 to authorise a mediocre Florentine painter named Alessandro Bardelli to 'touch up with his hand the painting that [Artemisia] has done for the Grand Duke . . . with full reign to do what he sees fit'.[6] Presumably, at the moment Artemisia was given the commission of the *Jaël and Sisera*, she was also supplied with the Grand Duke's ultramarine blue in order to employ it in the painting. Since the costly pigment did not belong to her, she had been obliged to leave it behind in Florence causing great delays to her progress on Cosimo II's commissions, as noted by Pierantonio Stiattesi in April of 1620 when protesting that the pigment be sent to Rome: '[. . .] [N]ot having received the blue has resulted in delays on the painting'.[7] Under these challenging circumstances,

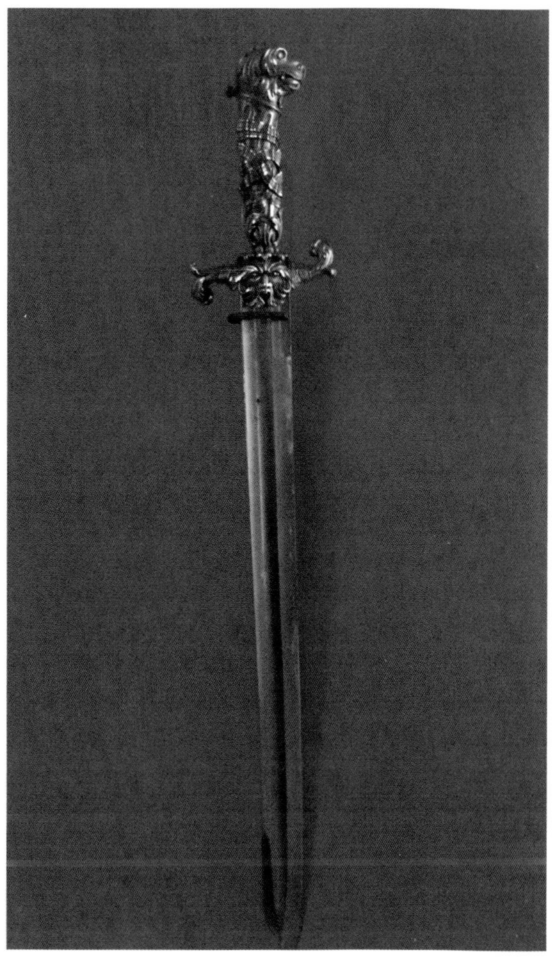

36 Hunting dagger, steel, length: 45 cm (17 ¾ in), Historical Hunting and Territorial Museum, Cerreto Guidi

Artemisia must have decided to let Bardelli finish her *Jaël and Sisera* in Florence, even while she worked on completing another canvas for the Grand Duke that she had managed to bring with her to Rome.

The *Jaël and Sisera* does not appear in the Medici inventories, and one can only suppose that it was given away as a gift shortly after being received by the court. If indeed the work never took its intended place in the Medici collections, the reason for its rejection could reasonably be ascribed to a risqué detail in its imagery, namely Sisera's hand tucked naughtily underneath Jaël's skirt. Not present in any other artist's rendering of this subject, this indecorous action would have surely displeased the Archduchess Maria Magdalena and the Dowager Grand Duchess Christine de Lorraine. Given the 'KK' stamp of the Viennese emperor on the back of the canvas, it seems that the Archduchess may have redirected the work to her brother Ferdinand II, Holy Roman Emperor, who could have seen in Sisera his own enemy: Frederick V, the Calvinist King of Bohemia.

Like the strange, straight-armed hammer-blow mentioned above, the erotic gesture of Sisera's groping hand was Artemisia's own innovation with respect to the traditional iconography of the subject. According to Mary D. Garrard's recent analysis of this painting's feminist content, the placement of Sisera's hand implies that Jaël used sexual favours to ensnare Sisera, following a standard rabbinic interpretation of the Biblical story.[8] Thus, with this eye-catching detail, Artemisia portrayed male carnal desire as a fatal weakness that subjects men to defeat by women. As Garrard argues convincingly, Sisera's gesture brings Artemisia's image in line with the *Weibermacht* [Power of Women] tradition in art and literature that served to warn men about the danger of falling victim to women's deceits, manipulations and seductions. Indeed, a lost painting of a *Hercules and Iole* that the Grand Duke commissioned from Artemisia on 16 January 1620 (and which Pierantonio Stiattesi mentioned in a letter to Maringhi of 20 March 1620) represented a myth that similarly admonished viewers about women's ability to bring about the demise of even the strongest of men.

In previous years, Artemisia's explicit depiction of Sisera's capitulation to Jaël's carnal enticements might very well have been welcomed as an innocuously sportive gesture by Cosimo II, himself an admirer of female talents like Artemisia, Francesca Caccini and Adriana Basile. But the spring of 1620 was a lugubrious period at the Medici court, and Cosimo's mother Christine was gradually taking over the reins of government due to the rapid decline in her son's health.

As Christine – together with Maria Magdalena – assumed greater authority, they imposed a strict moral code upon the Florentine court and scrupulously enforced a cultural program that, as shown by Kelley Ann Harness, indicated God – and not physical charms – to be the source of women's power.[9] There was a political exigency behind the co-Regents' prudish taste. Malicious gossip in Florence charged Christine and Maria Magdalena with pressuring Cosimo II to exclude Cosimo's brother from government and to put the regency in their hands alone. Rumours of a plot to overthrow the regency must have further intensified their anxiety, as pointed out by Janie Cole.[10] To deflect these attacks on their character and to justify the holding of power by women, Christine and Maria Magdalena encouraged cultural representations of strong women who were obedient, chaste and disinterested instruments of God's will.

This insistence upon godly and pious representations of womanhood was already evident in 1619. In that year, Michelangelo Buonarroti the Younger, Artemisia's convivial ally at the Florentine court, found himself in hot water with the Grand Duke's mother because of his raunchy play, *La Fiera*. The Dowager Grand Duchess' moral indignation at his play's 'double meanings of the words and actions' and its 'overstepping of the boundaries of modesty and purity' made Michelangelo a virtual pariah at court for the next fifteen years.[11] Under the influence of the female regency, the climate at the Florentine court was palpably different and Artemisia must have realised, perhaps with some irony, that her fiercely self-reliant heroines would fare better in papal Rome.

THROWING DOWN THE ARTISTIC GAUNTLET IN ROME

It is not known if the sanctimonious female regents at the Medici court appreciated Artemisia's *Hercules and Iole*. We do know, however, that as Artemisia finished up that canvas, it caught the eye of one of the most ardent art collectors in Rome, Alessandro Peretti Damasceni, also known as Cardinal Montalto (1571–1623), who requested a copy of it in March of 1620 or 1621. Encouraged by such shows of interest in her established repertoire, Artemisia continued to depict strong women during her period in Rome. Yet, at the same time, she showed a willingness to undertake experiments with painting materials, a receptivity to other artists' styles, and a readiness to modify her own approach in order to develop new expressive possibilities.

Now in the Burghley House Collection, the painting of *Susanna and the Elders*, signed 'Artemisia Gentileschi Lomi' and dated 'MDCXXII' (1622) is a case in point (fig.37). With its intensely luminous jewel-toned palette, fuliginous sky, broad and loose brushwork, sponge-painted trees and vertical piling of figures, the Burghley House *Susanna and the Elders* shows her mastery of the characteristic style of Guercino (1591–1666), who had arrived in Rome from Emilia in 1621 to serve the Bolognese pope elected that year, Gregory XV Ludovisi. In particular, Artemisia's *Susanna* mirrors the style of *The Penitent Saint Maria Magdalene* (fig.38), a work by Guercino which went on view in the same year of 1622 as the high altarpiece in Rome's church of Santa Maria Maddalena delle Convertite al Corso – a comparison first proposed by Richard Spear.[12]

It has been suggested that Artemisia adopted the style of the Bolognese pope's predilect painter for her Burghley House *Susanna and the Elders*, in order to make her art more saleable to the Ludovisi family members and allies who had followed the pope to Rome. This hypothesis has two flaws. First of all, it is undermined by the fact that this excellent imitation of Guercino's painting style is a one-off: the lack of similar works in Artemisia's oeuvre shows that she did not consider this borrowed style to be useful for attracting patrons. Additionally, there is no reason to believe that Artemisia's style was ever an impediment to her business, since the critical reception of her works had always been very positive. An alternative explanation for the salient Guercinesque appearance of the *Susanna and the Elders* of 1622 is that this astonishingly rapid and perfect assimilation of Guercino's style was a kind of publicity stunt intended to grab the attention of the Roman art world, and above all, that of the Emilian artist himself.

Artemisia's reason for appealing to Guercino in such a sensational fashion is easy to imagine. He was a close associate of Agostino Tassi, whose re-establishment in Rome had shocked Artemisia when she returned to the city in 1620, as we read in her husband's letter to Maringhi of 2 March 1620.[13] By 1622, all of Rome, in fact, must have been abuzz with praise for Guercino and Tassi's ground-breaking collaboration on the richly colored and boldly illusionistic frescoes in the Casino dell'Aurora in Villa Boncompagni Ludovisi, carried out during the previous year. In light of the close connection between Guercino and the man who had raped her, conned her and then maligned her, Artemisia's choice of Saint Susanna as the subject for her Guercinesque painting is highly significant. The picture provided her strongest testimony against Tassi yet: posed like an iconic martyr in the center of the image, a saintly Susanna rouses the viewer's pity and inspires scorn for the men who would slander her.

Apart from the motivation for the Guercinesque treatment of Artemisia's 1622 *Susanna and the Elders*, one consequence is undeniable: the experiment spurred Artemisia to dial up the chromatic intensity to a level never before seen in her oeuvre. The colors that she chose for the figures' clothing reflect the narrative with their symbolic content – Susanna's towel is white for purity, one elder's tunic is the red of passion, and his companion's tunic is the purple

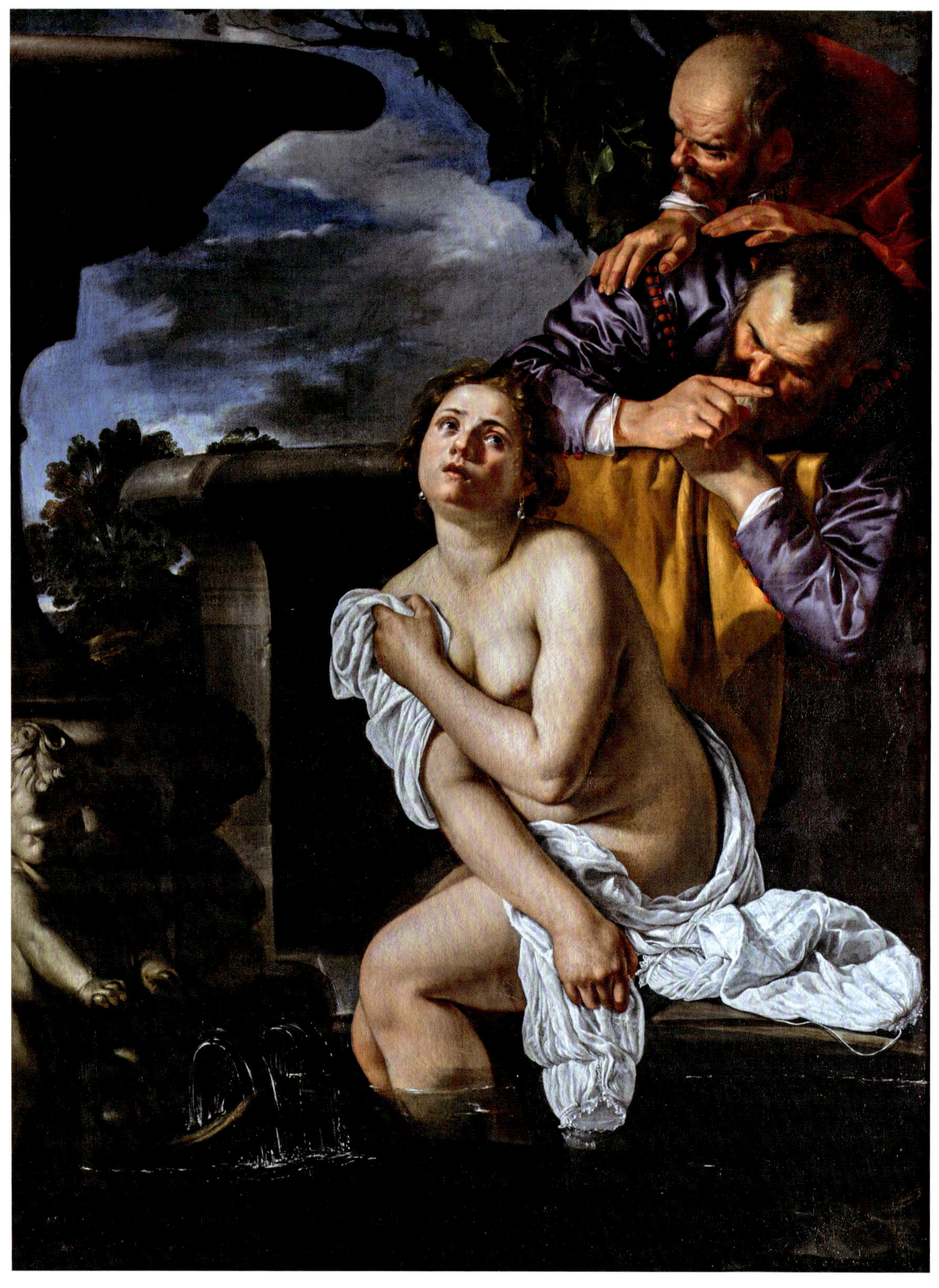

37 Artemisia Gentileschi, *Susanna and the Elders*, 1622, oil on canvas, 162.5 × 121.9 cm (64 × 48 in), The Burghley House Collection, Stamford, Lincolnshire

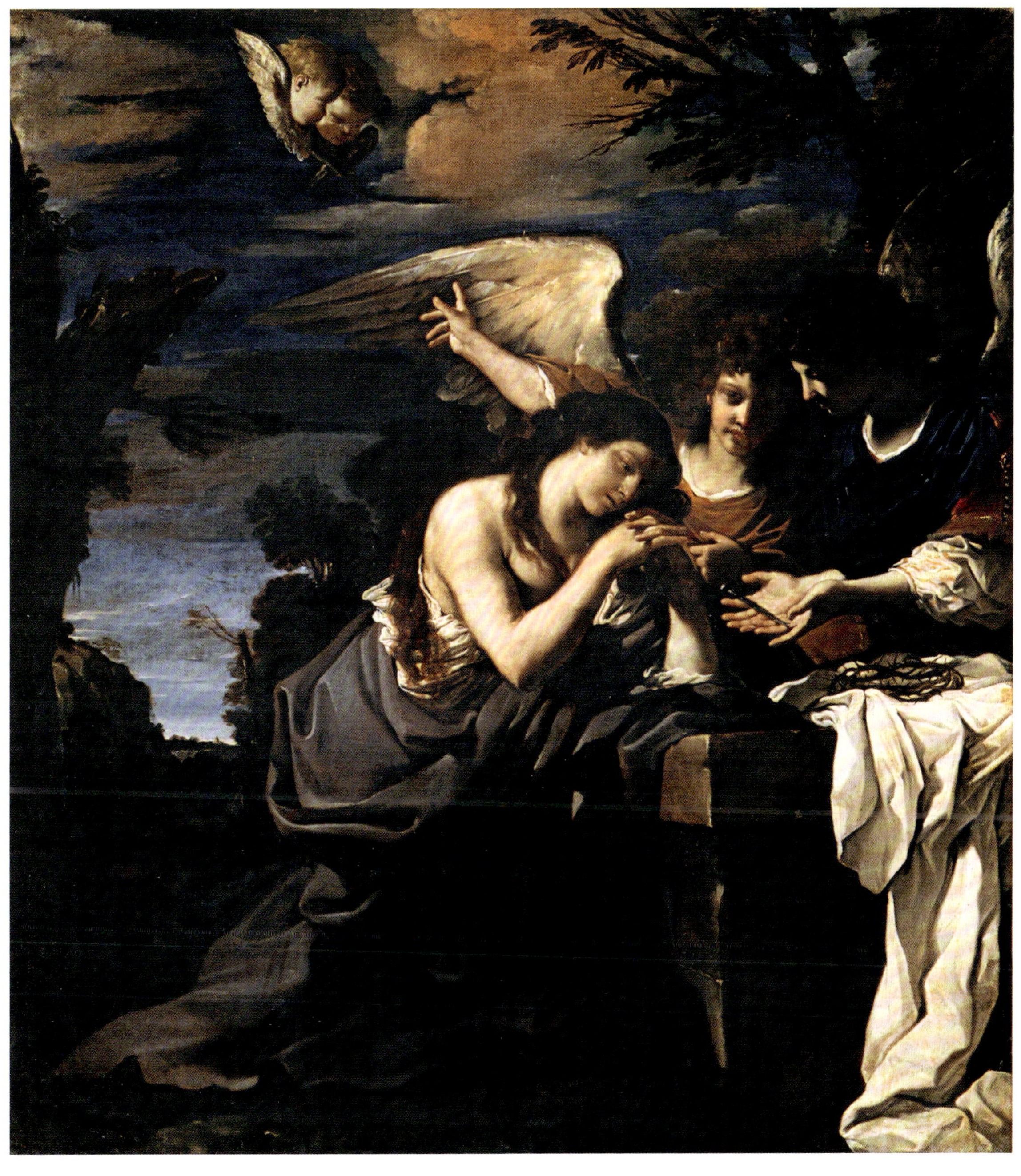

38 Guercino, *S. Maria Maddalena Penitente* [*The Penitent Saint Maria Magdalene*], 1622, oil on canvas, 222 × 200 cm (87 ⅜ × 78 ¾ in), Pinacoteca Vaticana (originally, Church of Santa Maria Maddalena delle Convertite al Corso), Vatican City

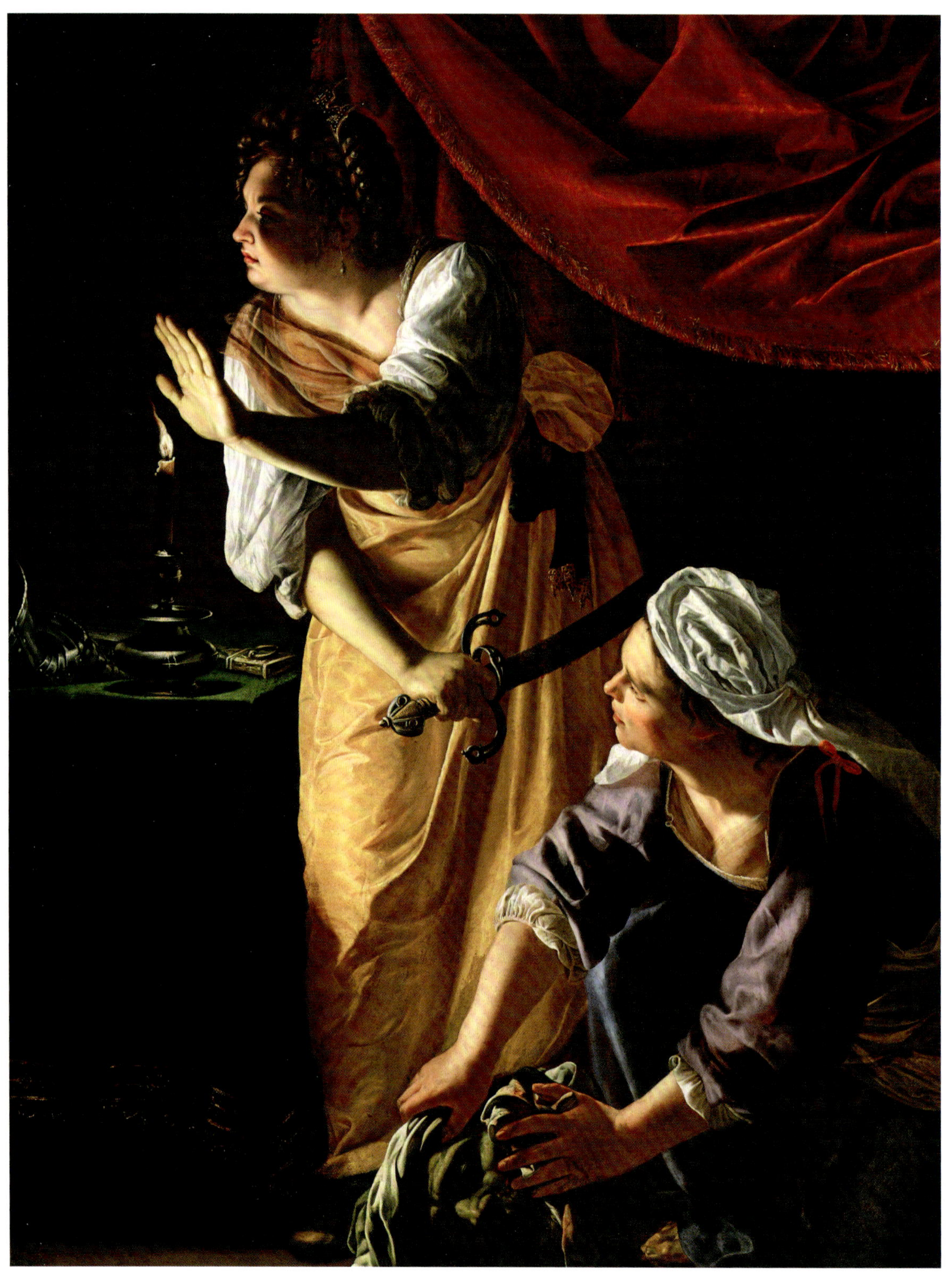

39 Artemisia Gentileschi, *Judith and Her Maidservant with the Head of Holofernes*, *c.*1624–7, oil on canvas, 187.2 × 142 cm (73 11⁄16 × 55 7⁄8 in), Detroit Institute of Arts

of the penitence that ought to follow sin – yet their material vibrancy gives them an inherent interest apart from the story. This is particularly true of the amethyst-purple color of the lower elder's tunic, a rich hue that seems never to have featured in Artemisia's palette before this moment.

Artemisia's new chromatic conquest immediately gave rise to a spate of paintings in which contrasting fields of purple and gold abut each other. Examples include the candlelit scene of *Judith and Her Maidservant with the Head of Holofernes* (*c.*1624–7) at the Detroit Institute of Arts (fig.39) and the *Mary Magdalene in Ecstasy* (*c.*1623–5) (fig.40) in a private European collection. Thanks to a technical study carried out on the latter painting in 2015 by the conservation department of the Royal Institute for Cultural Heritage (KIK-IRPA) in Brussels, we know that she achieved the purple coloring of the cloth – a symbolic allusion to the Magdalene's role as a model of penitence – by alternating between two hues, both made with a Mexican variety of cochineal scale insect recently introduced to the European market. One of these hues was a mix of carbon black and Mexican cochineal, and the other was a mix of the same cochineal and azurite blue. The significance of the composition of Artemisia's paints goes beyond questions of conservation. The evidence presented here points to Artemisia's enthusiasm for new artistic developments and her redoubtable technical know-how.

Amidst Artemisia's depictions of violent killings, music making and seductions, the *Mary Magdalene in Ecstasy* (*c.*1624–7) represents a momentary retreat into silence. Spurning the exuberant narrative impulses of the Baroque age, the image isolates the Magdalene's body in eremitic solitude. It shrouds her in darkness, it dispenses with her attributes, it minimises her action, and it eliminates almost all indication of her surroundings except for small plants on the cave wall, signaling that the Magdalene has entered Dante's 'selva oscura', the dark wood in which the penitent soul finds God. The tightly cropped composition brings us very close to the saint. This intimate connection with the Magdalene at first seems erotic due to the way her accidentally disordered chemise has exposed a plump, white shoulder draped with golden locks – a reminder of her former sins. Yet the Magdalene's body remains pure and inviolable under the seal of her lips, her tightly shut eyes, her clasped hands and her chastely locked knees. These subtle clues, together with a painfully rigid, sleep-inhibiting posture that no sentient body could maintain for long, an expression of perfect intellectual clarity, and a warm light that bathes her torso, all suggest she has departed the sensorial world in a most supernatural way. In the iconography of ecstatic female mystics, Artemisia's *Mary Magdalene in Ecstasy* furnishes the critical middle link between Caravaggio's brutally gaunt and ascetic representation of an insensate saint in his widely copied *Mary Magdalene in Ecstasy* of 1606 and Gian Lorenzo Bernini's disquietingly sensual sculpture of *Saint Theresa of Avila in Ecstasy* from 1642–57.

The significance of *Mary Magdalene in Ecstasy* within Artemisia's oeuvre cannot be overstated. With its pregnant solitude and resplendent interiority, the image succeeds in giving visual expression to the divine ardor held up by her era as its highest spiritual ideal. The work does not merely represent a mystic in prayer; it also conducts the viewer into the meditative quiet that is the initial stage of ecstatic prayer. This process begins when the viewer's eye surveys the sea of white linen that ripples, puckers and coils with a dizzying complexity. The tired eye finds refuge from this tumult within large and languorous purple folds. Finally, the eye fathoms the surrounding darkness. In the process of making this image with repetitive movements and unwavering concentration, hour after hour, Artemisia must have had to achieve her own interior vision and perhaps even shut off her senses to the world beyond her canvas.

Multiple commissions of religious subjects given to Artemisia in these years attest to the suitability of her devotional imagery to the spiritual dispositions of her contemporaries – particularly

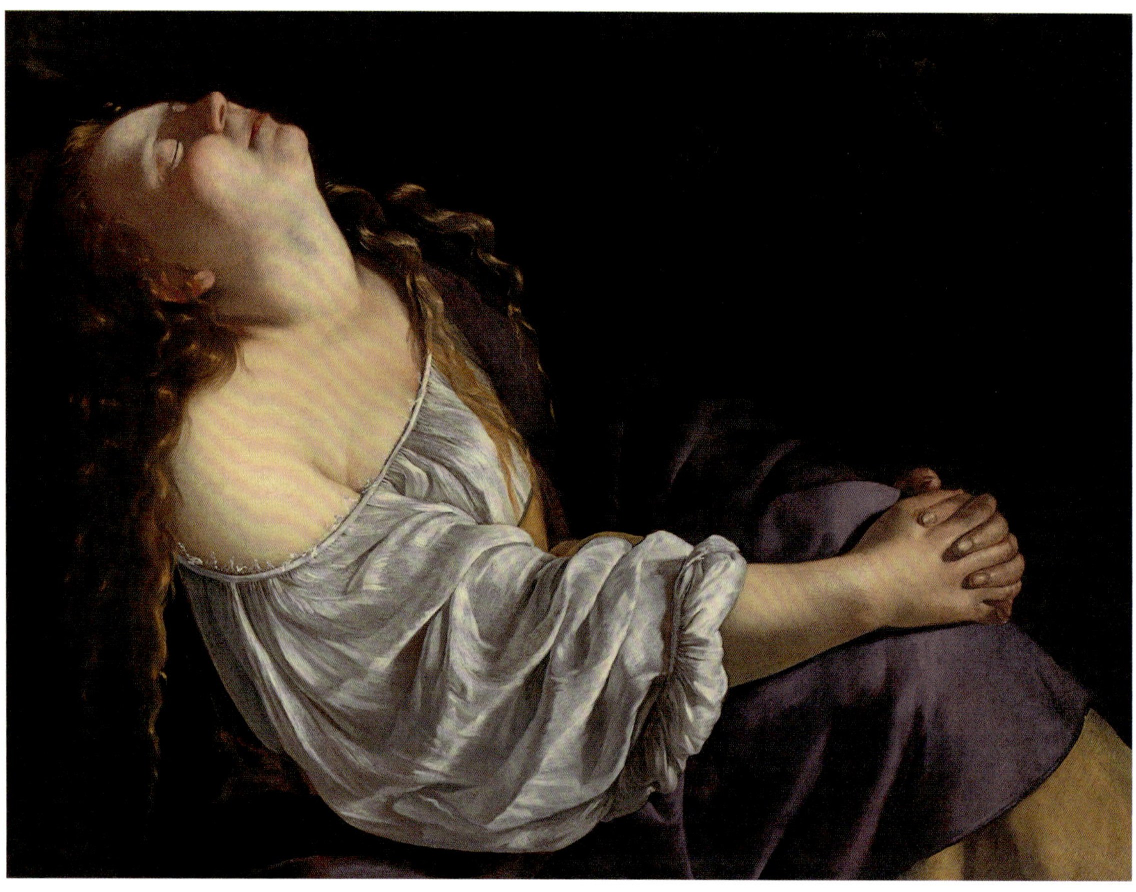

40 Artemisia Gentileschi, *Mary Magdalene in Ecstasy*, *c.*1623–5, oil on cavas, 81 × 105 cm (31 ⅞ × 41 5⁄16 in), private European collection

the Spanish nobility. Between 1625 and 1626, the Spanish ambassador to the Holy See, Fernando Afán Enríquez de Ribera, 3rd Duke of Alcalá, gave Artemisia three commissions for religious subjects: *The Penitent Magdalene* at the Cathedral of Seville, *Christ Blessing the Children* (now at the Arciconfraternita dei Santi Ambrogio e Carlo in Rome, signed and dated '1626' on the back), and a lost *David with His Harp*. While the patrons were largely responsible for choosing the subjects, it is nonetheless remarkable that penitential imagery – particularly the Magdalenes, but also David as the repentant psalmist – played such a prominent role in her religious imagery of this period. It is merely a suggestion, but perhaps her own religious expressions of contrition or her practice of penitence had led her patrons in Rome to single her out for interpretations of penitential saints.

Any one of a number of personal crises could have nudged Artemisia towards a more devout religious life. However, serendipity also factored into her newfound appreciation of affective piety and meditative prayer, since the 'bella casa' [stately home] that she and Pierantonio rented happened to be very close to the church of Santa Maria in Vallicella, also known as the Chiesa Nuova.[14] The Chiesa Nuova served as the Roman headquarters of the Oratorian Congregation founded by Saint Filippo Neri (1515–95), the charismatic spiritual leader known for his asceticism and frequent ecstasies, much like Saint Theresa of Avila. Through the encouragement of the Ludovisi pope, both Neri and Theresa were canonised in 1622, a process that led to widespread interest in their visionary experiences of God through ecstatic, non-verbal meditations.

Artemisia's artistic affinity with Oratorian spirituality should not surprise us. The two great artistic polestars of her youth both gave visual expression to the Oratorian movement with deeply affective paintings: Caravaggio painted his celebrated *Entombment of Christ* (1603) for the Chiesa Nuova, whereas Orazio Gentileschi painted his *Saint Francis Supported by an Angel* (1612) (fig.41) for Filippo Neri's earlier Oratorian church, San Girolamo della Carità. Upon her return to Rome as an independent artist, Artemisia must have looked with fresh eyes at her father's *Saint Francis Supported by an Angel*, a canvas that Ward Bissell hailed as Orazio's first truly Caravaggesque work.[15] She must have also appreciated its use of light to convey Saint Francis' mystical union with God during his ecstatic vision, the near-total elimination of any setting, and the chilling impenetrability of the dark night that envelopes the figure.

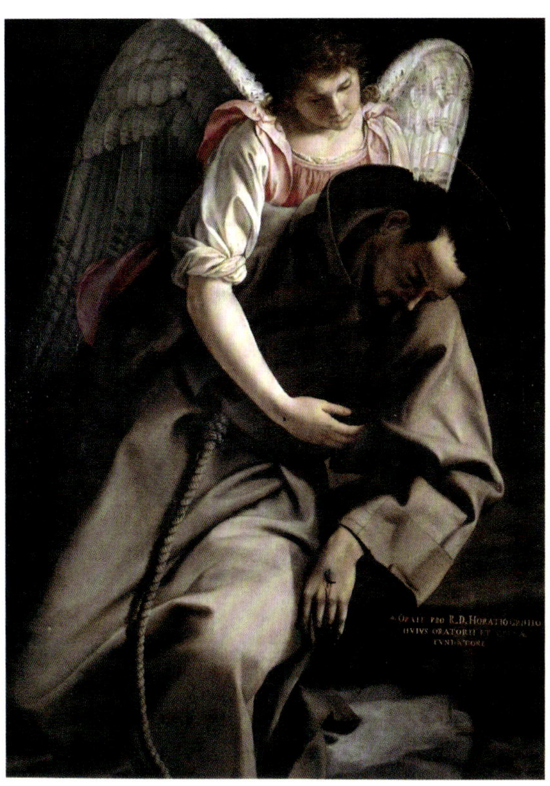

41 Orazio Gentileschi, *Saint Francis Supported by an Angel*, *c.*1612, oil on canvas, 139.4 × 101 cm (54 ⅞ × 39 ¾ in), Galleria Nazionale d'Arte Antica di Palazzo Barberini, Rome

Sharing Artemisia's interest in the religious life at the Chiesa Nuova was the nobleman Pietro della Valle (1586–1652). After a twelve-year journey through India, Turkey, Persia and the Holy Land, Della Valle settled back in his family's large Roman palace on 28 March 1626. He lived here with his second wife, Tinatin de Ziba of Georgia, while gravitating to the court of the reigning pope, Urban VIII Barberini (*r.*1623–44), who honored Della Valle with an appointment as a Gentleman of the Papal Bedchamber. Like other broad-minded members of the Barberini entourage, including his friends Cassiano dal Pozzo and Athanasius Kircher, Della Valle nurtured a deep curiosity about other civilisations. The notes in his travel journal cover such erudite topics as the differences between Egyptian and Hindu beliefs in reincarnation and his discovery of cuneiform inscriptions among the ruins of the ancient Sumerian cities of Nineveh and Ur. Della Valle also composed musical scores, and his involvement in Oratorian spirituality culminated in his contribution, in 1641, to the genre of musical oratorios, a mode of performance that did away with costumes, scenography and staging, in order to focus on the stories told with words and music alone.

A discovery made by music historian Eric Bianchi of an exchange of sonnets between Artemisia and Pietro della Valle – two by her, and two by him – confirms the painter's friendship with the Roman composer.[16] It also answers a lingering, and rather prophetic doubt of Roberto Contini, who mused in 2001 that 'the image of an Artemisia who was well read, intellectually engaged, and a fixture of cultural salons [. . .] would greatly increase the complexity of her personality'.[17]

The probable window for the dating of these sonnets is between April 1626, following Della Valle's return to Rome, and either late 1626 or early 1627, when Artemisia left Rome for Venice. Their content could be termed a 'mutual admiration society', since both poets speak of the desire to celebrate the other's multiple and prodigious talents. Artemisia here is praised as a painter and a singer, while Della Valle is praised for his travels and his verse. Notably, Artemisia initiated this exchange of sonnets. As noted in the title of the first of the four sonnets, she did so on the occasion of Della Valle's visit to her workshop:

Al sig.r Pietro della Valle mio sig.re in venire a veder le mie opere

Valle, che gia tutt' il mondano chiostro
cauto varcasti sotto varie stelle,
ecco quì l'opre mie queste son quelle,
chè fan quasi vergognia al secol' nostro.
Se'l mio non è, chiaro, e famoso inchiostro,
ne le pitture son loquaci, e belle,
il vostro stil vorrei, l'arte d'Apelle,
sol per farmi più grata al voler vostro.
Ma non vole il pennel la voglia mia
far satia, e'l Dio che ha in vera il sacro fonte
mi troncha ognhor' i passi a mezza via.
Chè se d'allori mi ingesse il fronte,
hor cantando, hor pingendo spereria
erger voi VALLE piu d'ogn'alto monte.

To Lord Pietro della Valle my lord, upon his visit to see my paintings

Valle, you that already crossed cautiously under various stars
The cloister garden of the world,
Here are my works, which are those
That almost bring shame to our era.
Since my ink is neither splendid nor famous,
And my pictures neither loquacious nor beautiful,
I wish for your style and the technique of Apelles
Just to make myself more pleasing in my service to you.
But the brush does not want to satisfy
My desires, and God who truly has the sacred source
Always cuts off my progress half-way,
And so if you set laurels around my head,
Now singing, now painting, I would hope
To raise you, VALLE, above every high mountain.[18]

Artemitia Gentileschi

These exalted exchanges between Artemisia and Della Valle testify to Artemisia's subtle intellect and her attainment of a gloss of the poetic skills that were the delightful currency of polite society in Italy. They also confirmed her ambition to be associated with the greatest of all poet-artists, Michelangelo Buonarroti, whose sonnets about the making of art and his relationships with patrons, lovers and God were compiled, censored and published by Michelangelo Buonarroti the Younger in 1623 as *Rime di Michelagnolo Buonarroti: Raccolte da Michelagnolo suo Nipote*.[19] Artemisia's knowledge of Michelangelo's sonnets is not certain, although she did employ one of their key metaphors – the artist as a barren tree – in her letter to the Duke of Modena of 25 January 1635, as first noted by Francesco Solinas.[20] It is quite possible that Artemisia owned a copy of Buonarroti the Younger's edition of his great-uncle's *Rime*.

Artemisia's dexterity in the verbal arts would later be recognised by two literary academies in Venice. For Artemisia, however, writing poetry was no mere divertissement: it was serious business. Like her expensive clothes, jewels and the house she kept 'fit for a gentleman to visit and to live in', with expensive gold-embossed leather wall panels, Artemisia's ability to converse adroitly, to write compelling business letters, and to compose clever sonnets facilitated her access to the circles of the moneyed patrons who might give her commissions.[21] Indeed, a similar motivation lay behind her frequent engagement with portrait painting during the period she spent in Rome. As Artemisia once explained to the Neapolitan painter Massimo Stanzione, painting portraits 'served only as a means of acquiring the good graces of those who might then give [the painter] more worthy kinds of commissions'.[22]

If Artemisia professed a disdain for portraiture, she nevertheless used self-portraiture to promote her celebrity and welcomed other artists' requests to depict her. Her likeness can be found in a sketch by Leonaert Bramer (1620); in Nicolas Régnier's *Cardsharps and the Fortune Teller* of *c.*1620–22 (Szépművészeti Múzeum, Budapest) (fig.42); in Simon Vouet's portrait (*c.*1623–6) from Palazzo Blu in Pisa (fig.43); in Pierre Dumonstier II's drawing of her hand (1625); in the bronze medal that an unknown artist crafted around the same year; and even perhaps in Valentin de Boulogne's *Herodias (or Salome) with the Head of Saint John the Baptist* (*c.*1626) at Galleria Spada. These, like the costumed self-portraits that she made in Florence, were vehicles for her fame. Yet, while these portraits undoubtedly benefitted Artemisia's career, they also should be recognised as evidence of her amicable nature, her social skills and the degree to which her colleagues sought her friendship well beyond pragmatic workshop collaborations. Artemisia's ability to strike up friendships first emerged in Florence, where she had asked the painter Cristofano Allori to serve as godfather to the son she named after him, and it would hold true for her future stays in Venice, where she befriended Giovanna Garzoni, and in Naples, too, where she offered Massimo Stanzione instruction and advice.

AN INTERLUDE IN VENICE INTERRUPTED BY PLAGUE

Despite this thickening skein of friendships with artists, intellectuals and patrons, Artemisia left Rome for Venice, either in late 1626 or early 1627, probably without her husband. (In fact, the Roman parish records published by Rossella Vodret show no trace of Pierantonio Stiattesi after 1622.[23]) The move to Venice is the only one of Artemisia's displacements for which no compelling explanation has yet emerged. As noted by Letizia Treves, two of Artemisia's painter-friends – Nicolas Régnier (1591–1667) and Simon Vouet (1590–1649) – also transplanted from Rome to Venice at this time, in 1626 and 1627 respectively.[24] Although Régnier's and Vouet's similar movements may have furnished Artemisia with convenient travel partners to share the expense and to diminish the dangers of the road, they do not suffice to explain why she embraced the risk, hassle and expense of an international move from the capital of the Papal See to the capital of the Venetian Republic. Of course, Venice, a vibrant port city, served as a launching pad for other destinations. It is thus also possible that Artemisia went to Venice with the intention of ranging even further abroad. Her conversations with Della Valle about his astonishing adventures in the Levant and south Asia may have even planted a bit of wanderlust in her heart.

If, indeed, Artemisia went to Venice in order press onward in her travels, then her ultimate plan may have been to join up with her father at the court of King Charles I of England. In October of 1626, Orazio had gone to London at the behest of George Villiers, the Duke of Buckingham. After carrying out diplomatic work in Brussels on behalf of the British crown, Orazio would remain in England

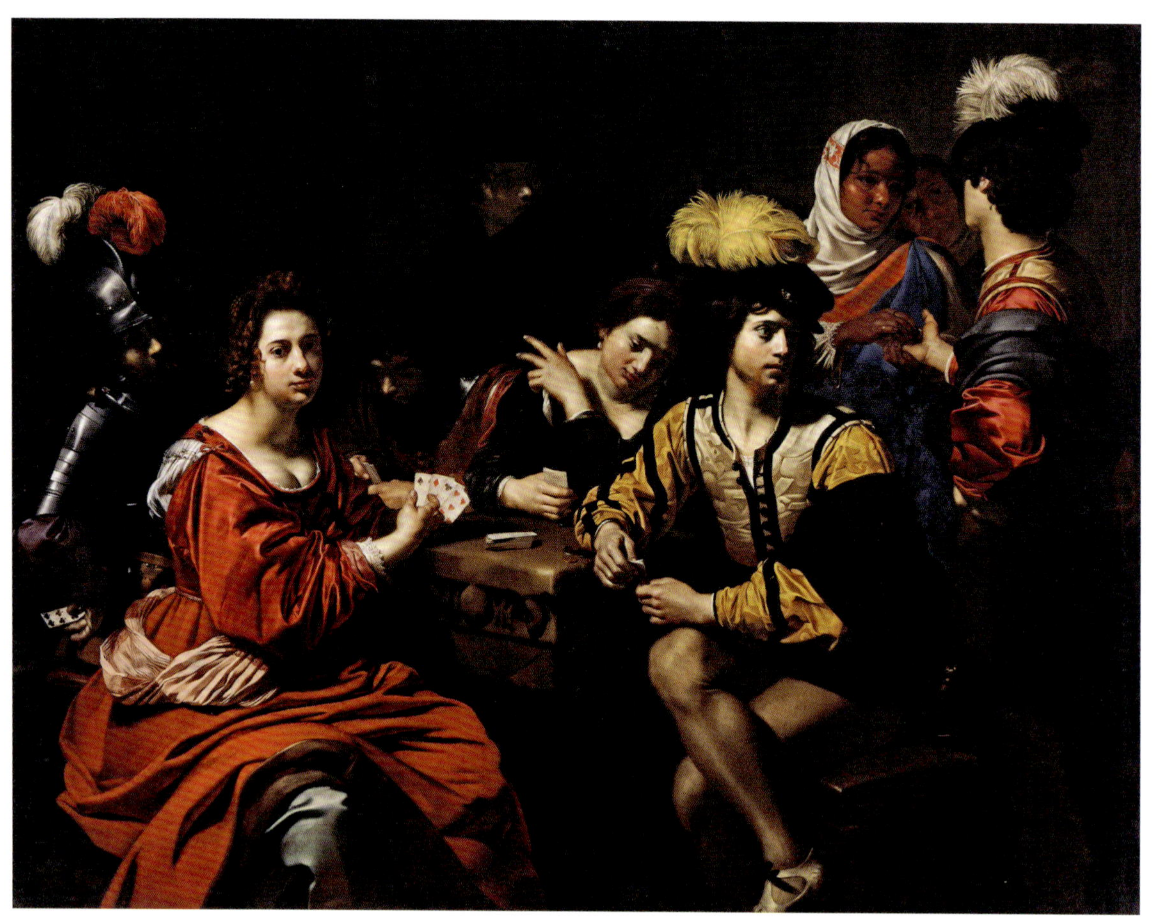

42 Nicolas Régnier, *Cardsharps and the Fortune Teller*, *c.*1620–22, oil on canvas, 174 × 228 cm (68 ½ × 89 ¾ in), Szépművészeti Múzeum/Museum of Fine Arts, Budapest

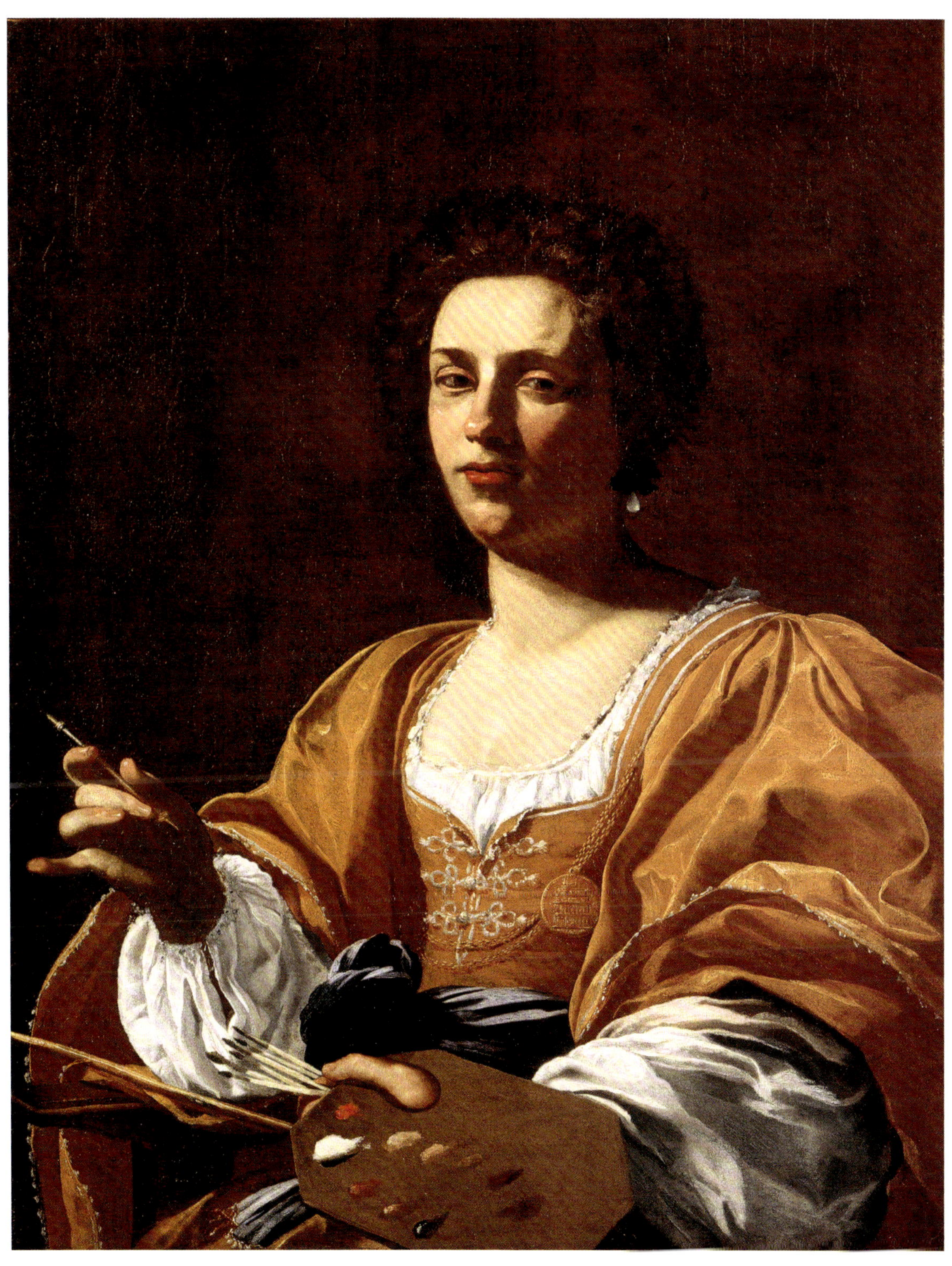

43 Simon Vouet, *Portrait of Artemisia Gentileschi with Painting Implements*, *c.*1623–6, oil on canvas, 90 × 71 cm (35 ½ × 28 in), Palazzo Blu, Pisa. Property of the Fondazione Pisa

with his sons for the rest of his life, although not always contentedly.

Orazio's sons Giulio and Francesco were employed by the King to make courier trips between London and Italy, and for this purpose they made at least two trips to Venice after Artemisia's arrival in the city, first in September through November of 1627, then again in April of 1628. While in Venice, Giulio and Francesco were supplied with money by Nicholas Lanier, a musician and amateur painter whom Charles I had sent abroad to buy the best available Italian paintings for his collection. These business meetings with Lanier afforded Artemisia's brothers many opportunities to pressure the English musician into recommending Artemisia to his King. Lanier met Artemisia at this time and even fell 'in love' with her, according to the diary of Richard Symonds.[25] Thus, in Venice the seeds were sown for Artemisia's eventual invitation to the court of London.

Two acts of fate thwarted Artemisia's early plans to go to England. One was the assassination in August of 1628 of Orazio's primary patron in England, the Duke of Buckingham, an event that created serious economic problems for Artemisia's father and generally disquieted the London court. The other was the lucrative commission for a lost *Hercules and Omphale* that she received that same year from Philip IV of Spain – Charles I's greatest rival in art collecting – through the Conde de Oñate, the Spanish Ambassador to Rome. Thanks to Véronique Gerard's archival discovery, we know that the King paid Artemisia 1,467 *giulii* for that work – a princely sum well in excess of the annual wages of the average artisan, and more than enough money to make her rethink any previous travel plans.[26]

Artemisia's reputation was soaring at this time. Her *Hercules and Omphale* was part of a series for which the Conde de Oñate had also commissioned paintings from the highest earning painters in all of Europe: Domenichino and Guido Reni, rival exponents of the Bolognese School of painting. Once Artemisia's canvas arrived in Madrid, the King had it hung in the Salón Nuevo of the Alcázar in Madrid directly across from a pendant of the same size: Van Dyck's *Achilles Discovered by Ulysses and Diomedes*. However, around a decade later Philip IV changed his mind about Artemisia's work, replacing it with Rubens' *Hercules and Antaeus* in 1641 – this being the date when Artemisia's painting disappeared from the record. Steven N. Orso has suggested that Artemisia's painting, formerly valued so highly, was later deemed inappropriate because its subject invoked the *Weibermacht* theme of the emasculated male, thus undermining the celebration of ruling Habsburg men.[27]

The discomfiture that Artemisia's *Hercules and Omphale* must have caused in the context of a deeply patriarchal propaganda program stemmed from the subject itself, one which had been determined by the patron and which cannot be blamed on the artist. Moreover, this is not the case of a mistake: it is unthinkable that a sophisticated man like the Conde de Oñate could have been unaware of the humorous reversal of normative gender hierarchy in the subject that he assigned to Artemisia. Perhaps the Conde de Oñate even meant for the pairing of her *Hercules and Omphale* and Van Dyck's *Achilles Discovered by Ulysses and Diomedes* to stand in opposition to each other and simulate a gender *paragone*, or a battle of the sexes, as fodder for entertaining conversations at the Spanish court in which the ladies could certainly participate.

We can be sure that the Conde de Oñate's assignment of this subject to a female artist took into account Artemisia's personal character – her charm, spirited nature and self-assurance – as a way to galvanise the piquant subject and bring it to life. Artemisia herself had encouraged her patrons to think of her not just as a painter but also as an alluring and celebrated woman. She did this by unabashedly proliferating her own likeness, appearing frequently in self-portraits, in costumed self-portraits and in portraits of her by others. She may have even instigated Jérôme David's engraving of *c.*1627–8 after her self-portrait, one that celebrates her as both a literary academician and as a painter.

The commission from the Conde de Oñate shows that Artemisia's imagery of courageous, self-possessed and spirited women enjoyed remarkable success among the male luminaries of her era. Nevertheless, it did not always please other women of her time, including those most invested in the literary defence of women's equal status. Mary D. Garrard's research has recently shed light on the surprising ideological division between Artemisia and Venice's famous contemporary feminist writers. As Garrard explains with penetrating clarity, 'in both life and art, [Artemisia] embraced contradictions the feminist writers tended to compartmentalise into virtue and vice'.[28] This was the case with the Venetian writer and polemicist Lucrezia Marinella (1571–1653). Like Artemisia, Marinella lived her own ideal vision of womanhood. For Marinella, however, this meant a life of chastity, strict morality, pure customs and a scrupulous avoidance of anything that might sully her reputation.

The feminism that Marinella promoted was a constricting, narrow path that would not have allowed Artemisia to exercise her art with the latitude that her creative genius required, nor could she have taken advantage of her carefully cultivated charisma, charm and beauty when struggling to promote her career. It is thus understandable that Artemisia instead found female companionship in Venice with a kindred artist-spirit like herself. This friend was Giovanna Garzoni (1600–70), a talented young woman who had already mastered a number of artistic arenas, from large-scale religious painting, to calligraphy, to portrait miniatures.

Artemisia and Garzoni were initially brought together by their decision to pursue art professionally. Soon they must have discovered that they also shared disillusionment with married life and a touch of scandal as a result of their disappointing entanglements with men. Moreover, both women had visited the Medici court, and both had attempted to gain Archduchess Maria Magdalena's favour with no luck. Then, unexpectedly, their destinies were temporarily united by an unforeseen danger. Beginning in late 1629, terrifying rumours began arriving in Venice of an outbreak of bubonic plague among the soldiers returning home from a campaign in Germany, and it suddenly seemed prudent to pack up and move south ahead of the deadly epidemic. On horseback or by carriage, the two women left town together in early 1630 with an entourage that included Garzoni's brother, Artemisia's daughter and Artemisia's unnamed 'consort' (who seems more likely to have been her lover, Francesco Maria Maringhi, rather than her husband, Pierantonio Stiattesi).[29] Whereas Garzoni hung back in Rome a bit to make botanical illustrations for the *virtuosi* of the papal court, Artemisia pressed on until she reached Naples, the pullulating capital of Spanish Italy.

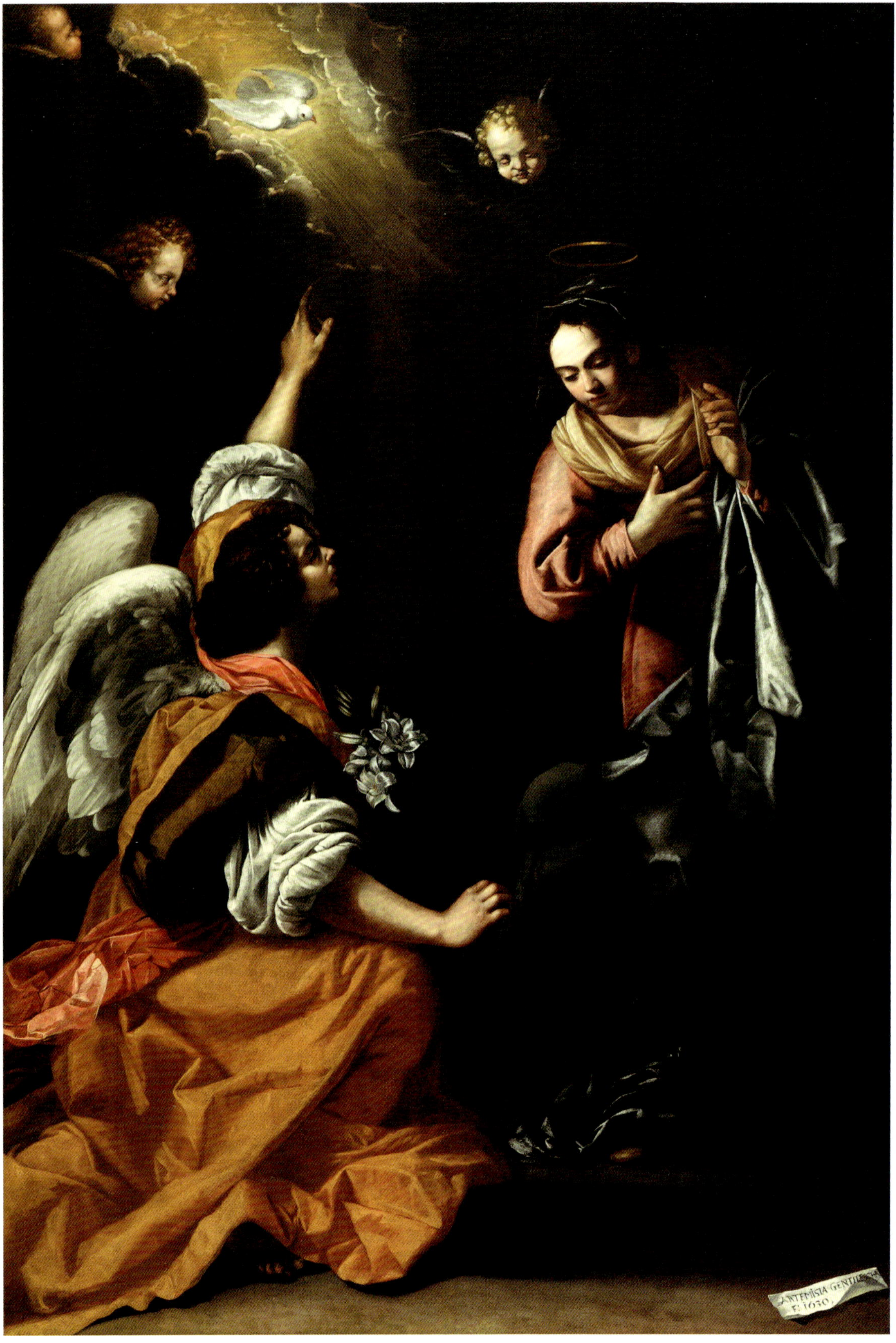
ARTEMÌSIA GENTIL
F: 1630,

4

Operating on a World Stage: Naples to London and Back

Artemisia's decision to go all the way to Naples, where her father had never set foot, was probably not meant to be definitive. Nevertheless, except for her stay in England between 1638 and 1640, Naples would be her home for the rest of her life. Following a suggestion first made by Jonathan Brown and Richard L. Kagan, Artemisia's willingness to venture so far from family can surely be attributed to an invitation to join the court of the powerful Spanish viceroy, the Duke of Alcalá, who envisioned that she and her companion Garzoni would enrich the entourage of the Infanta María Ana of Spain (1606–46) during her imminent visit to Naples to receive the honor of the Golden Rose from Pope Urban VIII Barberini.[1]

Upon settling in Naples, Artemisia put all her energy into this new opportunity for Spanish patronage. As she explained to Cassiano dal Pozzo in a letter of 24 August 1630, his own commission for her self-portrait would have to wait, because she needed first to finish several pictures for the aforementioned Infanta, daughter of King Philip IV and bride of the future Holy Roman Emperor Ferdinand III, who was expected to arrive by sea the next month.[2] The Duke of Alcalá had already acquired three paintings of religious subjects by Artemisia during his two-year post in Rome as the Spanish ambassador to the Holy See. Before the end of his viceroyalty in May of 1631, he commissioned from Artemisia yet another religious subject – a lost *Saint John the Baptist* – as well as several portraits, which, as noted above, were an art form she undertook as a means of encouraging new patrons to entrust her with more challenging and more costly commissions.

A PLAGUE-TIME ALTARPIECE FOR THE GENOESE IN NAPLES

One such commission – her first altarpiece in fact – came to her very shortly after her transfer to Naples: *The Annunciation* in the Capodimonte Museum that is signed and dated 'Artemisia Gentilescha F. 1630' on a *cartellino* in the bottom right of the image (fig.44). Once associated with the Neapolitan church of San Giorgio dei Genovesi, it is now unclear for which church this altarpiece was made. Ward Bissell has proposed that its patron – whom I suspect was a Genoese resident in Naples – asked Artemisia to repeat the subject and even the poses used in her father's altarpiece of the *Annunciation* in the church of San Siro in Genoa, which Orazio had painted around 1622 while living in that city (fig.45).[3] Although it has been established by Anna Orlando that Artemisia never travelled to Genoa, she could have known something of her father's San Siro *Annunciation* from drawings. Such drawings could have easily been made and sent to her by her brother

44 Artemisia Gentileschi, *The Annunciation*, signed and dated 1630, oil on canvas, 257 × 179 cm (101 ⅛ × 70 ½ in), Capodimonte Museum, Naples

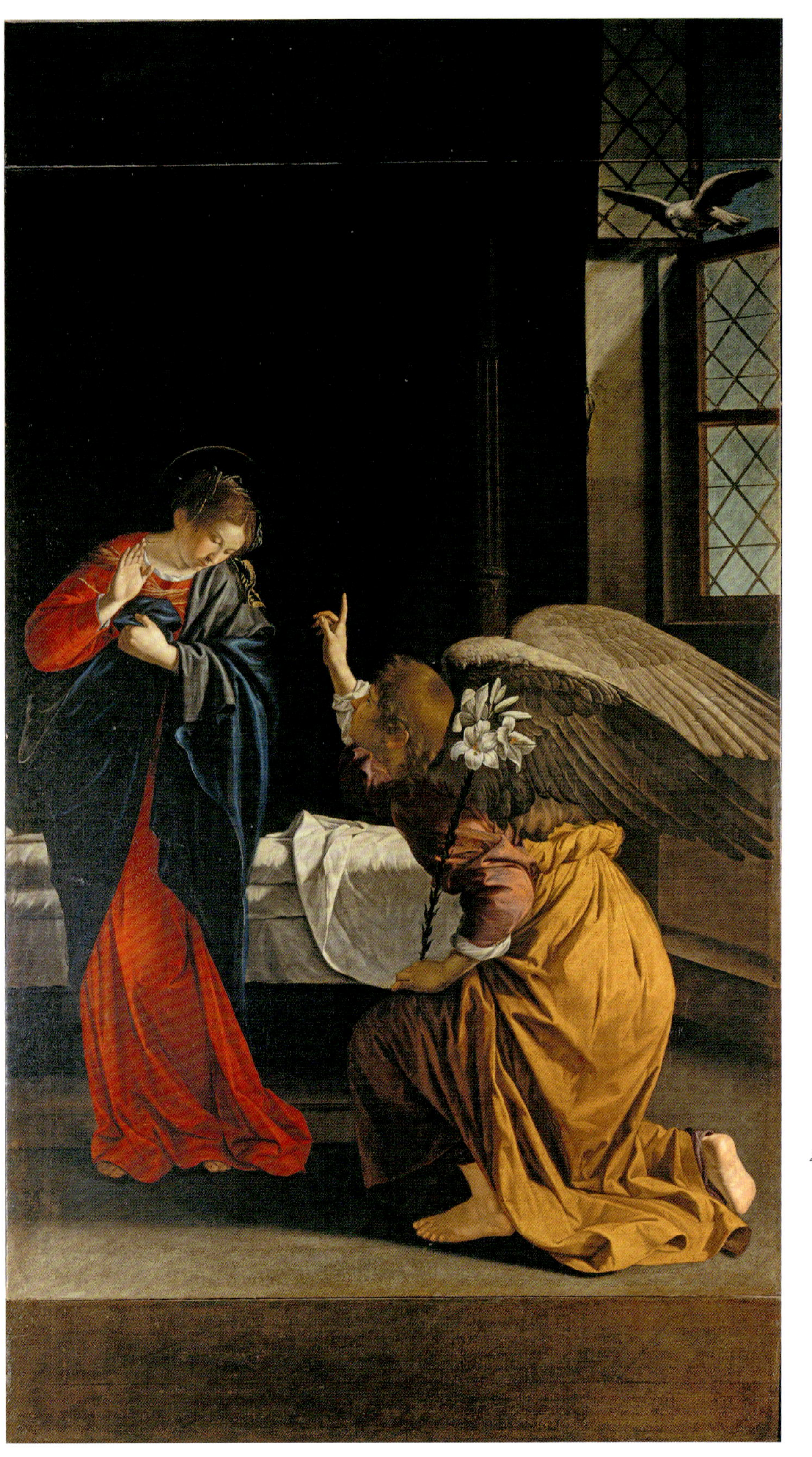

45 Orazio Gentileschi, *The Annunciation*, *c.*1622, oil o canvas, 281 × 157 cm (110 × 61 13⁄16 in) (original size 225 × 157 cm [88 5⁄8 × 61 13 in]), Basilica di San Siro, Genoa

Giulio, who settled in Genoa in 1630, the year that Artemisia made her altarpiece.[4]

In both Artemisia's and Orazio's treatments of the Annunciation subject, the angel kneels on the ground and points to the dove of the Holy Spirit. Mary, by contrast, remains standing, dipping her head in deference to her celestial messenger while holding one hand out and bringing the other to her chest. The patron who asked Artemisia to replicate the actions of the figures in Orazio's Genoese altarpiece evidently did not request her to replicate its style, since Artemisia's painting deviates notably from the style of her father's prototype, as will be discussed below. The patron's interest in maintaining the poses appears to have been motivated by their theological associations. As first noticed by Riccardo Lattuada, Artemisia's and Orazio's paintings differ from the vast majority of sixteenth- and seventeenth-century Annunciation scenes in which the angel Gabriel flies in the air with his head well above Mary's head.[5] Harkening back to a composition-type popular in the Quattrocento (such as in Filippo Lippi's *Murate Annunciation* of 1443, now in the Alte Pinakothek in Munich), Orazio's design puts Mary's head substantially higher than Gabriel's head. In an era when genuflection and bowing were strictly observed ceremonial protocols, and relative head positions were direct indicators of status, Orazio's compositional poses would have been understood by contemporary audiences to accord Mary a superior status in the hierarchy of divine Creation. This had far-reaching religious implications, for it would only be possible for her to be superior to an angel under the then-controversial dogma (which became an official doctrine only in the nineteenth century) of the Immaculate Conception, that is, the belief that Mary was conceived without sin.

Artemisia replicated Orazio's composition, yet she made it her own by means of a stylistic overhaul that transformed his historical narrative into a visionary experience. With a keen sensitivity to the admixture of asceticism and emotional intimacy at play in mystical piety, she eliminated Orazio's mundane setting of realistic furniture and architecture, leaving nothing except a hint of a green bed canopy; she cast the scene in utter darkness and omitted the window, perhaps to match the funereal shade of Domenico Fiasella's *Crucifixion* on the high altar; and she enlarged the figures to fill the frame, overspilling its edges. In this windowless interior, the sudden eruption of light illuminating Mary's ivory skin takes on a miraculous connotation: it is God's divine presence. In contrast to the lifeless fabrics in Orazio's pedestrian enactment of the scene, the robes of

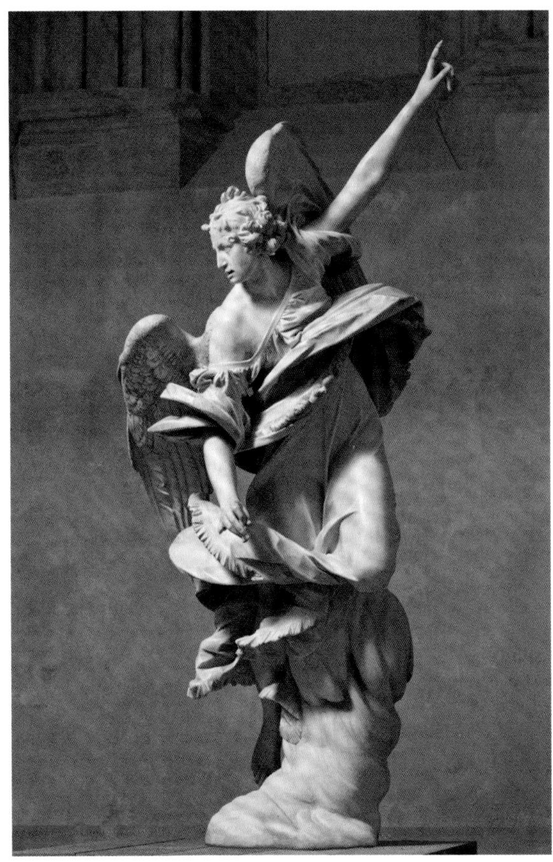

46 Francesco Mochi, *The Angel of the Annunciation*, c.1603–5, marble, height: 185 cm (72 ⅞ in), Museo dell'Opera del Duomo, Orvieto

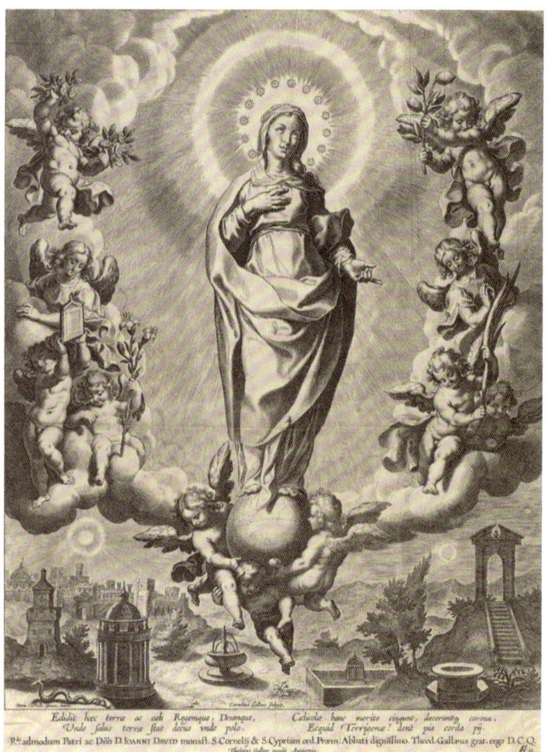

47 Cornelis Galle, *Virgin Immaculate (The Virgin in Glory)*, *c.*1602, engraving, sheet (trimmed): 36.9 × 27.5 cm (14 ½ × 10 13⁄16 in), The Metropolitan Museum of Art, New York

Artemisia's angel – the sleeves in particular – billow and coruscate with no apparent natural cause, evoking the riotous, anti-gravitational pirouettes of the angels' costumes sculpted by Francesco Mochi (fig.46) and Pietro Bernini around the turn of the century. Even Mary's blue mantle seems to ripple and flutter near the floor as if filled with divine wind, flashing brightly and evoking the open cloak that symbolized the protection (*tutela matris*) offered by the Virgin as Mater Misericordia.

As noticed first by Riccardo Lattuada, in the aspects where Artemisia departed most boldly from her father's model, she looked instead to an older altarpiece by a local artist: Scipione Pulzone's 1578 *Annunciation* (fig.48).[6] Perhaps Artemisia's patron brought Pulzone's work – which once hung in the church of San Domenico in Gaeta – to her attention; otherwise, as Lattuada has pointed out, she may have come upon the painting during her recent journey to Naples, since Gaeta is a natural overnight stop between Rome and Naples. But if her encounter with Pulzone's altarpiece was accidental, her use of it was purposeful: all three of the motifs she gleaned from it furnish visible proof of God's presence: the heavenward pointing gesture of the angel, the effulgent golden clouds and the uncanny electric charge that warps the angel's sleeve.

Along with these stylistic adaptations, Artemisia also introduced a subtle change in the Virgin Mary's pose that held theological significance. Instead of following Orazio's precedent of having the Virgin Mary use her interior arm to cover herself in a gesture of pudor, she instead makes Mary hold her heart. This gesture of solemn declaration seems to allude to Mary's participation in the redemption of mankind's sins ('I am the handmaid of the Lord'). Artemisia may have culled this motif not only from Pulzone's painting, but also from a key image for the cult of the Virgin Mary that her patron may perhaps have seen: Cornelis Galle's widely circulated *Virgin Immaculate* engraving from *c.*1602 (fig.47), which is roughly based on Bernardo Castello's altarpiece of that name in the church of San Francesco d'Albaro in Genoa, as shown by Jamie Gabbarelli.[7]

At this time, theological debates made it controversial to dedicate new altars to the polarizing Feast of the Immaculate Conception. Nevertheless, with the plague of 1630 concurrently ravaging not only Venice as mentioned before, but also Genoa, perhaps a Genoese resident of Naples sought to invoke the Immaculate Virgen's protection through Artemisia's altarpiece. The Genoese Republic had made vows to the Immacolata during the plagues of 1450 ('ut Virgo Urbem nostram liberet a pestilentia') and 1579, as noted by Laura Stagno.[8] Answering her patron's dilemma, Artemisia's ambivalent iconographical interpretation presented an

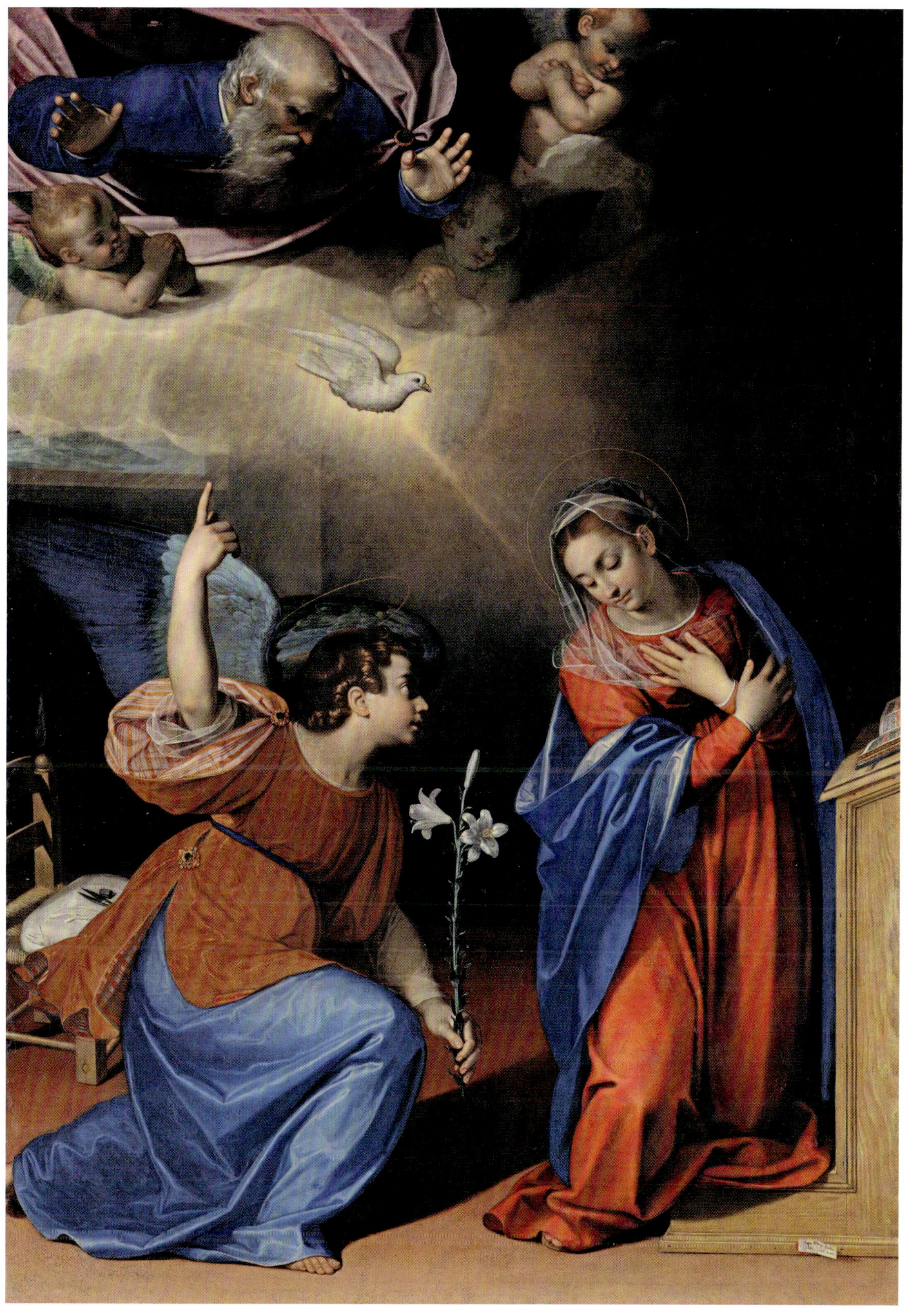

48 Scipione Pulzone, *The Annunciation*, 1578, oil on canvas, 52 × 39.5 cm (20 ½ × 15 ½ in), Capodimonte Museum, Naples

Annunciate Virgin who has all the regal dignity and visionary splendour of an Immacolata. Thus, amidst fears of a deadly epidemic, the people of Naples could pray at the hem of their female defender's coiling mantle. Indeed, the plague was averted and Naples was spared.

This *Annunciation* altarpiece in a time of plague inaugurated Artemisia's life in Naples under a favourable star. The enthusiastic reception it received would spawn many other commissions in the following years. It was thus as a painter of devotional images that Artemisia's fame spread among her Neapolitan patrons, reaching the attention of the Spanish viceroy from 1631 to 1637, Manuel de Acevedo y Zúñiga, Count of Monterrey. A description of some of these early Neapolitan commissions was made by the German painter Joachim von Sandrart when he visited her studio in the autumn of 1631 to deliver her father's greetings – and perhaps his letters and drawings, too – from London:

> She showed me her lovely paintings: among others one life-size picture of a graceful David holding in his hands the horrifying head of gigantic Goliath, and near it the many other works very cleverly wrought by her hand. She had also produced some exceptionally fine portraits.[9]

These were soon followed by three altarpieces for the church of San Procolo (*Saint Januarius in the Amphitheatre at Pozzuoli*, *Saints Proculus and Nicea* and the *Adoration of the Magi*) that she carried out between 1635 and 1637 as well as works for the King of Spain that she vaguely mentioned in her letter of 20 July 1635 (by then, Philip IV had already received the *Hercules and Omphale* that she painted in Venice).[10]

THE WASHERWOMEN AND THE KING

Only one of those works that Artemisia made for Philip IV while based in Naples is extant today: *The Birth of Saint John the Baptist* (fig.49). Sometime around 1635, it joined the four paintings by Massimo Stanzione and one by Paolo Finoglio to constitute a series of the Life of John the Baptist, which is thought to have decorated the hermitage of the King's newly built Buen Retiro Palace (fig.50). We do not know whether the three artists were commissioned separately or whether one of them – in all likelihood, Stanzione, who had the most canvases in the group – subcontracted components to the other two artists in order to meet a deadline. In either case, it is clear that certain formal characteristics of the series were carefully coordinated to give it stylistic uniformity and to harmonise the different personal styles: the standing figures are roughly the same height; the illusionistic space is relatively shallow; the main action as well as the vanishing points are displaced to one side of the center of each canvas; about seven to ten figures appear in each scene; and the earthy tones of the settings contrast with the pure, intense palette reserved for drapery and fabrics, these being painted in hues created with pigments of the highest quality: ultramarine blue, vermilion, orpiment and malachite.

The close involvement with Stanzione in this Life of John the Baptist series had a lasting impact on Artemisia's art. To some degree, the high-keyed palette of *The Birth of Saint John the Baptist* surely responds to Stanzione's overall vision for the series. Nevertheless, the solution she arrived at – involving pairings of complementary colors like red with green and blue with gold – belongs to her alone, just like the scene-stealing veil on the shoulders of the central wet nurse, made of a crinkled shot silk that vibrates between yellow and violet. Henceforth, Artemisia's colors took on an uninhibited, jewel-like intensity that is exalted through contrasting combinations, such as in the triad of violet, curry and aquamarine in the costume of the nymph in her *Corsica and the Satyr* of *c.*1635–7, or the confectionary hues of pink, yellow, ultramarine blue and plum set against a flaming sky in *Lot and His Daughters* of *c.*1640–45 (see fig.69 below). The sonorous deep green that she

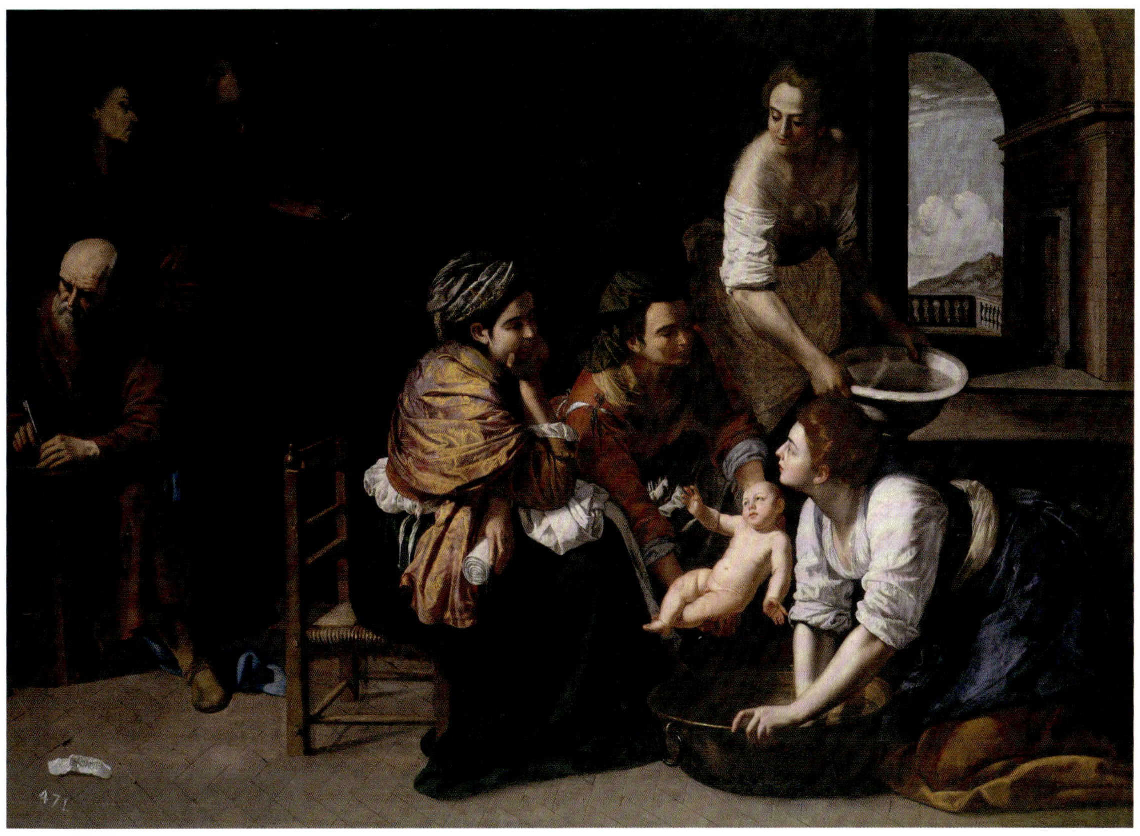

49 Artemisia Gentileschi, *The Birth of Saint John the Baptist*, *c.*1635, oil on canvas, 184 × 258 cm (72 7⁄16 × 101 9⁄16 in), Museo Nacional del Prado, Madrid

employed to great effect in the central part of *The Birth of Saint John the Baptist* would appear again as a protagonist in her *Self Portrait as the Allegory of Painting (La Pittura)* of about 1638–9 (see fig.61 below), and in her *Esther Before Ahasuerus* of *c.*1639 (see fig.62 below), which also reprises the violet and gold combination in the depiction of shot silk.

Artemisia, even while following Stanzione's lead, subtly asserted her own style. Whereas his fabrics are differentiated primarily by color, hers range across a variety of textures, fibres and weights: from wool, to fustian, to linen, to satin, to silk gauze. Unlike his bright hues that float decoratively on the picture surface, hers are muted to enhance the illusion of space, gradually subsumed by vaporous shadows in the background. By contrast, her simple white cloth steals the show with the variety of curling, coiling, twisting, pleated or folded arrangements. The same inventiveness inflects her representation of female beauty: each woman represents a distinct combination of age, skin color or hair color, such that they almost would seem to be painted by a variety of hands. With an ingenious touch, she grafted the rear of the room onto a balcony overlooking a large plain rimmed by a low mountain. That landscape, along with the salmon tinge of the masonry and the severe

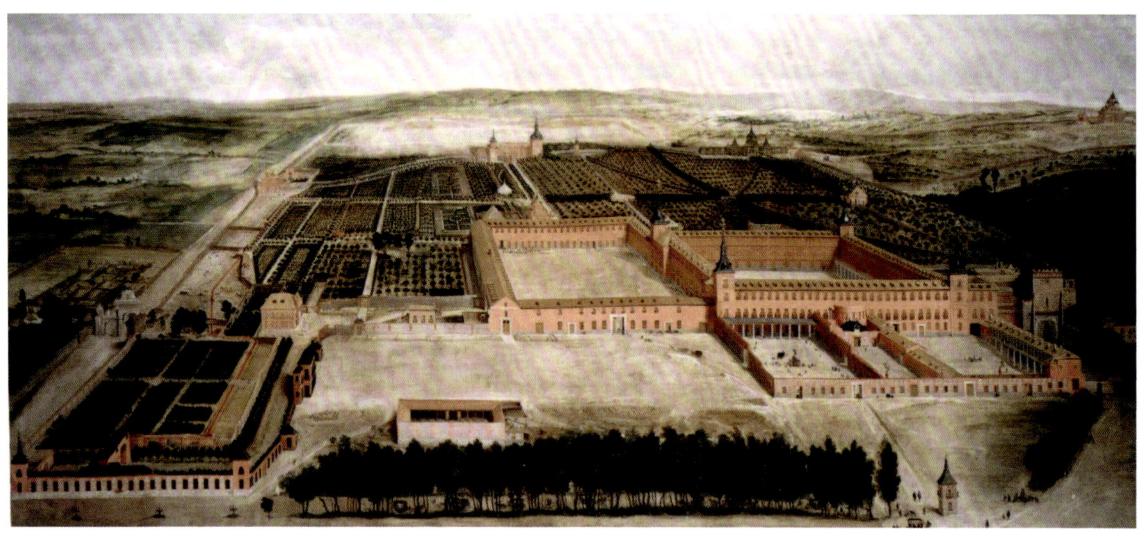

50 Jusepe Leonardo, *Buen Retiro Palace in 1637*, oil on canvas, 139 × 308 cm (54 ¾ × 121 ¼ in), Palacio Real de Madrid

stone doorframes, is highly suggestive of the Buen Retiro Palace itself (fig.50), where Philip IV surely intended to display this Life of John the Baptist series. Another thoughtful, personalising touch consists in the crumpled cartiglio carrying the artist's name: as noticed recently by Francesca Whitlum-Cooper, it lies on the floor near Zacharias' desk, as if he had discarded it before taking a new sheet to write down the name of his son.[11]

With this complex, multi-figure scene, Artemisia displays her full powers as a storyteller. Employing a surprising inversion, to the far left and cast in shadow are the most theologically important characters: Elizabeth in her birthing chamber and Zacharias at his desk while he writes out his son's name. By contrast, the more visually prominent action in the foreground – which is offset to the right of center, just like the conversion point of the orthogonal perspective lines (fig.51) – spotlights the nameless servants who are about to wash the newborn. The presence of the midwives is, in fact, called for by the account in the Gospel of Luke (1:5–80), and the way they huddle around the child in many depictions of the subject – including one by her uncle Aurelio Lomi (see fig.20) – loosely recalls a passage from the office of the Baptist's Feast Day: 'Among those born of women there is none greater than John' (Luke 7:28, 'Inter natos mulierum non surrexit maior'). Yet Artemisia's relegation of Saint Elizabeth to the picture's dingy edge tips the balance between the two parts of the image to an extreme, and her greater interest clearly lies with these lowly midwives and scullery maids.

Each servant woman strikes a graceful yet utterly natural pose suitable to her work, but the scattering of their looks speaks to the subject's underlying significance. The two servants in the rear of the group look reverently at the child, as if remembering that he was conceived through a miracle. The central servant on the chair holding a towel rolled up like an ancient scroll gazes very pensively at the newborn and the bath water, leading the viewer to realise that this purifying water prefigures the child's role as the Baptiser. The most radiant of these servants is the lowly washerwoman kneeling humbly on the ground to make ready the bath for the prophet who

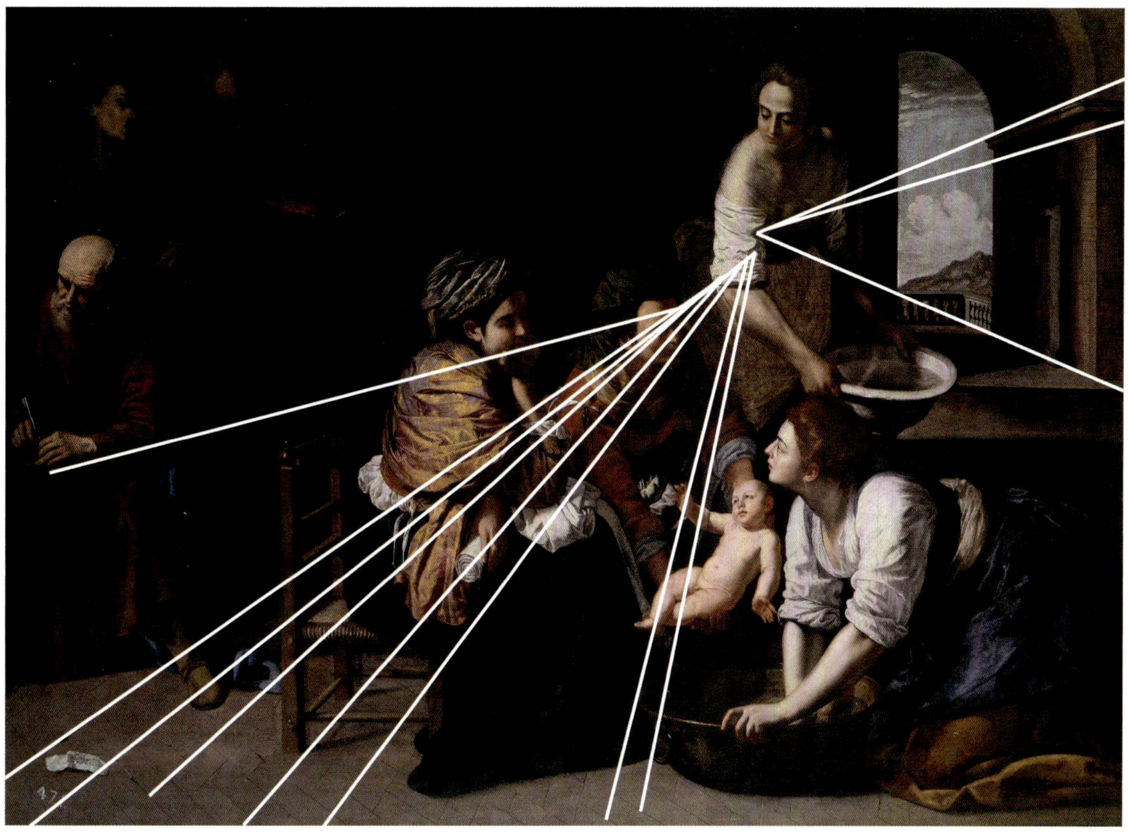

51 Perspective scheme of fig.49 (Artemisia Gentileschi, *The Birth of Saint John the Baptist*, *c.*1635), digital design, the Author

will prepare the way for Christ. Her face is transfixed as she looks across the room at Zacharias while he names the child 'John', recognising his faith in the miracle. Thus, each figure in this tightly composed group of ordinary women pauses in her performance of domestic chores in order to come to terms with the importance of the child in their midst.

Beginning with this painting, Artemisia revealed a proclivity to extend her sympathetic portrayal of womanhood universally, instead of just focusing on the exemplary heroes, saints and queens who figure in the *querelle des femmes* treatises. Anticipating by two decades the parallel elevation of humble women in Velázquez's *Hilanderas* of 1655, Artemisia's concern for women's lives encompasses average, imperfect women – women like the studio models she complained of once saying, 'one must suffer their pettiness with the patience of Job'. In the *Birth of Saint John the Baptist*, Artemisia acknowledges that even the humblest women can bear witness to God's miracles. From this perspective, her recasting of the Biblical story also served as a *sermo humilis* for the most powerful Catholic King on the planet.

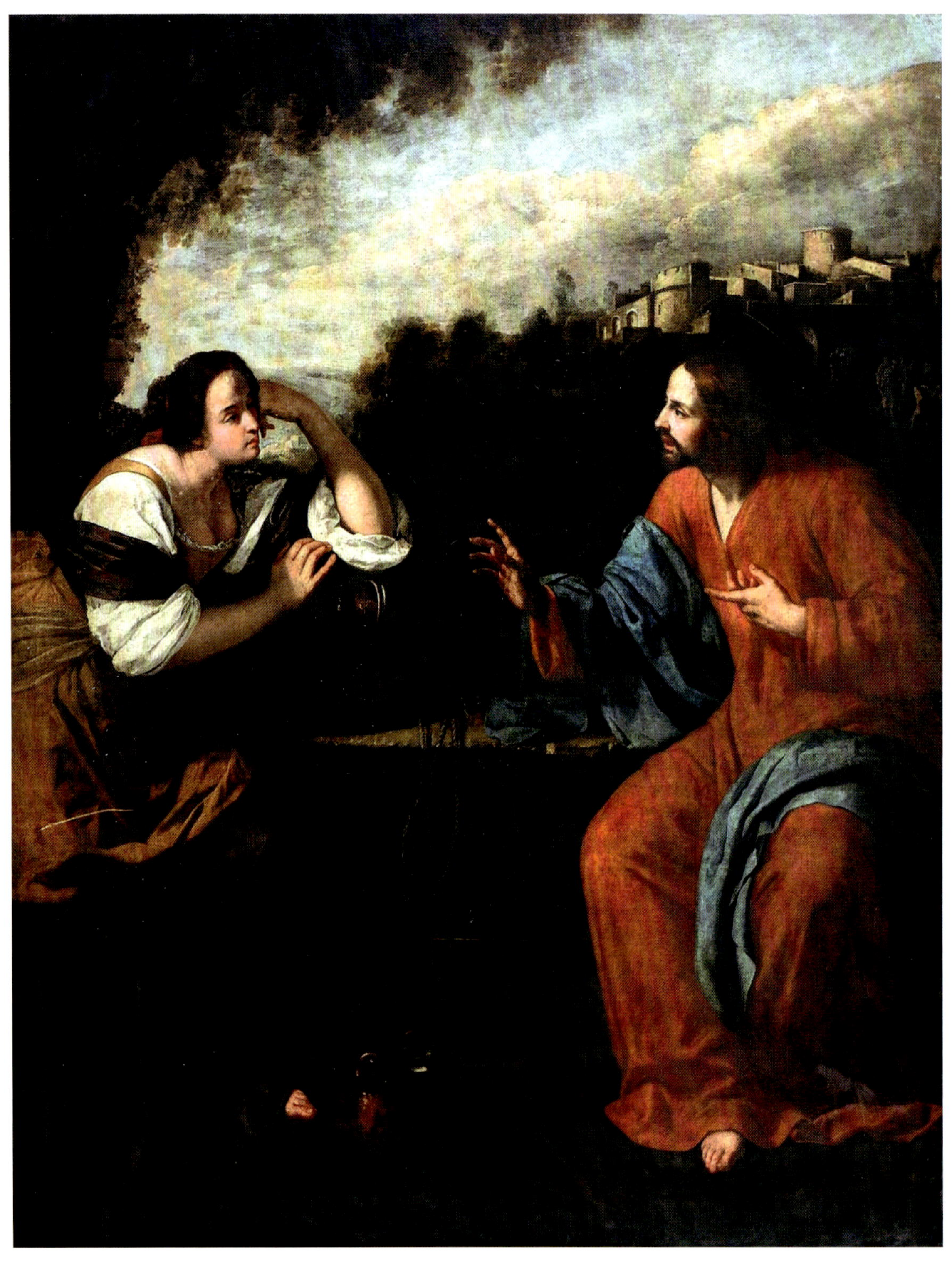

52 Artemisia Gentileschi, *Jesus and the Samaritan Woman at the Well*, 1637, oil on canvas, 267.5 × 206 cm (105 5⁄16 × 81 1⁄8 in), Palazzo Francavilla, Palermo

A WOMAN ARTIST'S INTERPRETATION OF A FEMALE EVANGELISER

Two years later, Artemisia would again underline the spiritual dignity of a woman with an inferior social station in *Jesus and the Samaritan Woman at the Well* (fig.52), a painting recently recognised as hers by Luciano Arcangelo.[12] In November of 1637 she sent two letters to Cassiano dal Pozzo, her friend at the Barberini court in Rome, to enlist his help in selling this work – as well as a *John the Baptist* – to the Pope's two Cardinal-Nephews, Antonio Barberini and Francesco Barberini. Pressing the urgency of the matter, she noted that the sale of the paintings would allow her to provide for her daughter's dowry.[13]

Surely Cassiano would have been amused by the choice of *Jesus and the Samaritan Woman at the Well* as a subject, since 'pozzo' means 'well'. Yet the painting is not about facile humour; it is about deeply challenging Christian concepts, including the role of women in the Church. Several aspects of the composition confirm Artemisia's interest in depicting the Samaritan woman – female, gentile, a labourer and a serial fornicator – as a fully dignified interlocutor when speaking with the Son of God about salvation. Her head is raised ever so slightly above the Savior's and, as explained previously in the discussion of Artemisia's *Annunciation*, such relative positions sometimes functioned as indicators of status. Thanks to the Samaritan woman's outstretched head, unblinking eyes and the knuckles-to-cheek pose that is familiar from the Michelangelesque philosopher in Raphael's *School of Athens* (1509–11) and the figure of the intellectual in Dürer's engraving of *Melancholia I* (1514), we are encouraged to see her as a deeply engaged thinker.

This ennoblement of the Samaritan woman accords not only with the Scriptures, where she is noted for her great efficacy as a proselytiser of the Christian faith after this meeting at the well (John 4:28–30, 4:39–42), but also with her saintly status in the Byzantine church as 'equal-to-the-Apostles' [*isapóstolos*]. Impressively, Artemisia found a way to indicate the Samaritan woman's near-apostle status by means of the landscape behind the two conversing figures in the foreground. To the far right in the landscape, the twelve Apostles are seen as they enter Jerusalem, set on a hill in the distance behind Jesus' head. Balancing that imagery on the Samaritan woman's side is a view of a sea that has no bearing on Jerusalem's real site, but which instead – like the well water beside her – symbolises the living water of eternal life that she has accepted from Jesus. Notably, Jesus tells the Samaritan woman that the religious role of Jerusalem will be superseded because 'the true worshipers will worship the Father in spirit and truth' (John 4:23), a reminder that Salvation will be available to all – men and women, gentiles and Jews. In the visual arrangement of the composition, the Samaritan woman is close to the living water and far from Jerusalem, just as the Apostles in the landscape are far from the living water yet close to Jerusalem, a visual chiasmus that expresses the parity of their evangelising work.

It has been overlooked until now, but Artemisia's decision to celebrate a female evangeliser in the painting she planned to give to the Barberini Cardinal-Nephews bore a direct connection to her desire to go to England. It evoked the journey's broader goal of converting Charles I to Catholicism, and it spoke of Artemisia's role of bringing about that conversion with the testimonial power of her art. How she arrived in England, and what she painted there, are questions still lacking complete answers, yet from the evidence already on hand, it is clear that this extraordinary and even dangerous episode catapulted her into a hotbed of politics.

A CATHOLIC ARTIST'S MISSION TO ENGLAND

Artemisia found plentiful work in Naples. At the same time, she continually nourished the hope of going to England. Her reasons for wanting to make

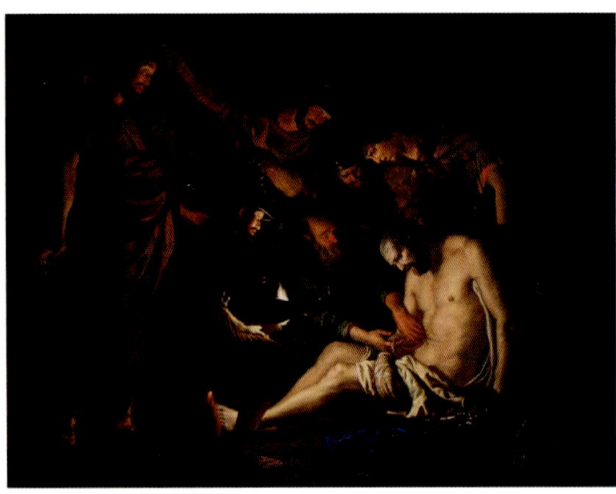

53 Joachim von Sandrart, *Death of Cato*, 1631, oil on canvas, 140 × 186.5 cm (55 1/8 × 73 7/16 in), Museo Civico, Padua

this journey may have included her sentimental attachment to her father, but surely of equal or greater consideration was the lucrative potential of becoming a court painter to either King Charles I or Queen Henrietta Maria de Bourbon, the Catholic daughter of Henry IV of France and Maria de' Medici. The need for money is, in fact, a leitmotif of her correspondence with patrons and contacts in the mid-1630s, as is her preoccupation with arranging a good marriage for her daughter Prudenzia, who by now could boast extensive experience in painting.[14] We know from Artemisia's letters that her husband Pierantonio had mysteriously disappeared some time before 1637, never to reappear, so she alone had to shoulder the entire expense of her child's dowry.[15]

In the previous chapter, we saw that Artemisia's plans to follow her father to England likely prompted her transfer to Venice in late 1626 or early 1627. From that time forward, Artemisia received a continual stream of visitors bearing ties to the English crown. For instance, while she resided in the Adriatic capital, her own brothers travelled from London to Venice several times in the service of Charles I, and presumably it was they who introduced Artemisia to Charles I's agent and their paymaster, Nicholas Lanier, who then spread word of Artemisia's talents at Charles I's court.

After settling in Naples, Artemisia was still in contact with visitors from England. Her brothers, who continued to work for Charles I as art agents and art couriers, visited her in Naples at least once. In 1631, the German artist Joachim von Sandrart brought her news from her father, to whom he had become deeply attached during his recent extended stay in London. Sandrart alighted long enough in Artemisia's studio to paint a gift for her at her insistence: a replica of his *Death of Cato* (fig.53) that he had first painted for the King of Spain. Surely Artemisia appreciated the technique Sandrart had used to create the illusion of candlelight and the insights that his painting afforded into King Philip IV's tastes; however, as the painter of Lucretias and Cleopatras, she also may have admired Sandrart's portrayal of Cato's resistance and Stoic virtue, for Cato chose to kill himself rather than to live under the thumb of a corrupt leader.

Again Artemisia received an English emissary in March of 1634. Bullen Reymes, the retainer of the Duke of Buckingham, paid a visit to her studio to deliver letters from her father. On that occasion, Reymes probably also purchased the first of Artemisia's paintings to enter the King's collection: a lost *Tarquin and Lucretia* that reached London by 1634, as documented by an order for a frame. Judging from Artemisia's later versions of the same subject, the painting must have featured a nude woman, thus allowing Artemisia to demonstrate her artistic strong suit. Indeed, the subject she chose for the recently married Protestant King reflected remarkably good judgment: *Tarquin and Lucretia* depicted a typical, if cautionary, epithalamic theme for bridal furniture (it can be found on wedding chests at the Ashmolean Museum and Mount Holyoke College, for example); moreover, the subject bore no traces of Artemisia's Catholic faith.

By 1635, a plan had been hatched. As Artemisia explained in a letter to Grand Duke Ferdinando II de'

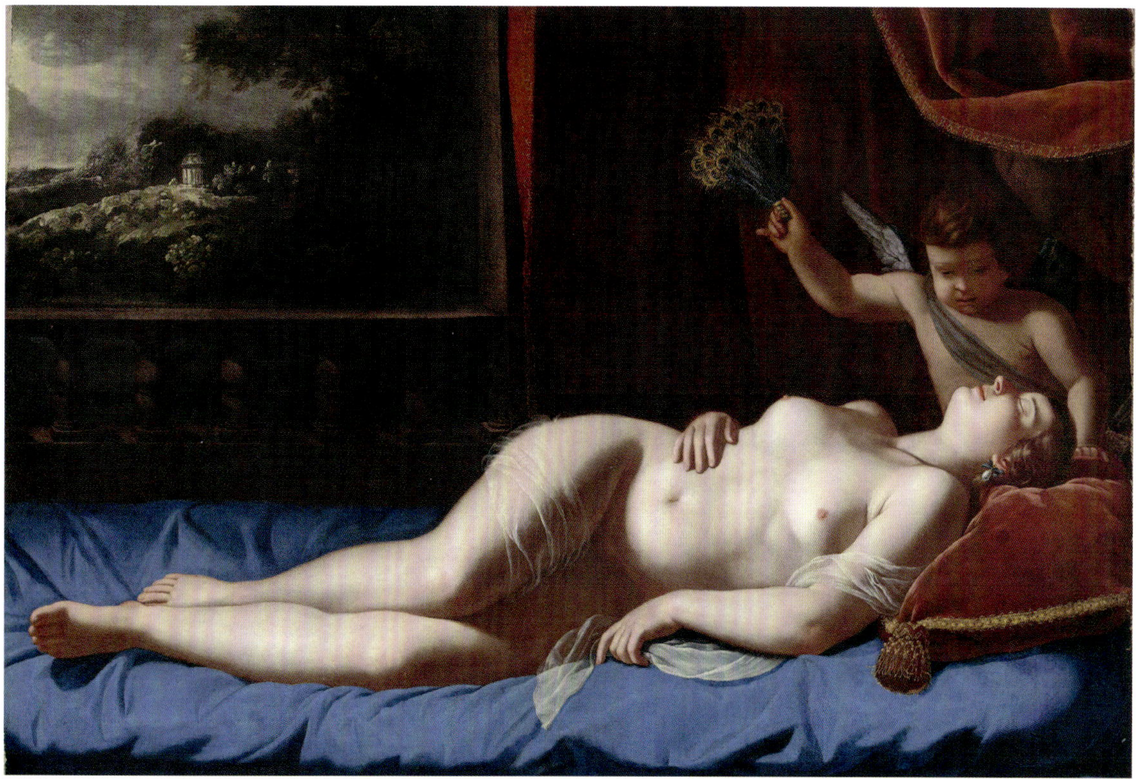

54 Artemisia Gentileschi, *Venus and Cupid*, *c.*1635–8, oil on canvas, 96.52 × 143.83 cm (38 × 56 ⅝ in), Virginia Museum of Fine Arts, Richmond, Virginia

Medici, her brother Francesco would rendezvous with her before going to Tuscany to deliver to the Grand Duke a gift of some paintings by her father. Then, Francesco would escort Artemisia to England:

> where many times before [the King of England] has requested that I serve him, and he even sent my brother [for this purpose], but because I was living in Naples in the service of this Viceroy in order to bring to completion some works begun for His Catholic Majesty [Philip IV], there was absolutely no way for me to satisfy the request of the [His] Majesty in England.[16]

It is clear from this letter to the son of her former patron Cosimo II, that Artemisia had learned from the sour experience with the Florentine court in 1620 that she could not leave the service of the Spanish Viceroy in Naples until all her commissions were complete. Duty, however, was not the only obstacle impeding her departure for England. She also needed a series of official letters of safe passage for each principality through which she would travel in the course of her journey. Additionally, she needed money to pay for carriages and inns along the way.

Artemisia addressed these problems with her pen and her paintbrush. Between 1635 and 1637 she wrote a flurry of letters to friends and dignitaries at the

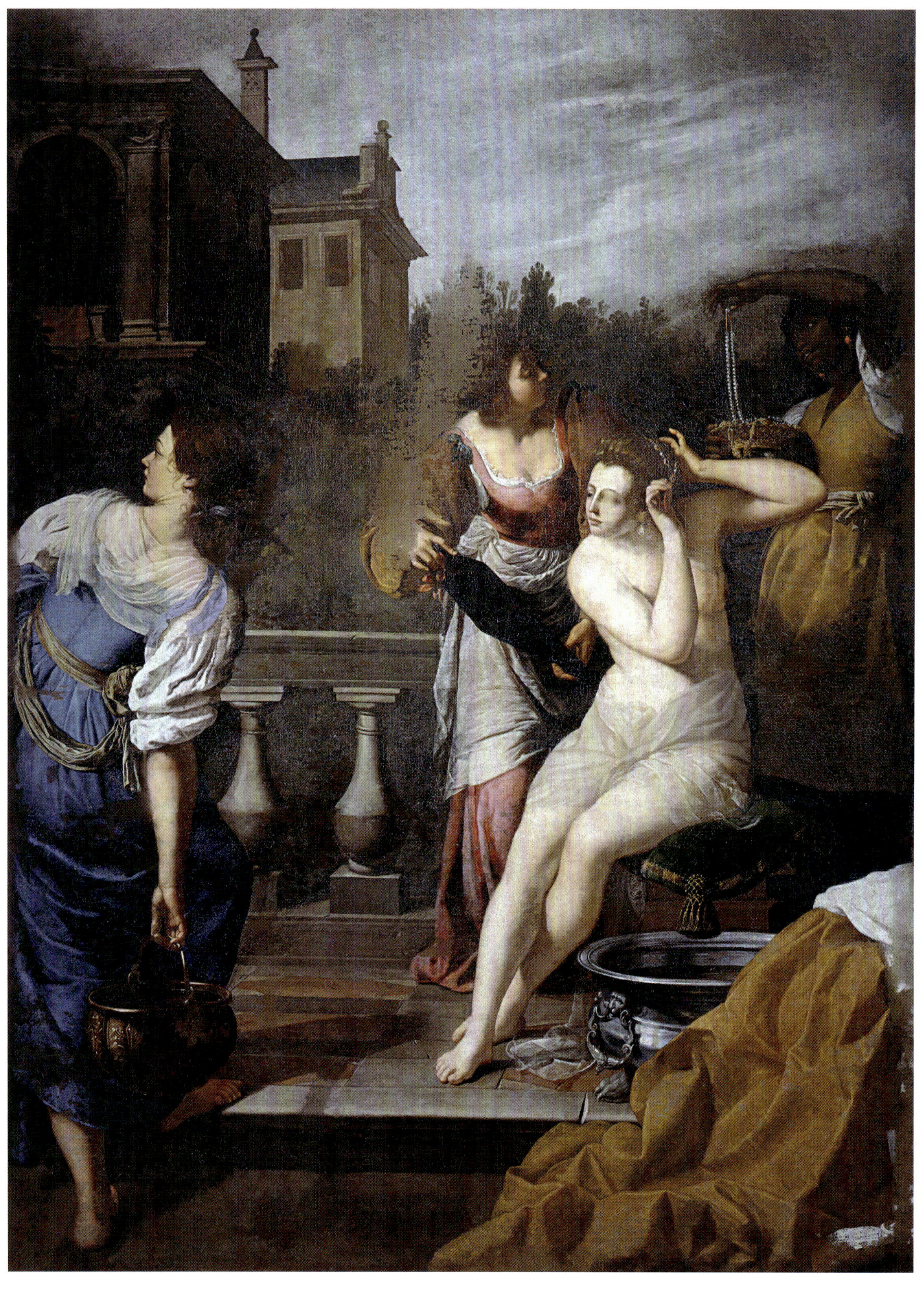

55 Artemisia Gentileschi, *Bathsheba at her Bath*, *c.*1635, oil on canvas, 286 × 214 cm (112 ⅝ × 84 ¼ in), Palazzo Pitti, Florence

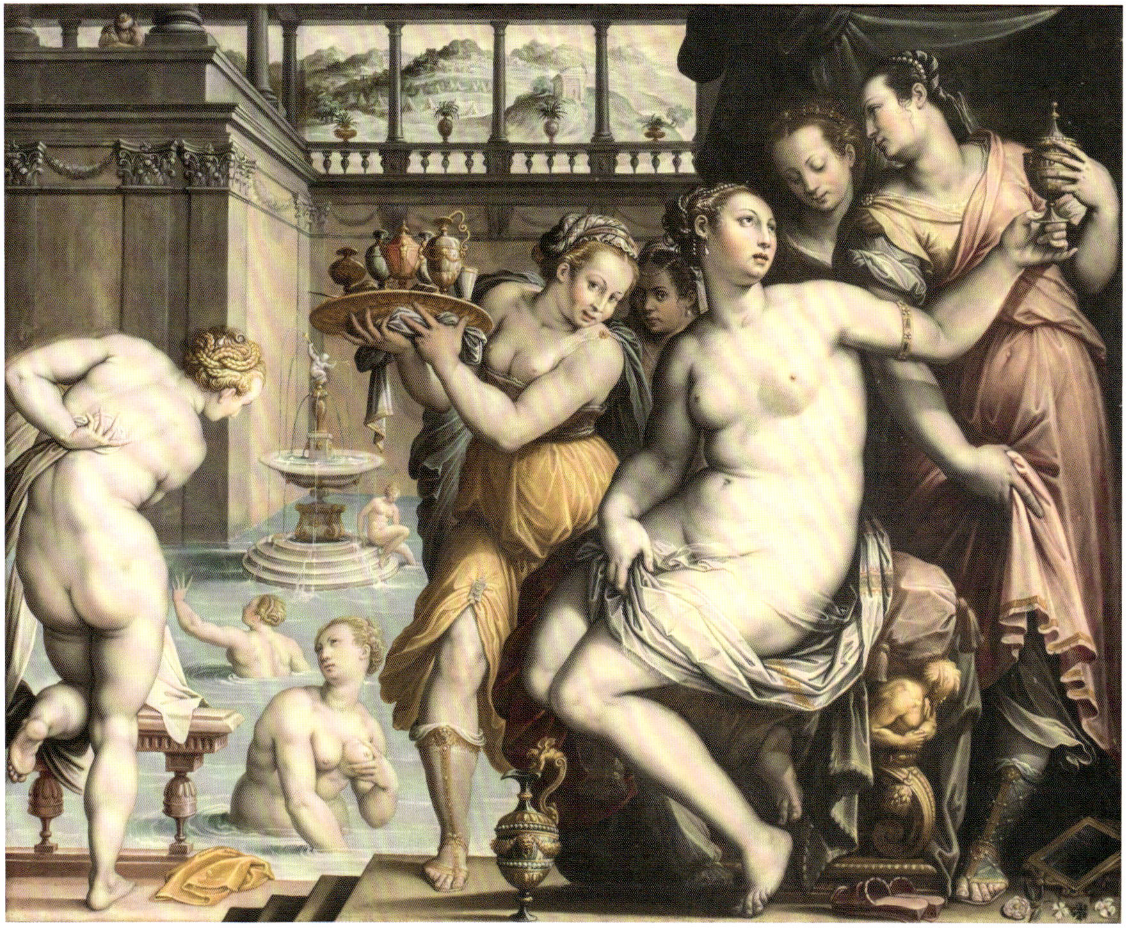

56 Jacopo Zucchi, *Bathsheba at her Bath*, *c.*1573, oil on panel, 115 × 145 cm (45 ¼ × 57 ⅛ in), Galleria Nazionale d'Arte Antica di Palazzo Barberini, Rome

courts of Rome, Florence and Modena, indicating a desire to travel to their cities for a few months in order to paint and earn money for her daughter's dowry (in actuality her daughter did not marry until 1649). Her letters also mention unsolicited paintings that she planned to send them and for which she hoped to be handsomely rewarded. These paintings include those she described to Cassiano dal Pozzo in her letter of 24 November 1637, namely the aforementioned *Jesus and the Samaritan Woman at the Well* (fig.52) and a lost *Saint John the Baptist* designated for Cardinals Antonio and Francesco Barberini.[17] Perhaps this was also the occasion when she sent Francesco Barberini the *Venus* that had entered his collection by 1644 – and which Mary D. Garrard has reasonably identified with the *Venus and Cupid* in the Virginia Museum of Fine Arts (fig.54).[18] Part of this same campaign, Artemisia's letter to Grand Duke Ferdinando II de' Medici of 20 July 1635, conveys her intention to pass through Tuscany on her way to Turin, where her brothers would meet her and accompany her across France. Although she did not name specifically the two paintings she had sent to the Grand Duke with her letter (described simply as 'le presente opere, le quali invio reverenti alli piedi di Vostra Altezza Serenissima' ['the present works, which I reverently send to the feet of Your Most Serene Highness']), one of them could very well be her *Bathsheba at her Bath* (*c.*1635, Palazzo Pitti) (fig.55). This last work, probably inspired by a Mannerist composition such as Jacopo Zucchi's earlier painting of the same subject (fig.56), is documented as being in the Medici collections since 1663. The date and circumstances of its commission are unknown, but perhaps it was made on the eve of Artemisia's departure for England, which would explain its strong relationship to the *Bathsheba* of Gosford House, Scotland – a canvas that Artemisia perhaps made in England and which was never documented outside Great Britain before it perished in a fire in 1940. Notably, several of the works made in these years leading up to the journey to England exhibit the same pasty, smooth hyper-idealisation of female flesh that can be seen in Guido Reni's paintings of this period. Emerging in her *Jesus and the Samaritan Woman at the Well* (fig.52), the tendency is fully evident in the *Bathsheba* at Palazzo Pitti and in the aforementioned *Venus* in the Virginia Museum of Fine Arts (fig.54).

So far, this account has suggested that Artemisia was pursuing these plans to go to England on her own, with the encouragement of her family. If that was the case initially, the situation may have taken a political twist in late 1637 or early 1638. Several scholars, beginning with Elizabeth Cropper, have promoted the hypothesis that Artemisia was selected by the Barberini for a diplomatic mission to shore up Catholic Queen Henrietta Maria's cultural influence and standing at the Stuart court, at a time when tensions were rising between the Protestants and Catholics in England.[19] Cardinal Francesco Barberini's role as Cardinal Protector to Henrietta Maria meant that he, more than anyone else at the papal court, was concerned that she should have Catholics in her retinue and in influential positions at court. Moreover, the Cardinal would also have been aware of the fact that Orazio Gentileschi himself had carried out diplomatic work in both Paris and London.

Adding more credence to this theory, there had already been attempts by the Barberini to enlist young women artists to join Henrietta Maria's retinue in London. Early on, the Florentine female botanical painter Anna Maria Vaiani had been identified as a possible candidate for the mission of expanding the Catholic cultural presence at Charles I's court. In 1630, in order to determine her suitability for such a delicate mission, Vaiani – still just a young woman – was interviewed by Cardinal Francesco Barberini during a face-to-face meeting in the presence of Michelangelo Buonarroti the Younger. During the interview, the Cardinal asked many questions about the artist who would eventually be sent to the English Court. He was keen to ascertain her level of learning; he wanted assurances regarding her character and comportment; and he wanted to see samples of her work (which is well represented by a decorative floral arrangement that she designed several years later and which exemplifies Vaiani's decorative style [fig.57]).[20]

Finally, in 1638, the conditions for Artemisia's journey were ripe and, at 45 years of age, she made the long journey over land to the court of Charles I. Only recently has it been possible to confirm that Artemisia was joined in this international adventure by her friend from Venice, Giovanna Garzoni. Since Garzoni had been in service at the Savoy court in Turin since 1632, it is reasonable to suppose that the two rendezvoused in Turin and then continued together from there. The coincidence of their journeys lends further support to the theory of a papal strategy, especially since Garzoni also enjoyed the protection of Cassiano dal Pozzo.

Upon arriving on British shores, the two women were presumably greeted either by George Conn, a Scottish Franciscan who advised Charles I on artistic matters, or by the Savoy Ambassador to England, Abbott Cesare Alessandro Scaglia di Verrua, an art collector as well as a friend of Cassiano dal Pozzo and Inigo Jones. Both of these men supported the

Roman Catholic cause in Great Britain. Artemisia may have opted to live with her father, although their time together was cut short when Orazio died on 7 February 1639, just a few months after Artemisia's arrival. Rather than returning to Naples immediately, however, she remained at the Stuart court for more than a year after her father's death, protracting her stay in England through early 1640. It is understandable why she wished to stay; Artemisia could expect to receive commissions not only from Queen Henrietta, but also from two other women in her immediate orbit: the Queen's mother, Maria de' Medici, who had been living in exile in England since 1639, and Aletheia Howard née Talbot, Countess of Arundel, a staunch Catholic and a fervent art collector.

A massive, chaotic sell-off of Charles I's enormous art collection followed his death by beheading in 1649. For this reason, we have lost track of many of Artemisia's works from her period in England. Lost but documented works of hers in Charles I's collection include a *Susanna and the Elders* that hung in the Queen's withdrawing chamber above the chimney, a *Saint with His Hand on Fruit*, a *Self-Portrait*, an *Allegory of Fame* and a *Diana at her Bath*. Artemisia is believed to have also contributed substantially to the *Allegory of Peace and the Arts*, a commission that Orazio had initiated for Henrietta in 1635, but which infirmity and then death prevented him from completing. The *Allegory of Peace and the Arts* consists of nine canvases originally installed in the ceiling of the Queen's House, Greenwich (fig.58), a project closely modelled after Rubens' Banqueting House ceiling at Whitehall, which had been installed in place in 1636. Orazio's health must have already been feeble from the outset of the project, for much of the work is weak and appears to have been carried out by Artemisia's brothers. She brought it to completion, adding such figures as the muses Polyhymnia and Terpischore and the allegory of Strength (fig.59), whose olive-colored skirt and partial armour recall David's dress in *David* in a British private collection

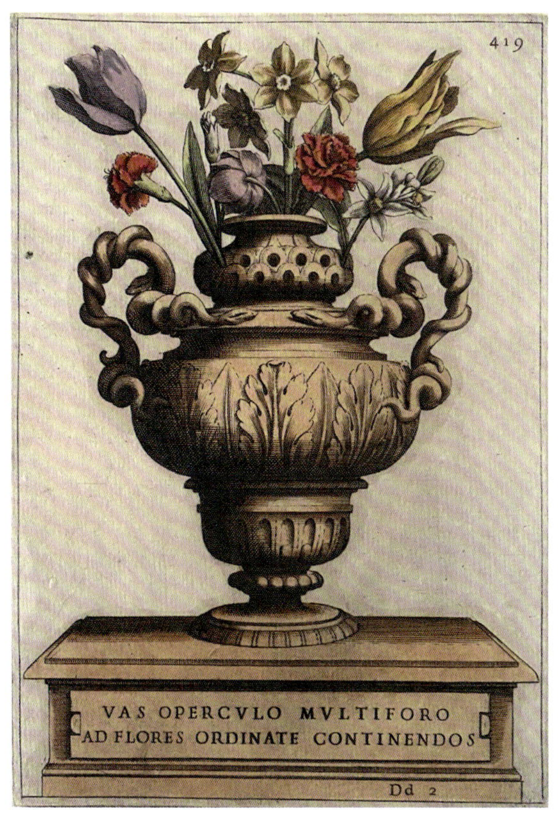

57 Anna Maria Vaiani, att., *Flowers in a Vase*, 1638, engraving, 19.4 × 13.8 cm (7 ¾ × 5 ⅜ in) (platemark), private collection, USA

(fig.60), a painting that, following Gianni Papi's recent arguments, dates from Artemisia's period in England.[21]

Of the works named in Charles I's inventories, one survives to this day in the Royal Collection: Artemisia's *Self-Portrait as the Allegory of Painting* (fig.61). Although this image looks like the portrait of a living woman, many scholars have noted that it follows – almost to the letter – Cesare Ripa's late-sixteenth-century instructions on how to figure the concept of painting as a female allegory.[22] While Artemisia clearly appreciated Ripa's association of the practice of painting with the activity of the intellect,

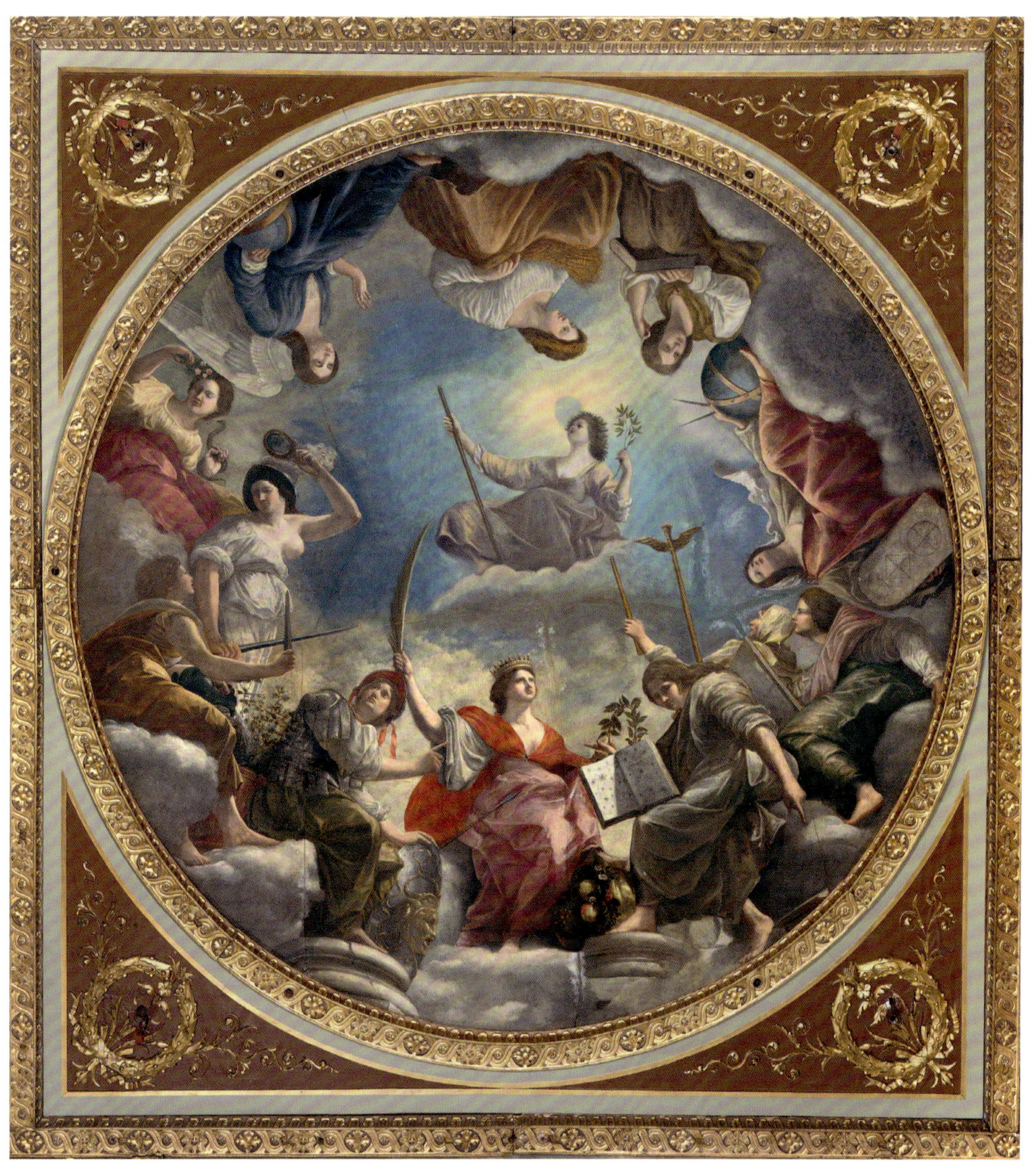

58 Orazio Gentileschi and Artemisia Gentileschi, detail of *Allegory of Peace and the Arts*, 1638, ceiling panel made for the Queen's House, Greenwich, oil on canvas, total scheme: 892 x 1070 cm (351 ⅛ x 421 ¼ in), inner circle diameter: 479 cm (188 ⅝ in), Marlborough House, London

which is symbolised by black and dishevelled hair, she disagreed with the notion that painting should be depicted as a mute art. Ripa had recommended illustrating painting's muteness by putting a gag in the mouth of the female allegorical figure so that she cannot speak.

The meaning behind this intriguing omission of the gag can perhaps be found in Artemisia's sonnet entitled 'Al sig.r Pietro della Valle mio sig.re in venire a veder le mie opere', in which she indicated her ambition to makes paintings that are '*loquaci*'. The use of the Italian adjective 'loquaci' (whose close cognate in English is 'loquacious') to describe paintings is highly anomalous in Italian art criticism. Artemisia's source for the word was surely '*Poema pictura loquens, pictura poema silens*' ['Poetry is a speaking picture, painting a silent poetry'], this being the Latin translation of the sentence that Plutarch first wrote in Greek and attributed to Simonides of Keos (556–468 BCE) in his *On the Fame of the Athenians*. Notably , in choosing the unusual term 'loquacious' – as opposed to the more typical 'poetic', for instance – she implied an analogy with spontaneous speech rather than the written word. There, in the living speech uttered in the multifarious intonations and accents of the ordinary people around her, she found inspiration for an art that speaks to us and grabs our attention; an art that is based on the movements of real, breathing bodies; an art that aims for immediate understandability over perfection; and art that crackles with spontaneous emotion and verve.

It is clear from the line in her sonnet and her iconographic detail in the *Self-Portrait as the Allegory of Painting* that Artemisia believed painting should be communicative, discursive, expressive and conversational. If paintings cannot talk for themselves, then they must tell their stories visually and inspire their viewers with the desire to converse with each other, explaining, querying, reasoning, riffing, disputing, praising and speculating. Moreover, Artemisia seems to have seized on the irony that while paintings were praised for speaking, as it were,

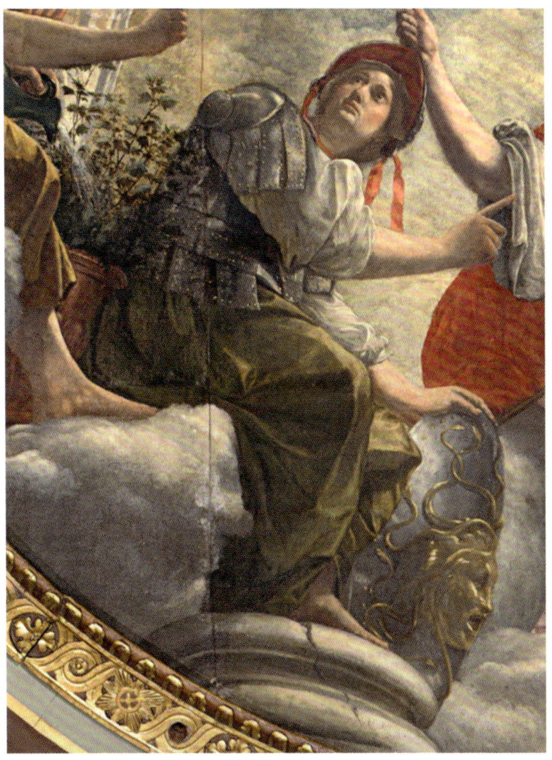

59 Artemisia Gentileschi, *Strength* (detail of fig.58), 1638, oil on canvas, Marlborough House, London

women were not. In Juan Luis Vives' widely read book from 1523, *The Education of a Christian Woman*, the author counsels his readership, 'I do not wish that a young woman be talkative, not even among her girl companions'.[23] In a society that discouraged women from speaking their own opinions in the presence of men, or even speaking at all, Artemisia's championing of a loquacious art would seem to be something more than just a theoretical reflection on her craft. For a woman to be loquacious in elite public spheres was an ungainly act of feminine defiance. However, for a woman to be loquacious in elite public spheres while expressing herself with artfulness and beauty was a winning strategy of early modern feminism.

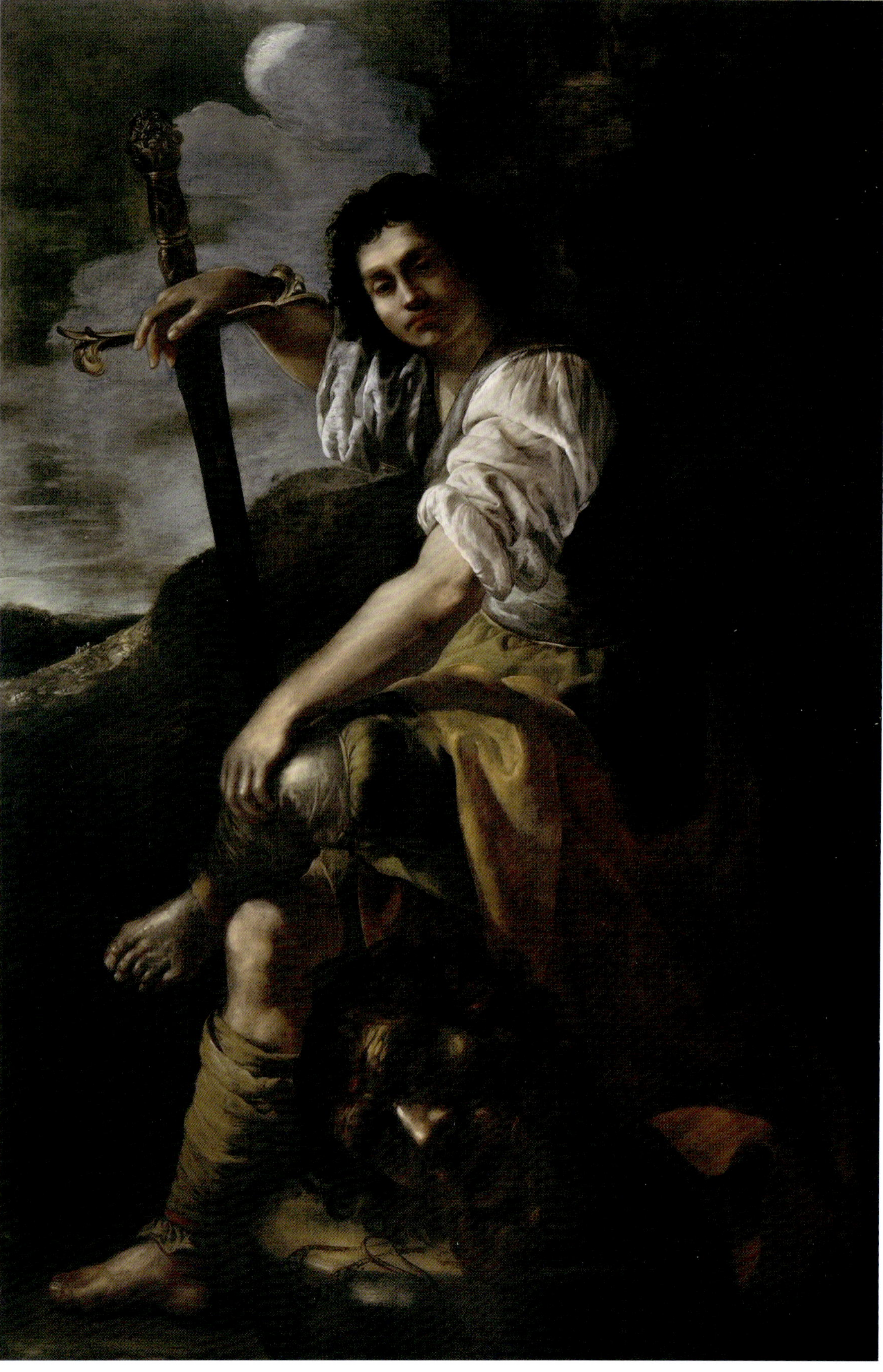

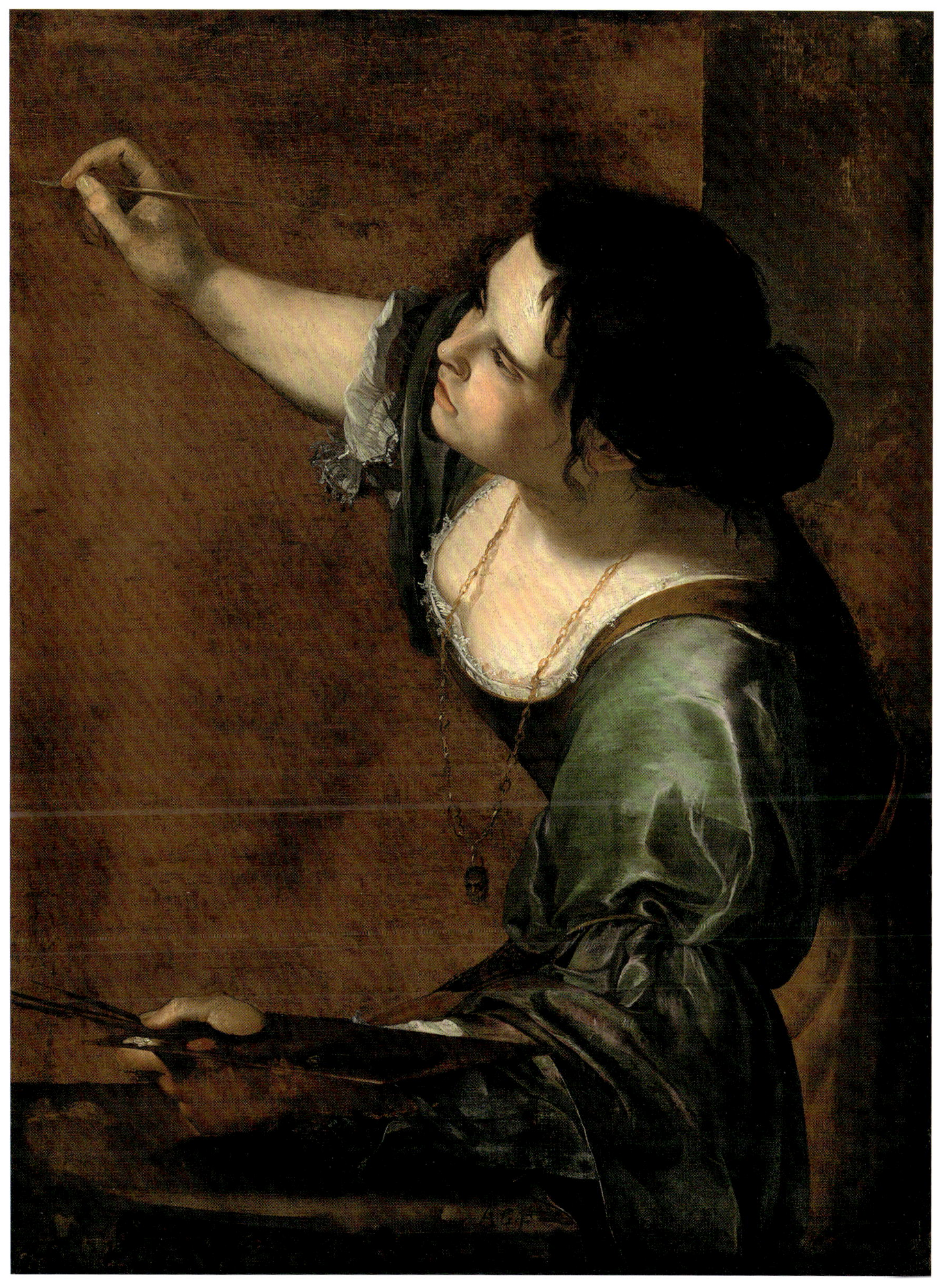

61 Artemisia Gentileschi, *Self-Portrait as the Allegory of Painting (La Pittura)*, *c.*1638–9, oil on canvas, 98.6 × 75.2 cm (38 13⁄16 × 29 5⁄8 in), The Royal Collection Trust, London

60 (opposite) Artemisia Gentileschi, *David*, *c.*1639, oil on canvas, 202 × 137 cm (79 1⁄2 × 54 in), private collection, UK

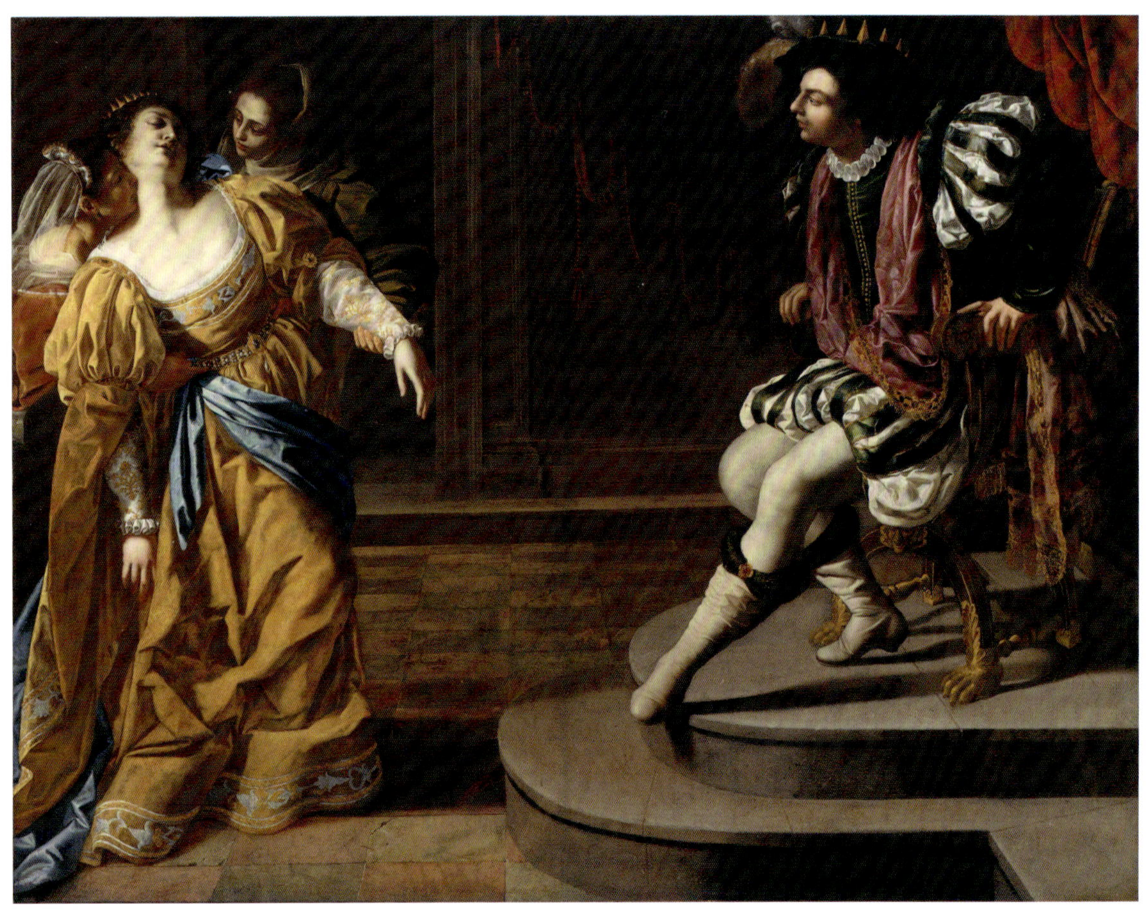

62 Artemisia Gentileschi, *Esther before Ahasuerus*, *c*.1639, oil on canvas, 208.3 × 273.7 cm (82 × 107 ¾ in), The Metropolitan Museum of Art, New York

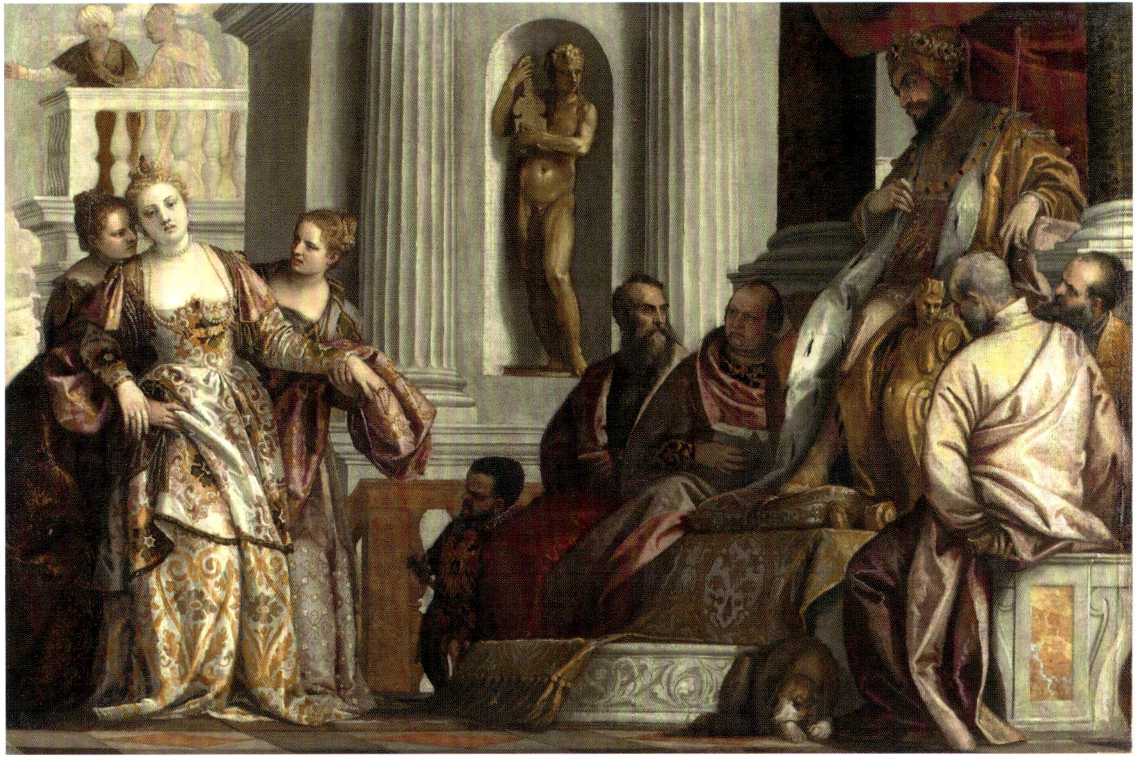

63 Workshop of Paolo Veronese, *Esther before Ahasuerus*, 1575, oil on canvas, 198 × 306 cm (78 × 120 ½ in), Musée du Louvre, Paris

A DANGEROUS MARRIAGE OF POLITICS AND ART

The large *Esther before Ahasuerus* (fig.62) should be added to the list of surviving paintings made by Artemisia while in England. Never one to shy away from controversy, Artemisia produced her most politically consequential work to date with this canvas. As will be explained shortly, its iconography was intimately linked to the current polemics that would eventually explode into the English Civil War and bring about Charles I's execution. It should be noted that many scholars now assume that Artemisia's canvas was completed in Venice since it bears similarities with a painting of the same subject that came out of Veronese's sixteenth-century workshop (fig.63). However, we cannot be sure that the sixteenth-century painting was in Venice while Artemisia was there. The latter picture is now at the Louvre, having been given to Louis XIV in 1662, its earliest known owner. We have no firm knowledge of the painting's location during Artemisia's lifetime.

There is a very real possibility that Artemisia saw the painting in question not in Venice, but in Charles I's collections, which were notoriously full of workshop replicas that had been acquired from unscrupulous agents who trumped up their attributions (indeed, the King's employment of Artemisia's brothers in his Italian art purchases may have been intended as a measure to halt this

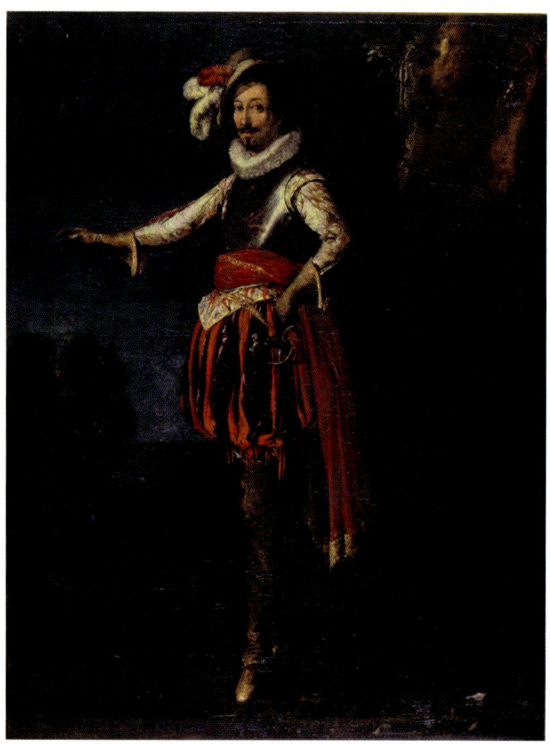

64 Filippo Napoletano, *Cosimo II*, 1618, oil on canvas, 67 × 52 cm (26 3⁄8 × 20 1⁄2 in), Museo Stibbert, Florence

chicanery). The inventories made after the King's death indicate several works having the subject of Esther before Ahasuerus but with no indication of the artist, and any one of these could have been the one from Veronese's workshop. Of course, it may also be that Artemisia encountered the painting by Veronese's workshop in Venice or even in a different location altogether, retaining a note of its composition and then making her own version of the subject long afterwards. Furthermore, if we recall that her *Annunciation* altarpiece in Naples was based on the composition of her father's painting in Genoa, and that she probably only knew of his painting by means of a drawing that had been sent to her, we should also admit the possibility that her knowledge of the *Esther before Ahasuerus* by Veronese's workshop could have come from a drawing in this case, too.

The early history of Artemisia's *Esther before Ahasuerus* at the Metropolitan Museum of Art is just as nebulous as that of the sixteenth-century painting that inspired it. Its provenance goes back only to 1856 when it was sold in Vienna. Before that date, it could have been one of the anonymous Esther and Ahasuerus paintings among the sales (and resales) of Charles I's art collection following his execution:

> At the Canary House near Exeter Exchange will be exposed to sale a curious collection of paintings, being about three hundred in number, most of them originals by the best masters of Europe [London, 1691]: lot 65. King Ahasuerus and Queen Hester by an Italian [Sold to Grafen von Harrach in Vienna]

> A collection of curious Italian and Flemish pictures [London, 1702]: lot 108 Queen Hester and Ahasuerus.

> An appendix to the auction of paintings, with other curiosities: Sale of paintings and Curiosities, most of which belonged to a person of quality, Canary House near Exeter Exchange [London, December 1691]: lot 253. Queen Hester Going to Pharoah.

> A collection of curious original paintings and other fine copies designed by the best masters. King's head Tavern in Southwark [London 8 July 1690]: lot 310. King Ahasuerus and Queen Hester, an original by Mr Boon.

Included in this list is a painting of 'King Ahasuerus and Queen Hester' by a 'Mr Boon' who cannot be identified with any known painter. It is proposed here that 'Mr Boon' may be a transcription mistake for 'Mrs Broom', noted in the following sales record:

> A curious collection of paintings by the best masters, ancient and modern. King's Head Tavern in Ratcliff

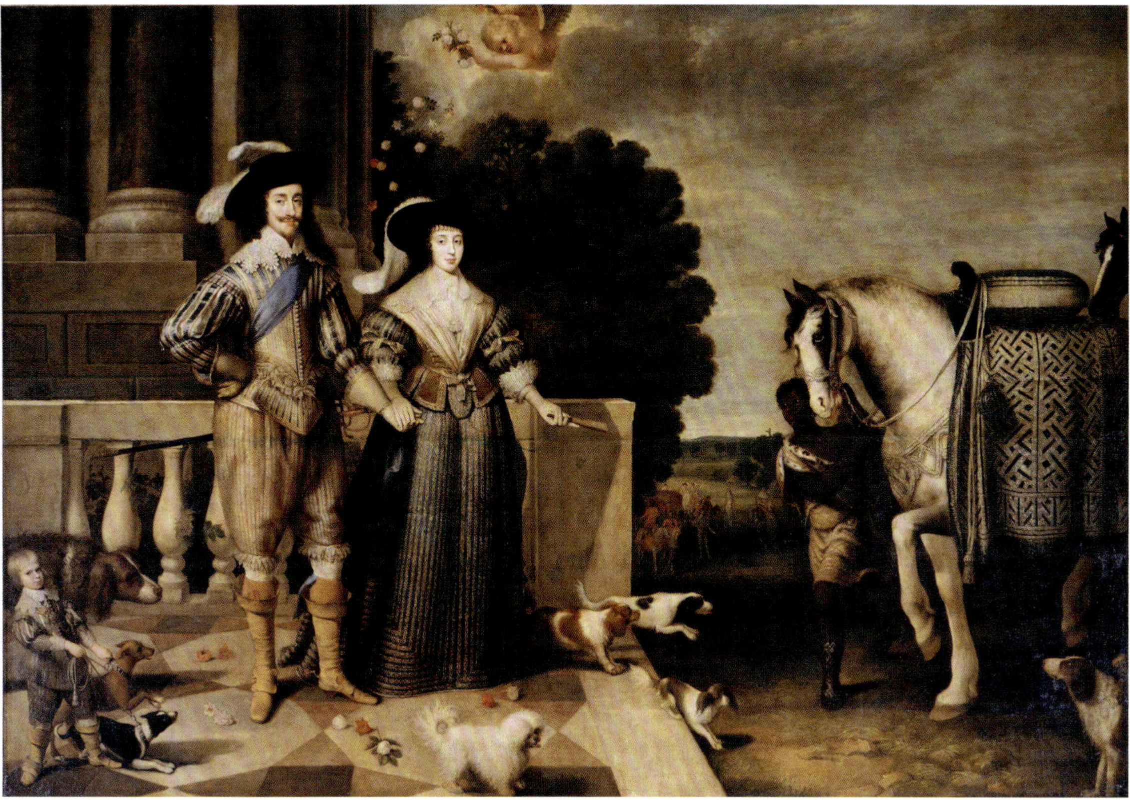

65 Daniel Mytens, *Charles I and Henrietta Maria Departing for the Chase*, *c.*1630–32, oil on canvas, 282 × 408.3 cm (111 × 160 ¾ in), The Royal Collection Trust, London

Broad Street [London, January 21, 1691]: lot 291. Mrs Broom the famous Paintress. Head.

Mrs Broom, I suggest, was Artemisia's nickname in England, perhaps given to her by detractors of the Queen and her Catholic retinue. The name 'Artemisia' to a seventeenth-century English herbalist or doctor was first and foremost a medicinal herb *Artemisia scoparia*, whose common name in English – given the taxonomic ambiguities of that age – was 'broom'.

With her *Esther before Ahasuerus*, Artemisia drew a comparison between Henrietta Maria – the protector of the persecuted Catholic minority in England – and the Old Testament heroine Esther – paladin of the Jews in Persia. The scene presents the moment right after Esther broke the rules set by the Persian King against appearing before him without a summons. She broke that injunction, and dressed in her finest clothes, for the sake of begging mercy for the Persian Jews who were being persecuted by the King's duplicitous minister Haman. Secretly, she herself was one of these Persian Jews. In the common apocryphal version, Esther fainted immediately upon appearing before the King, which spurred him to rush to her aid and take pity on her. The story of Esther and Ahasuerus was used many times by female rulers in Europe to legitimise their dissent from their husbands' religious authority, so Artemisia's allegorical

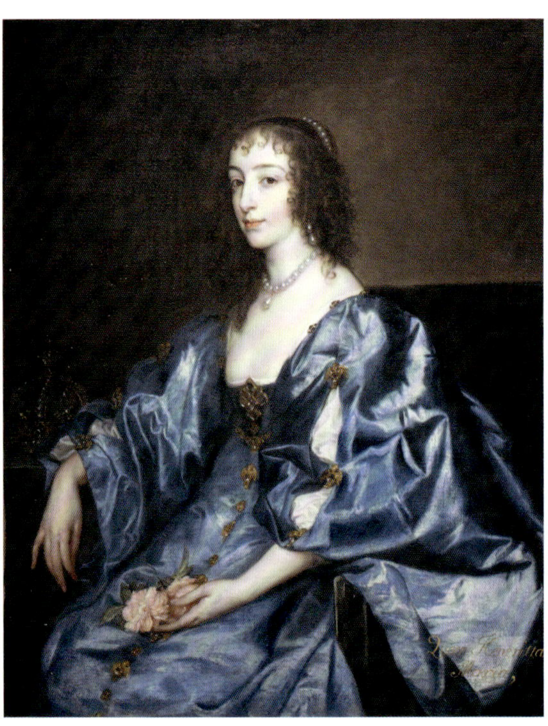

66 Anthony van Dyck, *Queen Henrietta Maria of England*, 1636–8, oil on canvas, 107.32 × 85.09 cm) (42 ¼ × 33 ½ in), San Diego Museum of Art

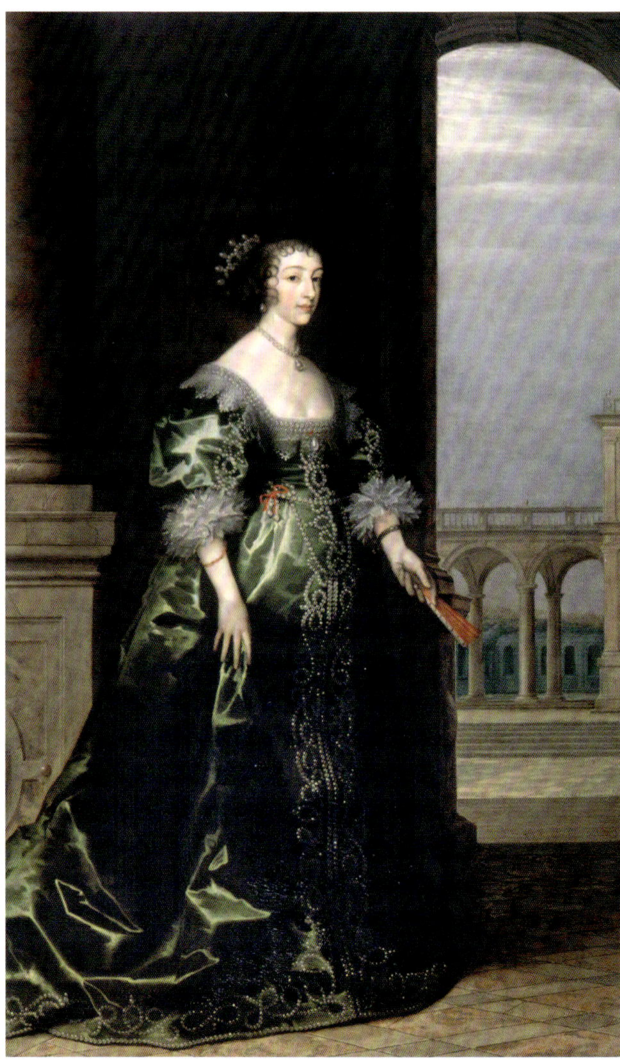

67 Unknown artist with background by Hendrick van Steenwyck, *Henrietta Maria*, c.1635, oil on canvas, 215.9 × 135.2 cm (85 × 53 ¼ in), National Portrait Gallery, London. Given by Henry Louis Bischoffsheim, 1899

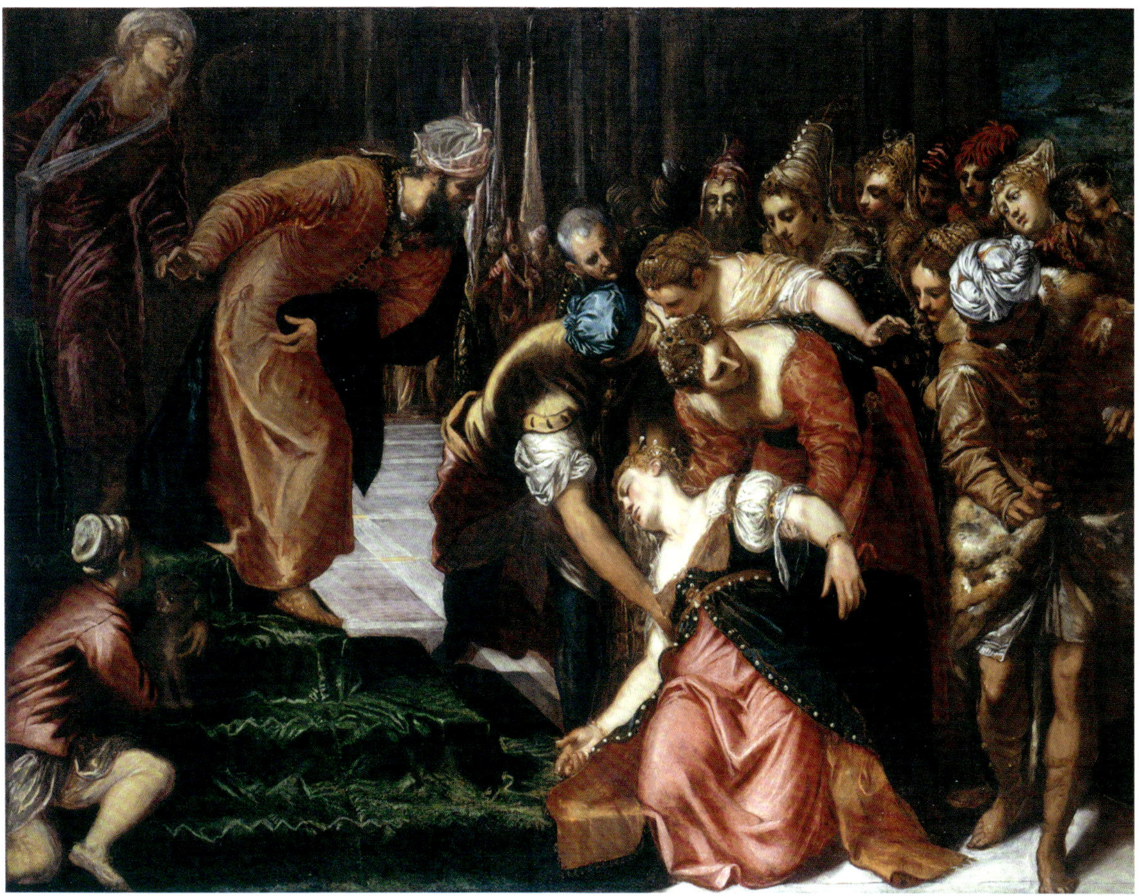

68 Tintoretto, *Esther Before Ahasuerus*, 1547–8, oil on canvas, 207.7 × 275 cm (81 ¾ × 108 ¼ in), The Royal Collection Trust, London

reference to Henrietta Maria's defence of English Catholics would have been widely understood by the original audience. Perhaps they would have also speculated that the Queen, like ancient Esther, would later seek the punishment of the modern-day Haman among Charles I's advisors.

Such a bold political statement has been missed until now, not only because the canvas was not placed in Artemisia's English period, but also because recent interpretations of the painting put it in a comic light. They point to the costume of King Ahasuerus in Artemisia's *Esther before Ahasuerus*, contending it was obsolete for the times and therefore the painting was meant to mock and ridicule the Persian King. Such interpretations ignore the fact that the very fashions worn by Artemisia's Ahasuerus – high boots, feathered cap, slashed pants and slashed doublet – had been worn by Grand Duke Cosimo II de' Medici when Artemisia was at the Florentine court (fig.64), and now, while she was in England, they represented the height of fashion. Charles I sports very similar ensembles in many of his official portraits (fig.65). In England at least, not only was Ahasuerus' clothing not a basis for ridicule, it was especially associated with the King. By the same token, Esther's curly hair was Henrietta's trademark. Likewise, Henrietta often

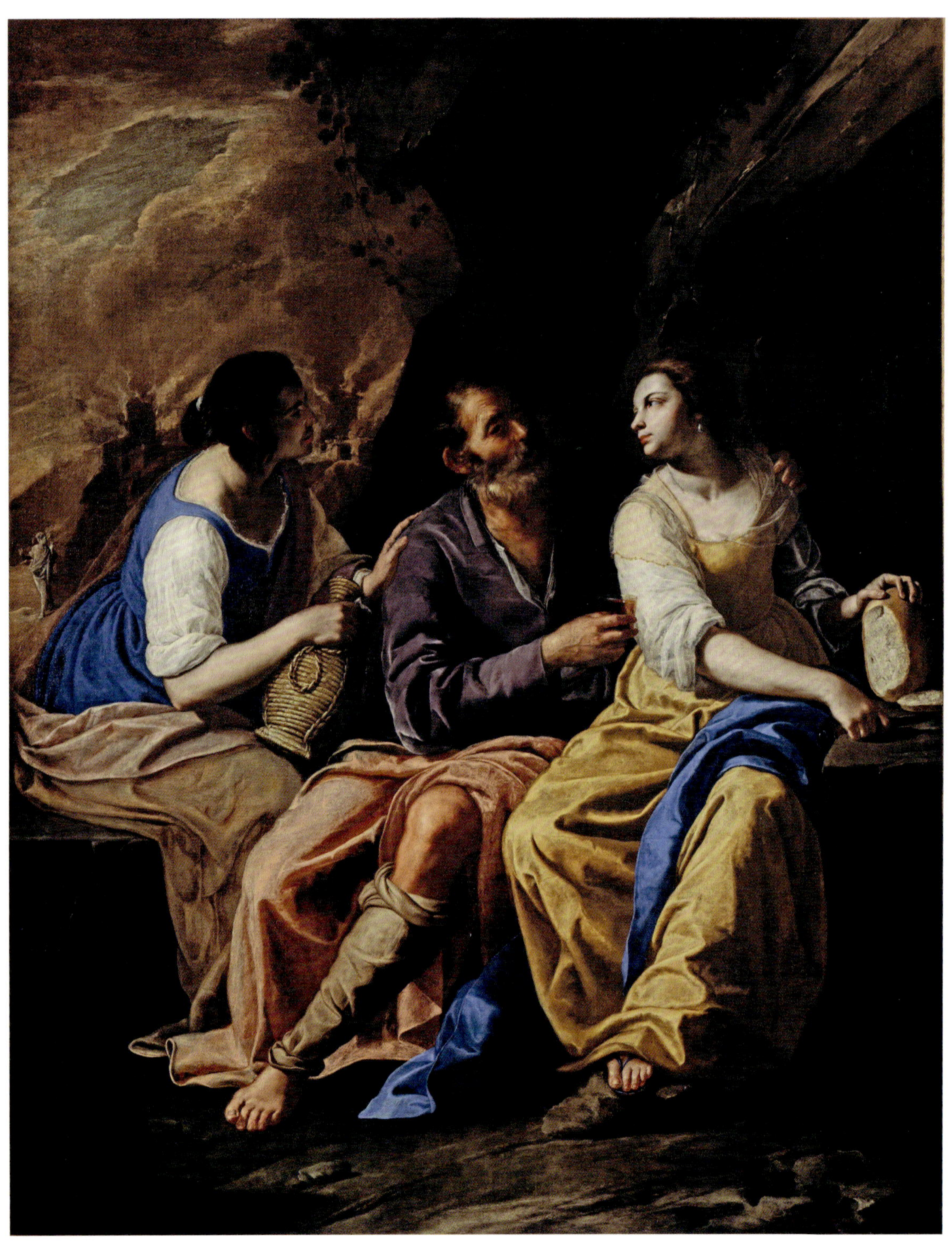

69 Artemisia Gentileschi, *Lot and His Daughters*, 1640–45, oil on canvas, 230.5 × 182.9 cm (90 ¾ × 72 in), Toledo Museum of Art, Ohio. Clarence Brown Fund 1983.107

wore golden and turquoise silk dresses like Esther's, and she was especially fond of deep bateau necklines as seen in portraits of her (fig.66, fig.67).

One additional point linking Artemisia's *Esther before Ahasuerus* to her time at the English court is its dimensions. Her painting measures 208.3 × 273.7 cm (82 × 107 ¾ in). Her father Orazio's *Joseph and Potiphar's Wife*, made for Charles I, is nearly the same size at 206 × 261.9 cm (81 ¼ × 103 ⅛ in). Another painting which it matches closely in size was also formerly in Charles I's collection: Tintoretto's *Esther and Ahasuerus* (1546–7, Royal Collection, Kensington Palace) (fig.68), one of the paintings of the Gonzaga collection that Charles I purchased in 1627 through his agent Lanier. Measuring 207.7 × 275 cm (81 ¾ × 108 ¼ in), Tintoretto's canvas was famous for being mentioned in Paolo Pino's 1548 art treatise as an ideal synthesis of Michelangelo's drawing and Titian's coloring.

It should not come as a surprise if Artemisia's theme repeats a subject already represented by Charles' collection. In several cases, Charles I commissioned Orazio Gentileschi and his daughter to paint, in similar dimensions, the subjects of the older Renaissance paintings he owned, especially his Tintorettos: *Tarquin and Lucretia*, *Apollo and the Arts*, *The Finding of Moses by the Pharaoh's Daughter*, and *Susanna* were all done again, to scale, by the Gentileschis. As a modern take on works done in the previous century by Tintoretto and Veronese's workshop, Artemisia's *Esther before Ahasuerus* was her artistic rejoinder to the Venetian masters. But it was also a commentary on the contemporary world. By portraying Henrietta Maria as a new Esther, protector of the persecuted Catholics of England, Artemisia became a player in a perilous political game. Serving as the agent of a Catholic strategy of soft diplomacy exposed her to dangers best appreciated from hindsight. Viewed from abroad, Charles' tolerance promised peace with Catholic Europe and inspired hope for his conversion, but in England that same tolerance ignited hostilities that exploded into a war over the religious policies of the English crown.

Artemisia seems to have enjoyed the favour of the Queen, for she stayed in England for nearly a year after burying her father. By late 1639, however, her letters show that she was anxious to return to Italy. Her distress was shared by other Italians. A letter found by Cristina Terzaghi indicates that Artemisia's brothers, Francesco and Giulio Gentileschi, returned to Rome in 1640 under the protection of Cardinal Francesco Barberini; presumably they provided the escort for their sister's return to Naples.[24] Giovanna Garzoni also left in 1640, taking shelter in Paris for several months. The next year, Aletheia Howard and her husband escaped with Maria de' Medici to the Dutch Republic. Civil war officially broke out in England in 1642. The Queen tarried, however, even as the House of Commons impeached her in 1643 for crimes of high treason. Finally, in 1644, Henrietta fled England to save her life.

It is tempting to frame Artemisia Gentileschi's *Lot and His Daughters* (Toledo Museum of Art) (fig.69) in the context of this political conflagration that sent so many souls in search of shelter. The painting has often been dated to immediately before Artemisia's English period, but it takes on a new urgency when placed in the aftermath. Artemisia's picture captures the strangeness of this Biblical narrative (Genesis 19:30–36) about the family of a good man named Lot who manages to escape God's destruction of the evil city of Sodom, and how Lot's daughters agree to seduce their own father in order to perpetuate his line, from which the Messiah will be born. The graceful poses, courtly gestures and sweetly colored clothes of the three foreground figures, are made to look utterly irrational and improbable when placed against a cataclysmic fire that sears the entire sky, as winds carry belching smoke and smells of burning bodies wherever they blow. The lips of the daughter on the left, before they kiss her father, are aglow like embers radiating the heat of the dying city. Yet where other painters – her father included – might have reduced the sense of the embraces to mundane incest, Artemisia sublimates the actions of these good people into a reminder of the

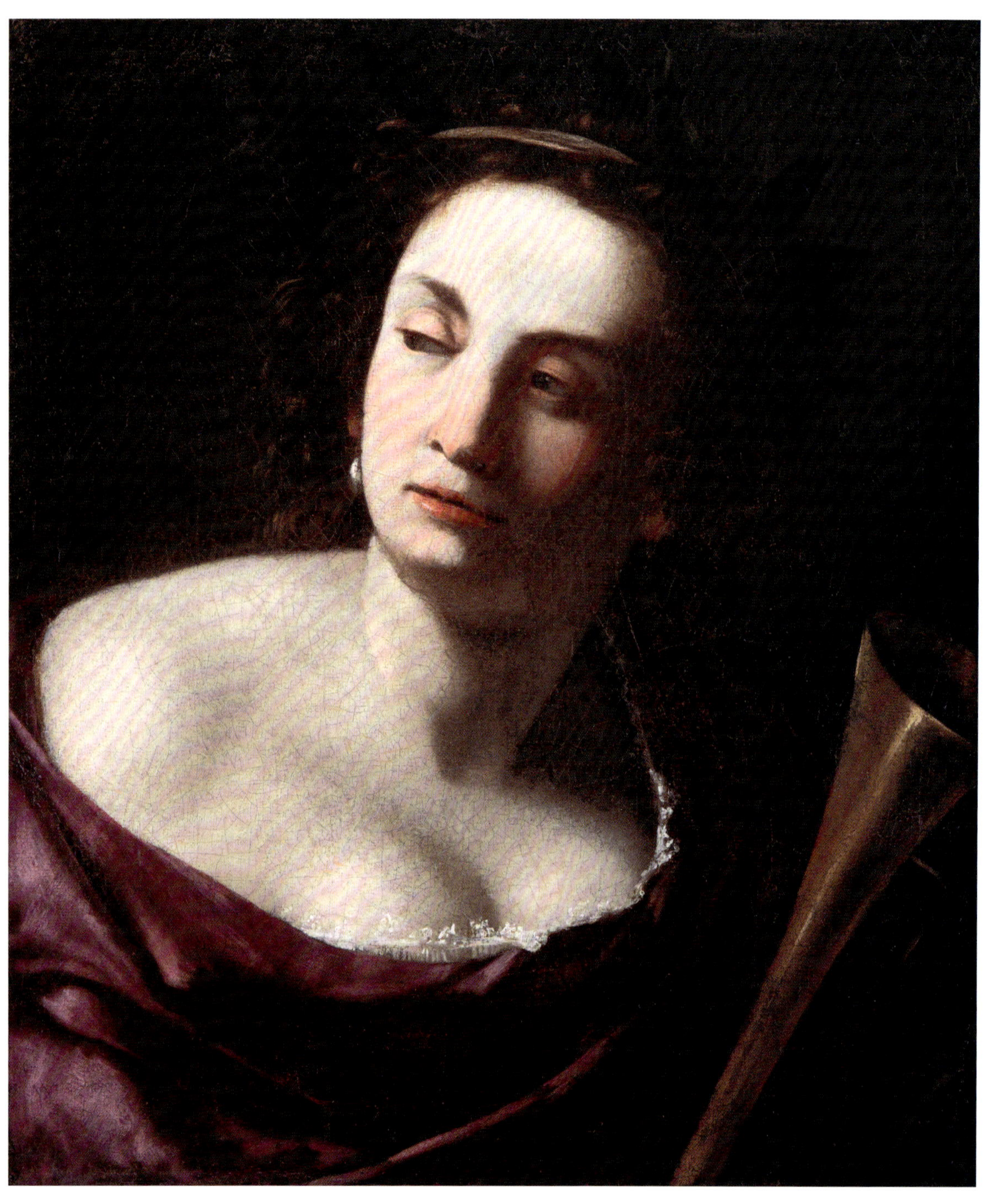

70 Artemisia Gentileschi, *Clio the Muse of History (Fame)*, *c.*1642, oil on canvas, 127.6 × 97.2 cm (50 ¼ × 38 ¼ in), private collection, USA

religious history of salvation and divine providence to which they belong. Wine and bread – symbols of the Eucharist – are solemnly offered as the bodies align in a trinitarian formation; the large dark form behind Lot is a tree that evokes the idea of a family tree, that is, the genitive line that links him, by divine plan, to Christ; and the rock on which one daughter places her foot suggests the metaphor for the foundation of Christ's church on earth.

As grand as such a pictorial narrative may be, Artemisia nevertheless found a way to weave into it a more personal one: the story of her last embrace with her father. Whether this painting is dated before her arrival in London, or after her departure, the painting must have reverberated with her thoughts about her own complicated relationship with a man who had given her both her life and her art. Moreover, if the painting does, in fact, date from immediately after her stay in London, then it is natural to speculate that Orazio's last appearance is imprinted on Lot's haggard and weathered face and in his clouded eyes, and that Artemisia remembered the feeling of his leathery hand on her shoulder. A similar dutiful tenderness that overrides other potentially conflicting feelings is seen in Artemisia's *Roman Charity*, from around 1645, now in a private collection in Puglia, in which the brave daughter Pero breastfeeds her imprisoned and starving father Cimon. This latter painting, which Viviana Farina has credibly linked to the incarceration endured by its patron, Count Giangirolamo II Acquaviva d'Aragona from 1643 to 1644, nonetheless bears the palpable imprint of Artemisia's personal memories, as the daughter who came to her irascible father's side in his hour of need.[25]

Like Lot's daughter, who was expected to continue her father's line, Artemisia, too, was charged with carrying forth her father's artistic legacy – something none of his sons was capable of doing in any significant sense. On some days, the unconventionality of Artemisia's status as a professional woman artist, and the loneliness and difficulty that came with it, must have felt like a burden or an inherited curse. One can only hope that, in the surreal setting of a distant British Babylon where neither father nor daughter spoke the language, Artemisia was able to turn to Orazio with the same grace as Lot's daughter, willing to forgive her father and willing to forgive herself, perhaps trusting in some larger destiny.

THE MYSTERY OF THE BODY

Artemisia's final period in Naples offered a respite from earlier pressures and provided at least some satisfactions. On 13 March 1649 she married her daughter to a 'knight of the Order of Saint James', thereby elevating Prudenzia's station in life. Artemisia ran a smoothly functioning studio in which several highly skilled painters – masters in their own right – might contract with her to collaborate on paintings. The arrangements with Onofrio Palumbo were particularly convenient, because they allowed her to leave the bulk of less important work to him while she drew, sketched and added her 'master's touches' to the near-finished canvases, much in the way Rubens divided labour with Jacob Jordaens or Anthony van Dyck.

The last decades of Artemisia's life are symbolised by the *Self-Portrait as Clio the Muse of History (Fame)* in a private collection (fig.70), in which Fame appears older, wiser and somewhat more cynical, as she looks askance at the society she must dutifully glorify. In these years, Artemisia dedicated more effort and consideration to her correspondence than ever before, as proven by her spirited letters to her Sicilian patron, Don Antonio Ruffo. At times the power of her writing and the intensity of her sentiment vastly exceed the ordinary purposes these letters served, suggesting that she anticipated her letters would be circulated one day among a curious and cultivated readership (as often did happen with the correspondence of famous individuals of her era). Although she frequently complained about her need for money, she clearly was not destitute, since those

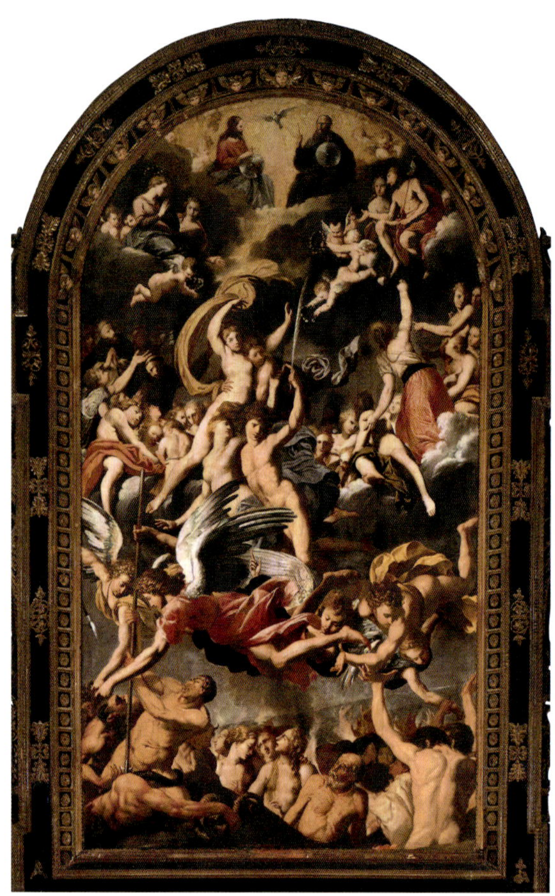

71 Giovanni Andrea Coppola, *Purgatory*, *c.*1649, oil on canvas, dimensions unknown, Co-Cathedral of Sant'Agata, Gallipoli, Italy

letters were written by scribes who did not assist Artemisia for free. Aside from financial issues, her missives occasionally address Artemisia's concerns about men's biases against women. Her letters to Ruffo in fact have furnished some of the most defiant feminist statements of her literary life, statements that still stir feelings today:

> 'I will show your Lordship what a woman can do'; 'A woman's work raises doubts until her work is seen'; 'You will find the spirit of Caesar in this soul of a woman'; 'If I were a man, I can't imagine it would have turned out this way'.[26]

Several of these impassioned expressions may have sprung from the argot of educated, well-read women; however they were triggered by instances of professional frustrations and obstacles that even artisan-class women of Artemisia's time could relate to.

For instance, the last complaint, 'If I were a man, I can't imagine it would have turned out this way', followed her account of having been cheated with regard to a presentation drawing of the *Souls in Purgatory* for her patron, the Bishop of Sant'Agata in Gallipoli, Consalvo de Rueda. The Bishop had taken the drawing that she gave him in good faith, but then he turned around and hired a cheaper artist – Giovanni Andrea Coppola, a Florentine painter who was a relative of Rueda's vicar – to execute it. Thus, in around 1642, Coppola completed a large painted altarpiece for Sant'Agata in Gallipoli on the basis of Artemisia's composition (fig.71). Clearly, many costly hours of drawing male and female models had gone into the preparation of her composition, so her anger is understandable.

Rueda, an esteemed theologian who promoted recourse to the viaticum for mere cases of illness, must have warned his flock frequently about the importance of taking measures to lessen one's time in Purgatory. He was also well known for his frugality, and for skimping on church expenses in order to help the poor. In light of the latter, Artemisia should have anticipated such chicanery from him, and perhaps Rueda would have cheated a male artist the same way – we shall never know – but what counts is that Artemisia habitually perceived and metabolised such disappointments as the consequence of a deep disparity in society between the sexes.

This crystallisation of Artemisia's ideas about the treatment of women in her society roughly coincided with a boom in her clients' demand for images of female nudes, painted true to life and

72 Artemisia Gentileschi, *Aurora*, *c.*1635, oil on canvas, 218 × 146 cm (85 ⅞ × 57 ½ in), private collection, Italy

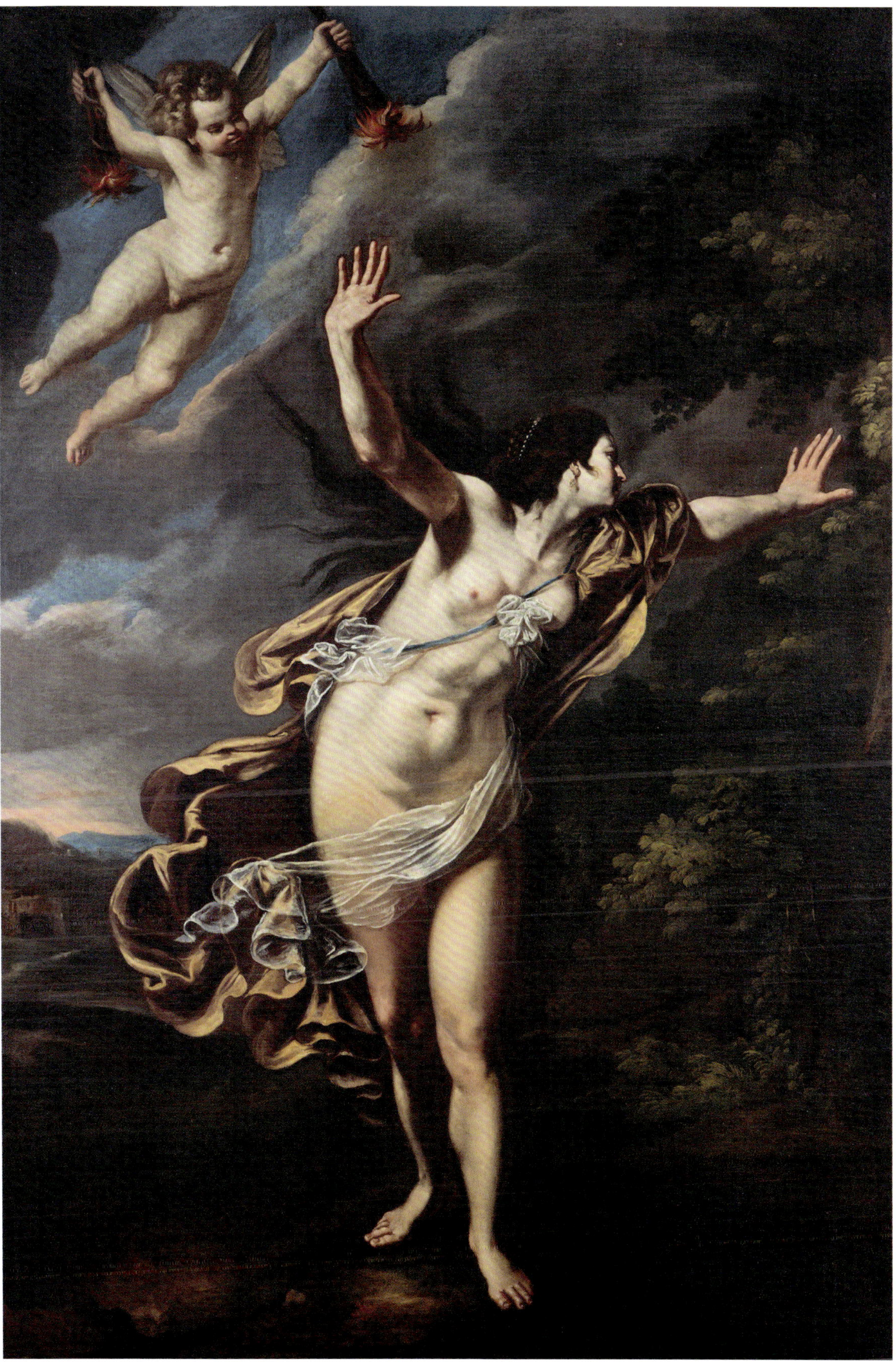

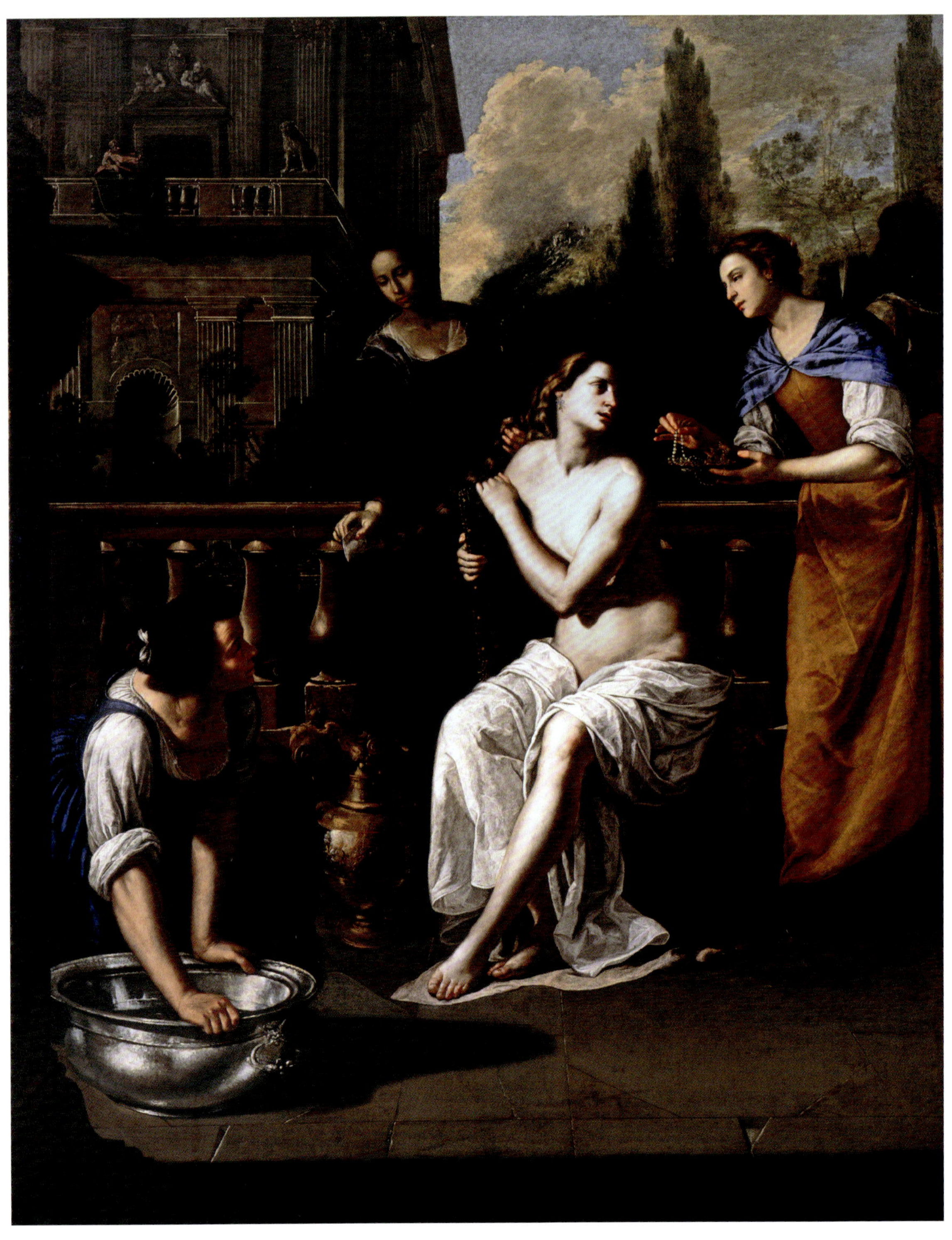

73 Artemisia Gentileschi, Viviano Codazzi, and Domenico Gargiulo, *Bathsheba at her Bath*, *c.*1642–5, oil on canvas, 265.43 × 209.55 cm (104 ½ × 82 ½ in), Columbus Museum of Art, Ohio. Acc.no.1967.006

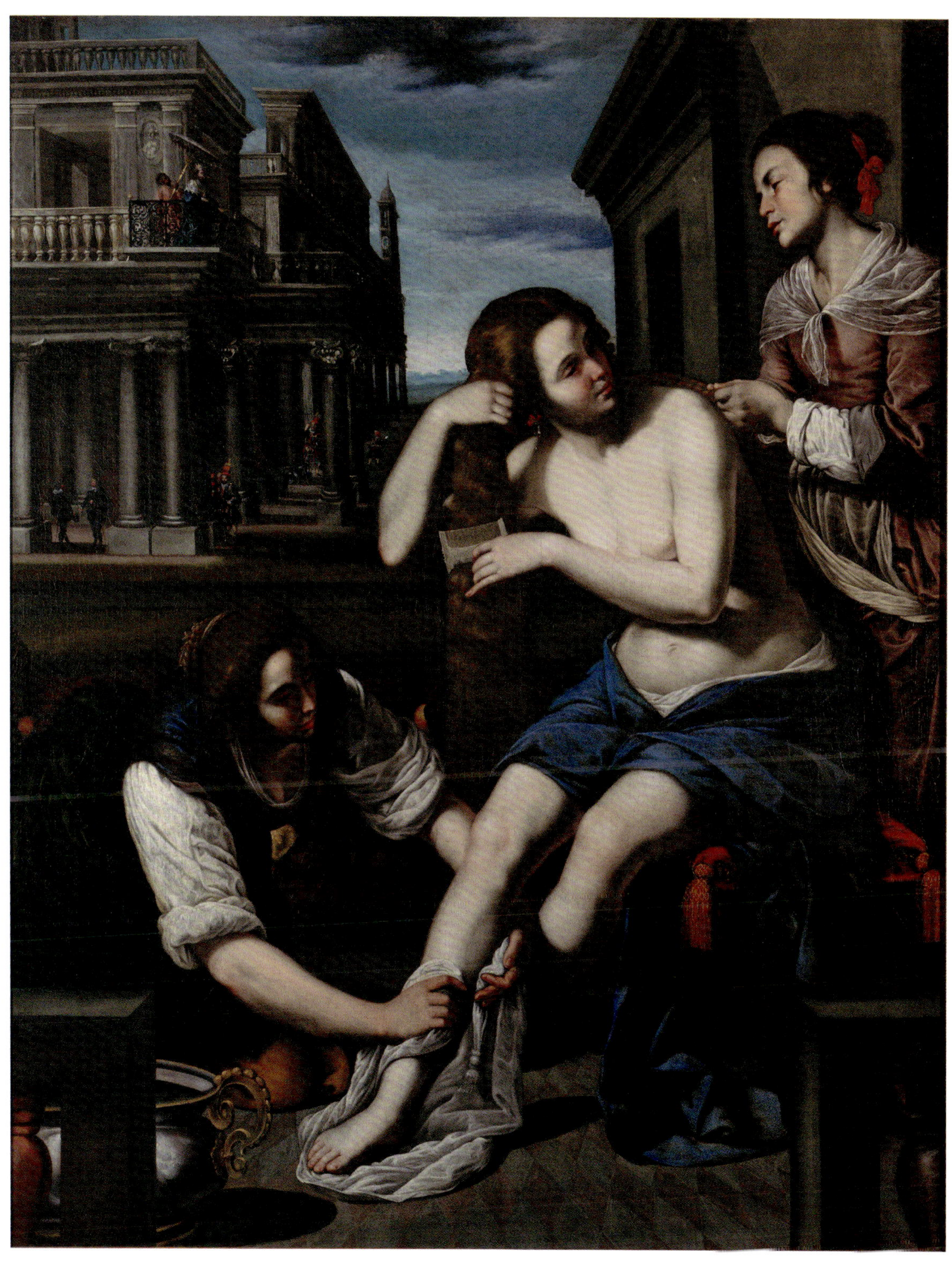

74 Artemisia Gentileschi and Bernardo Cavallino, *Bathsheba at her Bath*, *c.*1645–7, oil on canvas, 185.2 × 145.4 cm (73 × 57 ¼ in), Cesare Lampronti Gallery, London

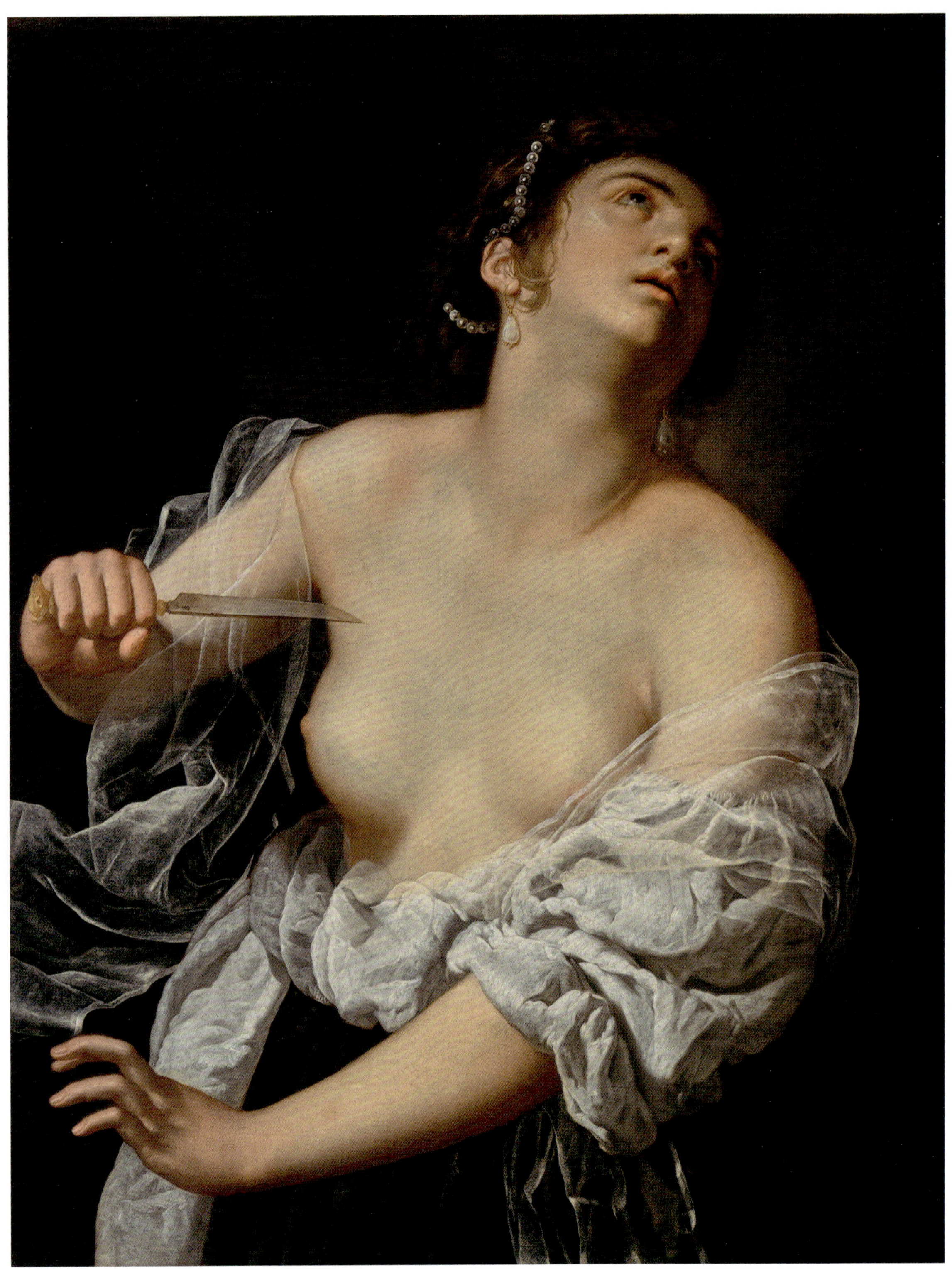

75 Artemisia Gentileschi, *Lucretia*, *c.*1635–45, oil on canvas, 92.9 × 72.7 cm (36 ⅝ × 28 ⅝ in), The J. Paul Getty Museum, Los Angeles

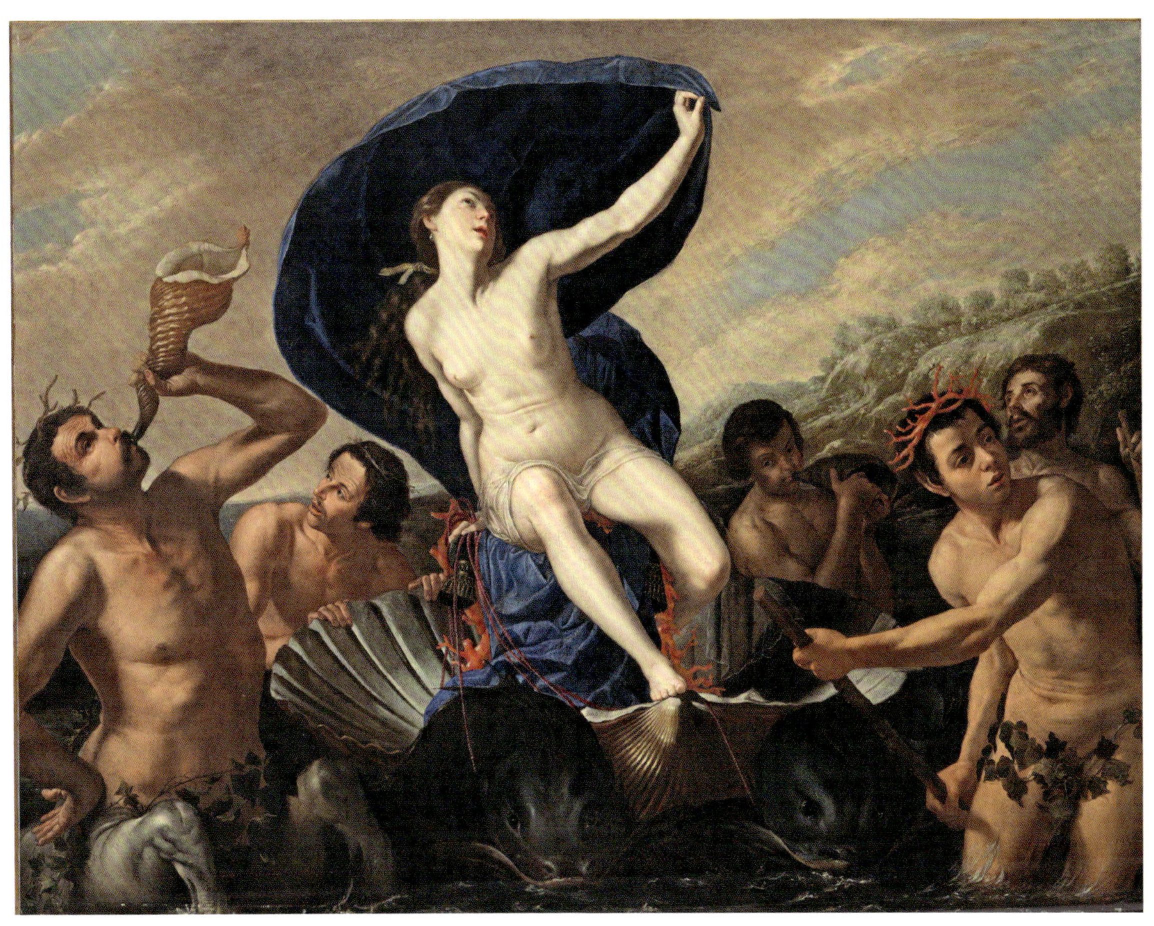

76 Artemisia Gentileschi, *The Triumph of Galatea*, *c.*1649, oil on canvas, 196.8 × 254.5 cm (77 ½ × 100 ⅛ in), private collection

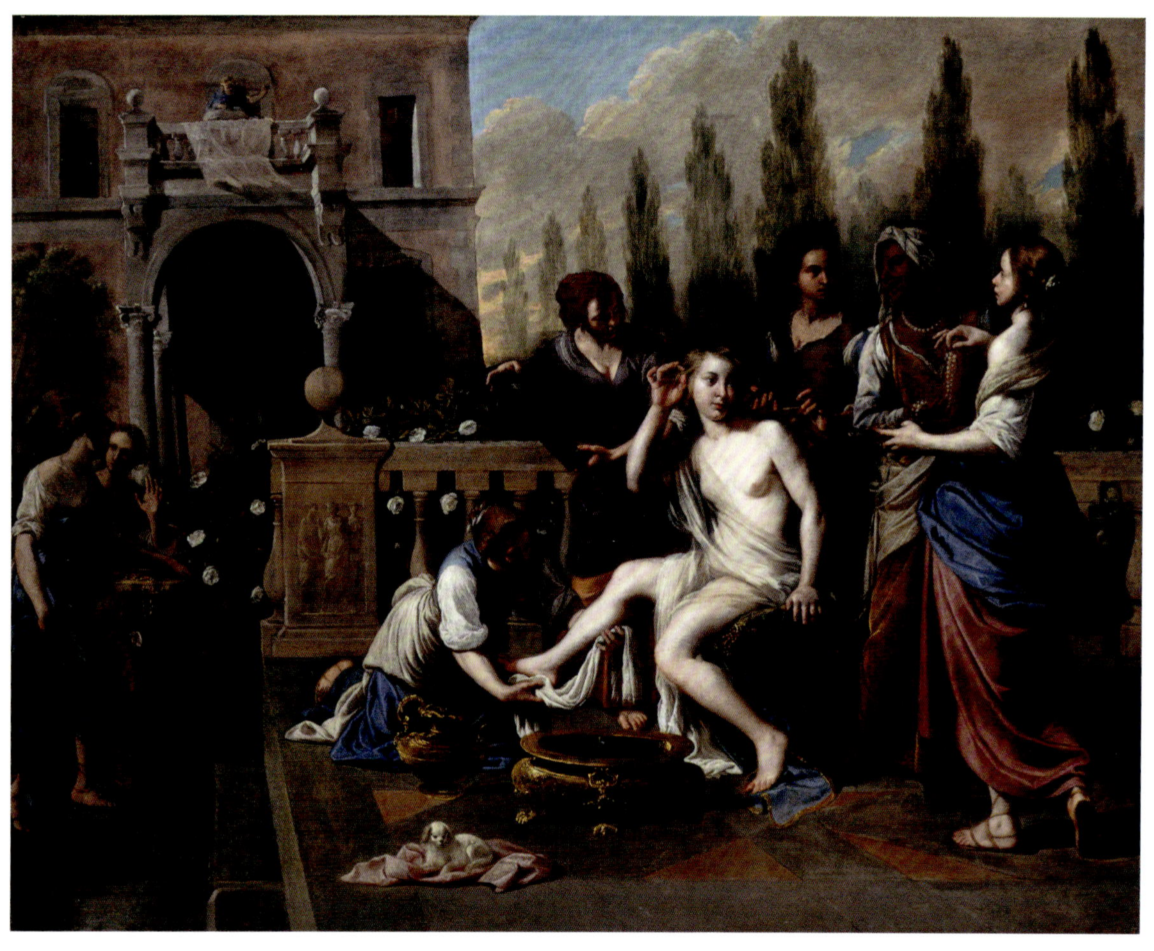

77 Artemisia Gentileschi and Domenico Gargiulo, *Bathsheba at her Bath (David and Bathsheba)*, 1650s, oil on canvas, 84.5 × 115.6 cm (33 ¼ × 45 ½ in), The Ringling Museum, Sarasota, Florida

life-sized. Images of multiple nude women grouped together in subjects, like *Diana at her Bath*, fed her clients' aesthetic appetites with the 'various kinds of beauty' that she achieved by using different models and, perhaps, on some occasions, different workshop assistants. To justify the high price-tag she put on her *Diana and Actaeon* for Don Antonio Ruffo in 1650, she explained how many different views of womanhood he was getting for the price and how expensive it had been for her to find real women who could produce the effects of abundance and variety associated with the best works of art:

> The expenses are great on account of having these female nudes . . . the expenses are unbearable because fifty [female models] might take off their clothes and barely one of them makes the cut. In this painting I need more than just one model because there are eight figures and it is necessary to do various kinds of beauty.[27]

Passages such as this one in her correspondence show that Artemisia's evolving business model had led her to engage in a kind of mercenary commodification of painted flesh whose value could be mathematically calculated. She shamed her Sicilian patron Ruffo in 1649 for not knowing that formula: 'Everywhere else I have been paid one hundred scudi per figure. And this was in Florence, as well as Venice and Rome.'[28]

The rapport between Artemisia's painted female nudes and the real women who posed for her became more direct in the years leading up to her complaint to Ruffo about the high cost of models. Her truthful depiction of her models' imperfect bodies is very apparent, for example, in Artemisia's *Aurora* of *c.*1635 (fig.72). This painting of the swiftly moving goddess of the dawn bears such signs of feminine aging as stretchmarks, heavy thighs and lower-belly fat. Moreover, these are all the more discernible because of the crepuscular half-light that bathes them, an effect which particularly impressed Baldinucci. It is as if those blemishes were meant to assure her clients the prices she was demanding were justified: these 'accidents of nature' showed that she had painstakingly studied her live models, thus backing up her claims about the sizable outlays for modeling costs. But realistic nude figures, aside from being a basis for her pricing strategy, also played a role in her portrayal of 'various kinds of beauty', that was noted above. These late depictions of particularised women's bodies, with characteristic imperfections – so different from her highly idealised nudes of the 1630s – allowed Artemisia to diversify the canon of beauty in a way that celebrated real women, even as they aged.

Riccardo Lattuada has compellingly suggested that Artemisia deliberately shared the making of these paintings of nude women with one or more male collaborators (most probably Bernardo Cavallino, Domenico Gargiulo, Viviano Codazzi, Onofrio Palumbo or Massimo Stanzione), as a time-saving expedient, but also as a means of creating a visual bouquet of various artistic styles for connoisseurs who appreciated artistic ensembles the same way they might listen to a musical camerata.[29] (See for instance figs 74 and 77.) If this was the case, then perhaps Artemisia's art could no longer offer viewers the morally 'safe' spectatorship of women's bodies through a woman's eyes, as she had when young and proud to defend the autonomy of her artistic style, an impulse that was described above with regard to her very first *Susanna and the Elders*. Did Artemisia, we might wonder, feel uncomfortable about this high-volume production of nudes – nudes who might also be male, too, as in the case of the varied naked male figures forming the aquatic retinues of Tritons in her several late *Galatea* (fig.76) and *Amphitrite* paintings? Did her trade in nude imagery – such as in her oft-repeated representations of Venus (fig.54 above), Lucretia (fig.75),[30] or Bathsheba (figs 73 and 77) – ever lead her to a moral impasse or to a sense of surfeit? Or was she indifferent to everything but the artistic result?

Our own society's attitudes regarding the sensual allure of painted nude bodies do not always

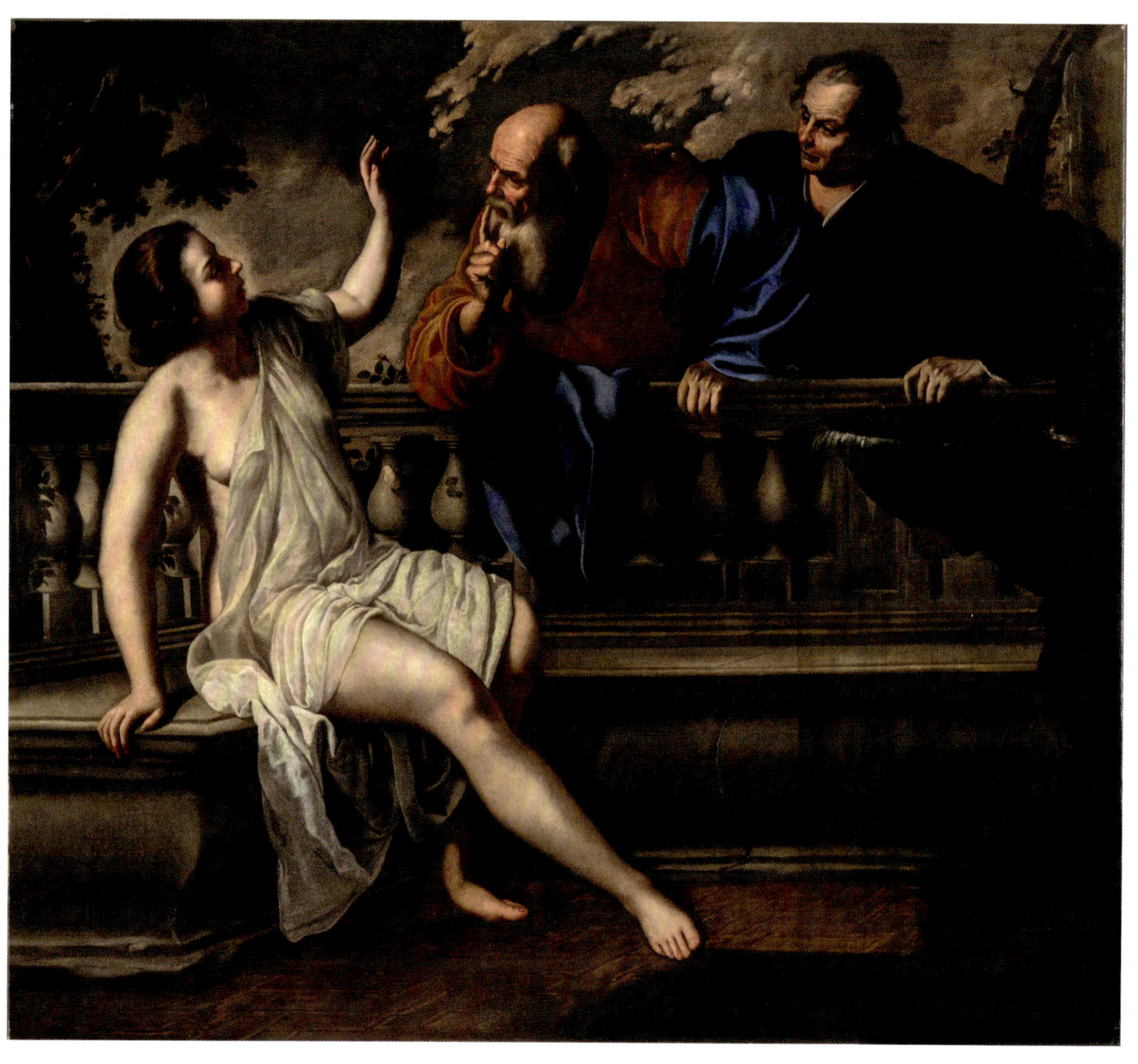

78 Artemisia Gentileschi, *Susanna and the Elders*, 1652, oil on canvas, 200.3 × 225.6 cm (78 ⅞ × 88 13/16 in), Polo Museale dell'Emilia Romagna, Pinacoteca Nazionale, Bologna

correspond to those of Artemisia's era. It is often difficult to determine whether an easel painting like Artemisia's *Susanna and the Elders* from 1622 (fig.37) was intended for a hedonistic eye, or a devout one, or both kinds simultaneously. Nude or nearly nude bodies of Adam, Eve, Christ, Saint Onofrius, Saint Agatha, Saint Laurence and others, frequently appeared in the decorations of Baroque churches, as well as in domestic devotional art. Moreover, we would do well to recall that around 1642, as described above, Artemisia had aspired to making a large altarpiece for a church in Puglia that depicted Purgatory as a thunderous, roiling cascade of naked human bodies. In this case, it is possible that she had contemplated the theological teaching that those bodies do not exist in Purgatory, meaning that the nude bodies on the canvas are merely the artist's metaphors for depicting the individual, invisible souls that carry us into eternity.

THE MYSTERY OF ARTEMISIA'S BODY

It is a deep irony that with regard to one of the most celebrated individuals of the seventeenth century we are completely at a loss to pinpoint the earthly remains of her body. Averardo de' Medici, a Florentine nobleman who had taken a deep interest in Artemisia after purchasing her last known work, the *Susanna and the Elders* of 1652 (fig.78), wrote this in 1792 about her last known traces:

> It is much more difficult to assert how long she lived, and where and when her days came to an end. With all likelihood, she died in Naples, not only because she carried out many paintings there but also because it is well known that she spent the better part of her life there. Moreover, although it has been written that she passed away in 1640, it is nevertheless certain that even in 1652 she was still painting brilliantly, as demonstrated by the inscription dated with that year on the acclaimed painting of the *Susanna*: and therefore it is unquestionable that she lived well into her sixties.
>
> Thanks to a distinguished Florentine citizen who presided over the sumptuous restoration of the church of S. Giovanni dei Fiorentini in Naples in 1785, we have the reliable notice that on that occasion a large marble gravemarker was lost, although it is not known whether it was destroyed or merely covered up under the new pavement; that stone, which had formerly been near the chapel of the Riccio family, was inscribed in its center with these words: HEIC ARTIMISIA. Perhaps this brief epigraph, like the famous one in Perugia reading 'ossa Bartoli', was meant to point to the location of her remains and to invoke simply by means of her first name a most fitting eulogy for the outstanding painter we are celebrating?[31]

Incredibly, although more than two centuries have elapsed since Medici wrote this ending to her biography, we cannot add much to his scenario. Riccardo Lattuada and Eduardo Nappi have shed light on the matter by publishing some dated financial documents regarding Artemisia's collaboration with Onofrio Palumbo, demonstrating that she lived at least until January of 1654.[32] And Adelina Modesti succeeded in discovering the present-day whereabouts of Averardo de' Medici's painting, long hidden from view under an incorrect attribution.[33] We still cannot say when her life ended, although the massive mortality spawned by the plague of 1656 has reasonably been proposed as the direct or indirect cause of her death.

In the absence of an explanation of what end was met by the artist's body, we can console ourselves with the marvels of the 'loquacious and beautiful' artworks she has left behind, works that still talk to their viewers – and still provoke their viewers to talk about her.

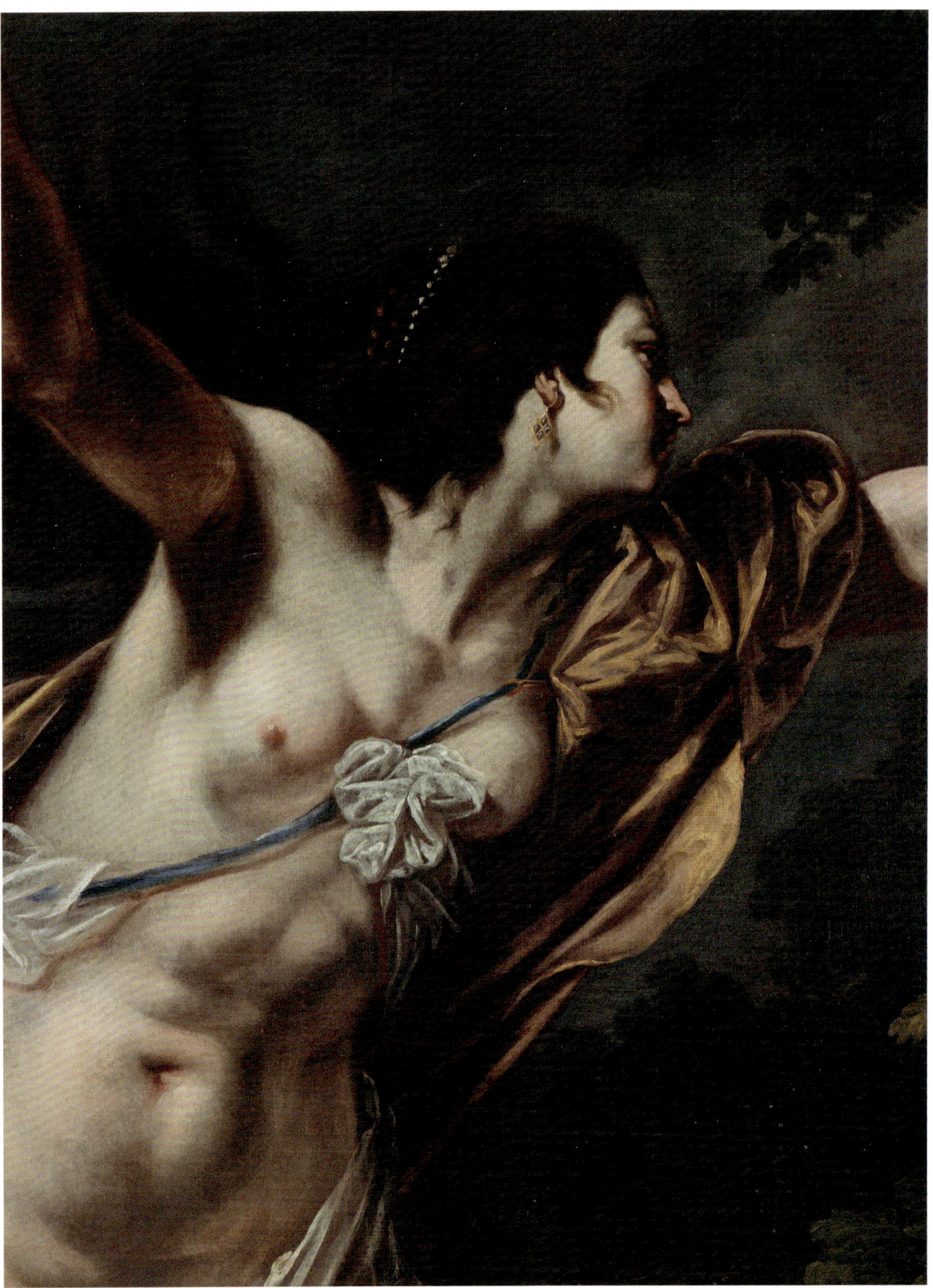

Epilogue

The passage of time, aided by scholarly diligence, may perhaps one day reveal the final resting place of Artemisia's body. In the meantime, each of us can look through her oeuvre and elect an ideal body from among her many painted ones that seems best to represent her spirit. For me, that ideal body is not one of her renowned self-portraits. It is, instead, her painting of the goddess of the dawn, *Aurora* (figs 72 and 79), a divinity who has momentarily left her post at the head of Apollo's blazing celestial chariot to walk on the earth among us humans.

Why she has come here, why she has removed the yellow gown she wears while leading the sun god's retinue, why she readily soils her ethereal white feet in the mud and sod of our dark realm is explained in a rather obscure ancient myth by pseudo-Apollodorus (1.4.4.): after Aurora flirted with Mars, who was Venus' beloved, Venus took revenge on Aurora by cursing her to constantly fall in love with one flawed earthling after another. The agony of the unwillingly concupiscent goddess was retold in 1629, in a Latin poem written by John Milton: Elegy 5, '*In his twentieth year. The coming spring*'. The poem tells us that Aurora has been unfaithful to her aging human husband Tithonus, in order to lie with the handsome young hunter Cephalus – also called Aeolides – in the grass under the cover of darkness, and it is here, wandering in the grass, that Apollo finds her, chides her for her infidelity, and reminds her that the deity Hymettus has been complicit in all this by carrying her torches – so that she can hold her lover. Milton's poem ends with the shamed goddess casting off her sensual reverie in order to rise to Apollo and return to her serious business of hastening the horses that speed the light of day across the sky.

Artemisia's painting is essentially set in the same narrative moment, but her portrayal of Aurora's last steps on earth before returning to heaven are interpreted very differently, in a way never anticipated by any poet or painter before her. We see Aurora on her own. Her earthly lovers are nowhere in sight, nor is Apollo; only her little heavenly helper, Hymettus, is present. Her unabashedly nude Amazonian body ripples with health and vigor as she courses surefooted and swiftly along her path. She is undeniably feminine, and yet she moves with the spirit of Caesar. This virago is not Milton's cowering Aurora, chastened and shamed into obedience. Instead, Artemisia's Aurora takes this time for herself and willfully tarries before answering Apollo's call. Turning her head from her destination, she looks upon the world, raises her powerful arms high, and uses her life-giving, rosy-fingered hands to instill nature with vitality.

Aurora's gesturing arms, one reaching to heaven and the other to the forest, recall the madrigals that

79 Artemisia Gentileschi, *Aurora* (detail of fig.72), *c*.1635, oil on canvas, private collection, Italy

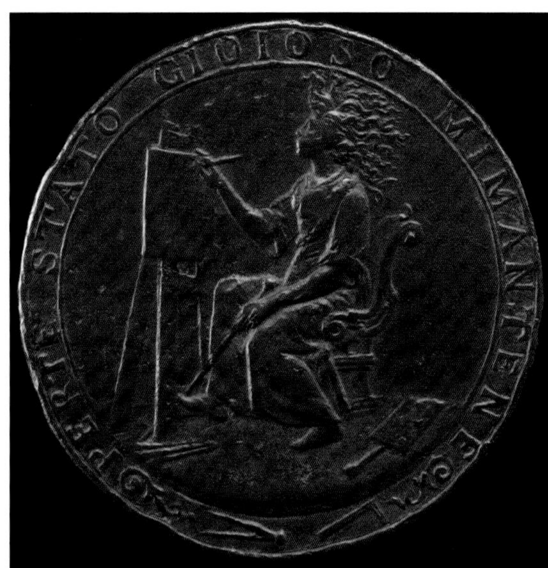

80 Reverse of Felice Antonio Casoni, portrait medal of Lavinia Fontana, 1611, bronze, diameter: 6.6 cm (2 9/16 in), National Gallery of Art, Washington, DC. Samuel H. Kress Collection, 1957.14.1071.a

Torquato Tasso wrote for the Medici Grand Duchess Bianca Cappello in the 1580s, which praise Aurora as the goddess who brings life to plants and flowers with her light. The life-giving arms also evoke Artemisia's role as a painter, giving color and beauty to the world with her gifted handiwork. Artemisia's craft is aptly represented by the goddess of the morning's earliest light because, as underlined in Meister Eckhart's interpretation of *aurora consurgens* in the Biblical Canticles 6:9, the rising dawn is a mixture of light and dark. Artemisia was thus in Aurora's realm when, as a Caravaggist painter, she built her forms at the meeting point between illumination and shadow. Additionally, linking Aurora to Artemisia's painting activity are the dark tresses streaming out in all directions from the goddess' head. Michael Levey was the first to connect the loose, dark locks falling around the head of the painter in Artemisia's *Self-Portrait as the Allegory of Painting* (fig.61), with the dishevelled black hair signifying 'imaginative thought' in the allegorical figure of Painting (*Pittura*) in Ripa's *Iconologia*, as mentioned above.[1] Just as Ripa described them, the flying locks of a female painter can also be seen in the allegorical figure of Painting on the reverse of a portrait medal – made in 1611 by Felice Antonio Casoni – to honor Lavinia Fontana (fig.80).

Artemisia could not have met Milton in England because in 1638–9, the Calvinist poet was in Florence. Throughout his long stay, Milton was an honored guest in Jacopo Gaddi's art-filled palace, a Parnassus on the Arno, where he recited his Latin poems in the company of Carlo Dati, Piero Frescobaldi, Antonio Francini and other members of Florence's Svegliati and Apatisti Academies, before eventually moving on to Rome as the guest of Cardinal Francesco Barberini. It is not known who commissioned Artemisia's *Aurora*. In the late seventeenth century, however, Filippo Baldinucci admired Artemisia's *Aurora* in Palazzo Arrighetti-Gaddi. This palace, adjoined to the palace where Milton lived and mingled with fellow poets during his halcyon sojourn in Florence, is as fitting a place as any to envision Artemisia's happiness – a happiness we hope was not as fleeting as that of her restless goddess of the half-light.

Notes

PREFACE

1 Sheila Barker, 'The First Biography of Artemisia Gentileschi: Self-Fashioning and Proto-feminist Art History in Cristofano Bronzini's Notes on Women Artists', *Mitteilungen des Kunsthistorieschen Institutes*, vol.60, no.3, 2018, pp 416–17.

2 The phrase 'di bellissimo, molto vivace, e fiero aspetto' was applied by Baldinucci specifically to *The Allegory of Inclination*; see Filippo Baldinucci, *Notizie dei professori del disegno da Cimabue in qua*, ed. F. Ranalli, V. Batelli e Compagni, Florence, 1846, vol.3, p.713.

3 Mary D. Garrard, *Artemisia Gentileschi: The Image of the Female Hero in Italian Baroque Art*, Princeton University Press, Princeton, 1989, esp. pp 13–138; Elizabeth Cropper, 'New Documents for Artemisia Gentileschi's Life in Florence', *The Burlington Magazine*, vol.135, 1993, pp 760–61; and R. Ward Bissell, *Artemisia Gentileschi and the Authority of Art: Critical Reading and Catalogue Raisonné*, The Pennsylvania State University Press, University Park, 1999, pp 1–102.

4 Francesco Solinas (ed.), with Michele Nicolaci and Yuri Primarosa, *Lettere di Artemisia. Edizione critica e annotata con quarantatre documenti inediti*, De Luca Editori d'Arte, Rome, 2011.

5 Eric Bianchi and Sheila Barker, '"Upon His Visit to See My Paintings": Artemisia Gentileschi's and Pietro della Valle's Exchanged Sonnets', *The Burlington Magazine*, (forthcoming).

6 Mary D. Garrard, *Artemisia Gentileschi and Feminism in Early Modern Europe*, Reaktion Books, London, 2020.

7 Ann Sutherland Harris and Linda Nochlin, exh.cat., *Women Artists: 1550–1950*, Los Angeles County Museum of Art and Alfred A. Knopf, Los Angeles and New York, 1976, p.41.

8 Francesco da Sangallo to Benedetto Varchi in Giovanni Gaetano Bottari, *Raccolta di lettere sulla pittura, scultura ed architettura scritte dai più celebri personaggi che in dette arti fiorirono dal secolo XV al XVII*, Pagliarini, Rome, 1757, vol.I, p.35.

9 Arezzo, Casa Museo Vasari, Archivio Vasari 31, fol.57v.

INTRODUCTION

1 Fredrika H. Jacobs, 'Woman's Capacity to Create: The Unusual Case of Sofonisba Anguissola', *Renaissance Quarterly*, vol.47, no.1, Spring 1994, p.76. 'Virtuous envy' is the phrase used by Dionisio Atanagi to describe Spilimbergo in 1561; see Anne Jacobson Schutte, 'Irene di Spilimbergo: The Image of a Creative Woman in Late Renaissance Italy', *Renaissance Quarterly*, vol.44, no.1, Spring 1991, pp 42–61.

2 Valerio Morucci, *Baronial Patronage of Music in Early Modern Rome*, Routledge, New York and London, 2018, p.14.

3 Rinaldina Russell (trans.), 'Margherita Sarrocchi and the Writing of the *Scanderbeide*', in Margherita Sarrocchi, *Scanderbeide: The Heroic Deeds of George Scanderbeg, King of Epirus*, University of Chicago Press, Chicago, 2007, pp 1–43.

4 Letter of Artemisia Gentileschi to Francesco Maria Maringhi, 26 June 1620, in Francesco Solinas (ed.), with Michele Nicolaci and Yuri Primarosa, *Lettere di Artemisia: Edizione critica e annotata con quarantatre documenti inediti*, De Luca Editori d'Arte, Rome, 2011, p.74; Letter of Artemisia Gentileschi to Cassiano Dal Pozzo, 21 December 1620, in Solinas, 2011, letter 39, p.96.

5 I have not been able to locate either of these treatises yet, despite a search in the Vatican Secret Archives where Bronzini reported seeing them. Ian Verstegen has kindly informed me that Girolamo Della Rovere published the brief treatise *Ad commendationem Sexus Muliebris*, Rome, 1540, written at age ten.

6 First published in 1532, the anonymous *Leg[g]endario delle Santissime Vergini, Le quali volsero morire per il Nostro Signore Giésu Christo & per mantenere la sua Santa Fede* [*Legends of the Holy Virgins Who Wanted to Die for Our Lord Jesus Christ & to Keep the Holy Faith*], F. Bindoni & M. Pasini, Venice, was published again in 1536, 1546, 1554, 1575, 1578, 1581, 1585, 1591, 1594, 1600, 1601, 1603, 1611, 1621, 1662, 1711 and 1731; see Gabriella Zarri (ed.), *Donna, disciplina, creanza cristiana dal XV al XVII secolo: studi e testi a stampa*, Edizioni di Storia e Letteratura, Rome, 1996, pp 580–82.
7 Antonio Gallonio, *Historia delle Sante Vergini romane* [*History of the Roman Holy Virgins*], Ascanio e Girolamo Donangeli, Rome, 1591.

CHAPTER I

1 Bronzini, BNCF, Magl. Cl. VIII, 1525, I, fol. 125 v, cited in Sheila Barker, 'The First Biography of Artemisia Gentileschi: Self-Fashioning and Proto-feminist Art History in Cristofano Bronzini's Notes on Women Artists', *Mitteilungen des Kunsthistorieschen Institutes*, vol.60, no.3, 2018, pp 415, 433.
2 As reported in the testimony of Tuzia Madaglia, in Mary D. Garrard, *Artemisia Gentileschi: The Image of the Female Hero in Italian Baroque Art*, Princeton University Press, Princeton, 1989, p.422.
3 Bronzini, BNCF, Magl. Cl. VIII, 1525, I, fol. 125 v, cited in Barker, 2018, pp 416–17.
4 Bronzini, BNCF, Magl. Cl. VIII, 1525, I, fol. 125 v, cited in Barker, 2018, pp 415, 433.
5 Bronzini, BNCF, Magl. Cl. VIII, 1525, I, fol. 125 v, cited in Barker, 2018, pp 415, 433.
6 Gian Paolo Lomazzo, *Idea del tempio della pittura*, Paolo Gottardo Pontio, Milan, 1590, p.166.
7 Deposition of Mario Trotta in Cavazzini, 'Documenti relative al processo contro Agostino Tassi', in Keith Christiansen and Judith W. Mann (eds), *Orazio e Artemisia Gentileschi*, exh.cat. Rome/New York/Saint Louis 2001–2, Milan 2001, The Metropolitan Museum of Art, New York, Yale University Press, New Haven and London, 2001, pp 432–45; p.434. Cf. depositions of Luca Penti (idem), Antinoro Bertucci (Garrard, 1989, p.485), and Tassi (ibid., p.455).
8 Biblioteca Nazionale Centrale di Firenze MS, Magl. Cl. VIII, 1525, II, Cristoforo Bronzini, 'Della dignità et della nobiltà delle donne', fols 119v–120r.
9 Deposition of Tuzia Madaglia, in Garrard, 1989, p.422.
10 Patricia Simons, 'Artemisia Gentileschi's Susanna and the Elders (1610) in the Context of Counter-Reformation Rome', in Sheila Barker (ed.), *Artemisia Gentileschi in a Changing Light*, Harvey Miller Publishers, London, Turnhout, 2017, p.47.

CHAPTER 2

1 Letter of Giovanbattista Stiattesi to Cosimo Quorli, undated, *c.*March 1612, published in translation in Mary D. Garrard, *Artemisia Gentileschi: The Image of the Female Hero in Italian Baroque Art*, Princeton University Press, Princeton, 1989, p.436 ('Appendix B').
2 ASF, Compagnie soppresse sotto Pietro Leopoldo 1195, f.83v. Alana O'Brien generously brought this unpublished archival notice to my attention.
3 ASF, Gabelli dei contratti, Scritte matrimoniali condizionati 736, ins. 219. This interpretation of the document's timed partition of the payouts supersedes what I stated incorrectly in Sheila Barker, 'A New Document Concerning Artemisia Gentileschi's Marriage', *The Burlington Magazine*, vol.156, December 2014, p.803.
4 Nicolay, Nicolas de, *Les quatres premiers livres des navigations et peregrinations orientales*, Guillaume Roville, Lyon, 1568; published in an Italian edition in 1577.
5 Jesse Locker, 'Artemisia Gentileschi: The Literary Formation of an Unlearned Artist', in Sheila Barker (ed.), *Artemisia Gentileschi in a Changing Light*, Harvey Miller Publishers, London, Turnhout, 2017, p.94.
6 Garrard, 1989, p.37.
7 'Servitio delle Serenissime Principesse'; see Archivio di Stato di Firenze ms, Guardaroba Medicea 309, fol.15v.
8 Translation from Suzanne G. Cusick, *Francesca Caccini at the Medici Court: Music and the Circulation of Power*, University of Chicago Press, Chicago, 2009, p.73.
9 Elizabeth Cropper, 'The Place of Beauty in the High Renaissance and its Displacement in the History of Art', in Alvin Vos (ed.), *Place and Displacement in the Renaissance*, State University of New York Press, Binghamton, New York, 1995, p.190.
10 In a contemporary lexicon of the Tuscan dialect, the *Vocabolario degli Accademici della Crusca*, G. Alberti, Venice, 1612, p.431, 'inclinazione' is defined firstly as 'Attitudine, e natural disposizione a cosa particolare' ('Orientation and natural disposition towards some particular thing'), with the example, 'Che benchè ciascuno huomo nasca sotto alcuna costellazione, la qual gli dia alcuna inclinazione, con la sua influenza, in sua podestà è d'acquistarla, o nò' ('Since each person is

born under some constellation, which gives him or her an inclination through its influence, it is that person's power to take possession of it or not'), and secondly as, 'Per declinazione, abbassamento' ('Meaning declination, descent'), referring to the technical astrological term for measuring a star's position in the sky.

11 This occurs for the first time in the record for the debt with Michele di Domenico, undated but bound near other records from April of 1615, in ASF, Accademia del Disegno 65, carta 40.

12 Barker, Sheila, 'Artemisia's Money: The Entrepreneurship of a Woman Artist in Seventeenth-Century Florence', in Sheila Barker (ed.), *Artemisia Gentileschi in a Changing Light*, Harvey Miller Publishers, London, Turnhout, 2017, p.75, doc.9; p.77, doc.24.

13 Barker, 2017, p.69.

14 Roberto Contini, 'L'indotto fiorentino di Artemisia Gentileschi', in Keith Christiansen and Judith W. Mann (eds), *Orazio e Artemisia Gentileschi*, exh.cat., Rome/New York/Saint Louis 2001–2, Milan 2001, The Metropolitan Museum of Art, New York, Yale University Press, New Haven and London, 2001, pp 313–19, p.314.

15 Elena Fumagalli, 'Florence', in Richard E. Spear and Peter Sohm (eds), *Painting for Profit: The Economic Lives of Seventeenth-Century Painters*, Yale University Press, New Haven and London, 2010, pp 172–203, p.174.

16 ASF, Mediceo del Principato 2950, fol. n.n., MIA doc. ID# 5620.

17 Garrard, 1989, p.307.

18 See Garrard, 1989.

19 Frima Fox Hofrichter, 'Artemisia Gentileschi's Uffizi *Judith* and a Lost Rubens', *The Rutgers Art Review*, vol.1, January 1980, pp 9–15.

20 Xenia von Tippelskirch, 'Die indexkongregation und die würde der frauen: Cristofano Bronzini, "Della dignità e nobiltà delle donne"', in Anne-Marie Bonnet and Barbara Schellewald (eds), *Frauen in der Frühen Neuzeit: Lebensentwürfe in Kunst und Literatur*, Böhlau Verlag, Cologne, 2004, pp 235–62.

21 Kelley Ann Harness, *Echoes of Women's Voices: Music, Art, and Female Patronage in Early Modern Florence*, University of Chicago Press, Chicago, 2006, pp 111–41.

CHAPTER 3

1 Artemisia Gentileschi to Cosimo II de' Medici, 10 February 1620, ASF, Mediceo del Principato 998, fol.204r, my translation.

2 Letter of Gino Ginori to Cosimo II de' Medici, 12 February 1620, in Francesco Solinas (ed.), with Michele Nicolaci and Yuri Primarosa, *Lettere di Artemisia: Edizione critica e annotata con quarantatre documenti inediti*, De Luca Editori d'Arte, Rome, 2011, appendix II, p.142.

3 Letter of Artemisia Gentileschi to Francesco Maria Maringhi, 14 February 1620, in Solinas, 2011, letter 10, p.34.

4 Letter of Pierantonio Stiattesi to Francesco Maria Maringhi, 11 April 1620, in Solinas, 2011, letter 21, p.54.

5 Letter of Pierantonio Stiattesi to Francesco Maria Maringhi, 2 March 1620, in Solinas, 2011, letter 11, p.37.

6 Letter of Pierantonio Stiattesi to Francesco Maria Maringhi, 20 March 1620, in Solinas, 2011, letter 21, p.54. Solinas does not explain why the date of this letter is not to be calculated by the Anno Fiorentino, as was done with all the previous correspondence.

7 Letter of Pierantonio Stiattesi to Francesco Maria Maringhi, 11 March 1620, in Solinas 2011, letter 15, p.46, translation my own.

8 Mary D. Garrard, *Artemisia Gentileschi and Feminism in Early Modern Europe*, Reaktion Books, London, 2020, p.161.

9 Kelley Ann Harness, 'Amazzoni di Dio: Florentine Musical Spectacle Under Maria Maddalena d'Austria and Cristina di Lorena (1620–1630)', PhD Dissertation, University of Illinois at Urbana-Champaign, 1996, pp 8–9.

10 Janie Cole, *Music, Spectacle and Cultural Brokerage in Early Modern Italy: Michelangelo Buonarroti il Giovane*, Leo S. Olschki, Florence, 2011, vol.I, p.298.

11 Michelangelo Buonarroti the Younger to Francesco dell'Antella, 14 February 1619, Archivio Buonarroti 39, ff 102–5, and Cole, 2011, vol.I, pp 292, 295.

12 Richard E. Spear, '"I have made up my mind . . . to take a short trip to Rome"', in Keith Christiansen and Judith W. Mann (eds) *Orazio and Artemisia Gentileschi*, exh.cat., The Metropolitan Museum of Art, New York, Yale University Press, New Haven and London, 2001, pp 338–9.

13 Letter of Pierantonio Stiattesi to Francesco Maria Maringhi, 2 March 1620, in Solinas, 2011, letter 11, p.37.

14 Letter of Pierantonio Stiattesi to Francesco Maria Maringhi, 2 March 1620, in Solinas, 2011, letter 11, p.37.

15 R. Ward Bissell, *Orazio Gentileschi and the Poetic Tradition in Caravaggesque Painting*, The Pennsylvania State University Press, University Park and London, 1981, pp 18–19, 140.

16 Eric Bianchi and Sheila Barker, '"Upon His Visit to See My Paintings": Artemisia Gentileschi's and Pietro della Valle's Exchanged Sonnets', *The Burlington Magazine*, (forthcoming).

17 Roberto Contini, 'L'indotto fiorentino di Artemisia Gentileschi', Keith Christiansen and Judith W. Mann (eds), *Orazio e Artemisia Gentileschi*, exh.cat. Rome/New York/Saint Louis 2001–2, Milan 2001, The Metropolitan Museum of Art, New York, Yale University Press, New Haven and London, 2001, pp 313–19, p.314.
18 The translation is mine.
19 Michelangelo Buonarotti, *Rime di Michelagnolo Buonarroti: Raccolte da Michelagnolo suo Nipote*, Giunti, Florence, 1623.
20 Artemisia Gentileschi to Francesco I d'Este, Duke of Parma, 25 January 1635, in Solinas, 2011, letter 41, p.94, n.5.
21 Artemisia Gentileschi to Francesco Maria Maringhi, 9 July 1620, in Solinas, 2011, letter 33, p.76.
22 De Dominici, Bernardo, *Vite dei pittori scultori ed architetti napoletani*, Francesco e Cristoforo Ricciardi, Naples, 1743, vol. 3, p.46; English trans. in Artemisia Gentileschi et al., *Lives of Artemisia Gentileschi*, ed. and intro. by Sheila Barker, J. Paul Getty Museum, Los Angeles, 2021, p.179.
23 Rossella Vodret, *Alla ricerca di 'Ghiongrat': Studi sui libri parrocchiali romani (1600–1630)*, 'L'Erma' di Bretschneider, Rome, 2011, p.234.
24 Letizia Treves, 'Venice, Naples and London', in Letizia Treves (ed.), *Artemisia*, exh.cat., National Gallery, London, 2020, p.186.
25 Alexandra Lapierre, *Artemisia: Un duel pour l'immortalité*, Robert Laffont, Paris, 1998, p.474, citing a diary of Richard Symonds which she found in the British Library, Harley MS 991.
26 Véronique Gerard, 'Philip IV's Early Italian Commissions,' *Oxford Art Journal*, vol.5, no.1, 1982, pp 11–13.
27 Steven N. Orso, *Philip IV and the Decoration of the Alcázar of Madrid*, Princeton University Press, Princeton, 1986, pp 55, 107–13.
28 Garrard, 2020, p.34.
29 Sheila Barker, 'Introduction', in Artemisia Gentileschi et al., *Lives of Artemisia Gentileschi*, ed. and intro. by Sheila Barker, J. Paul Getty Museum, Los Angeles, 2021, p.36 (with reference to p.176).

CHAPTER 4

1 Jonathan Brown and Richard L. Kagan, 'The Duke of Alcalá: His Collection and Its Evolution', *The Art Bulletin*, vol.69, no.2, June 1987, p.243.
2 Letter of Artemisia Gentileschi to Cassiano Dal Pozzo, 24 August 1630, in Francesco Solinas (ed.), with Michele Nicolaci and Yuri Primarosa, *Lettere di Artemisia: Edizione critica e annotata con quarantatre documenti inediti*, De Luca Editori d'Arte, Rome, 2011, letter 37, p.85.
3 R. Ward Bissell, 'Artemisia Gentileschi: A New Documented Chronology', *The Art Bulletin*, vol.50, no.2, June 1968, pp 158–9 n.50.
4 Anna Orlando, 'I Gentileschi a Genova. Dati certi e incerti per Orazio, Artemisia, Francesco e Giulio', in Anna Orlando (ed.), *Caravaggio e i genovesi: Committenti, collezionisti, pittori*, Sagep Editori, Genoa, pp 168–9.
5 Riccardo Lattuada, cat. entry no.72, 'Annunciation', in Keith Christiansen and Judith W. Mann (eds), *Orazio and Artemisia Gentileschi*, exh.cat., The Metropolitan Museum of Art, New York, Yale University Press, New Haven and London, 2001, p.394.
6 Riccardo Lattuada, cat. entry nos 72–84, 'Artemisia in Naples, Naples and Artemisia', in Christiansen and Mann, 2001, p.381.
7 Jamie Gabbarelli, 'Cornelis Galle I between Genoa and Antwerp', *Print Quarterly*, vol.34, 2017, pp 18–31.
8 Laura Stagno, 'Modelli iconografici per l'Immacolata a Genova nel Cinquecento', in Alessandra Anselmi (ed.), *L'Immacolata nei rapporti tra l'Italia e la Spagna*, De Luca Editori d'Arte, Rome, 2008, p.314.
9 Translation in Barker, 2021, p.33.
10 Artemisia Gentileschi to Ferdinando II de' Medici, 20 July 1635, in Solinas, 2011, letter 43, p.104.
11 Francesca Whitlum-Cooper, catalogue entry for 'The Birth of Saint John the Baptist', cat. no.29, in Letizia Treves (ed.), *Artemisia Gentileschi*, exh.cat., National Gallery, London, 2020.
12 Catalog entry, *Christ and the Samaritan Woman at the Well*, in Roberto Contini and Francesco Solinas, *Artemisia Gentileschi: Storia di una passione*, exh.cat., Palazzo Reale, Milan, 2011–12, Pero, 24 ORE Cultura, 2011, cat. no. 34, p 210.
13 Solinas, 2011, letter of 2 October 1637, letter 49, p.117.
14 Artemisia Gentileschi to Andrea Cioli, 1 April 1636, in Solinas, 2011, letter 48, p.116.
15 Artemisia Gentileschi to Cassiano dal Pozzo, 24 October 1637, in Solinas, 2011, letter 49, p.117.
16 '[D]ove molte volte prima mi haveva richiesto a suo servitio, et inviato l'istesso mio fratello, ma perché mi trovavo in Napoli, al servitio di questo viceré, per dare fine ad alchune opere comingiate per Sua Maestà Cattolica, non potei in nessuna maniera contentare la Maestà d'Inghiterra'. Translation mine. From Solinas, 2011, letter of 20 July 1635, letter 43, p.104.
17 Artemisia Gentileschi to Cassiano dal Pozzo, 24 November 1637, in Solinas, 2011, letter 50, p.118.

18 Mary D. Garrard, *Artemisia Gentileschi: The Image of the Female Hero in Italian Baroque Art*, Princeton University Press, Princeton, 1989, pp 108–9.

19 Elizabeth Cropper, 'Life on the Edge: Artemisia Gentileschi, Famous Woman Painter', in Keith Christiansen and Judith W. Mann (eds), *Orazio and Artemisia Gentileschi*, exh.cat., The Metropolitan Museum of Art, New York, Yale University Press, New Haven and London, 2001, p.270.

20 Letter of Michelangelo Buonarrotti the Younger to Galileo Galilei dated 3 June 1636, in Galileo Galilei, *Le opere*, ed. by Antonio Favaro, Barbèra, Florence, 1968, vol.14, letter 2012.

21 Gianni Papi with Tracey D. Chaplin and Simon Gillespie, 'A *David and Goliath* by Artemisia Gentileschi Rediscovered', *The Burlington Magazine*, vol.162, March 2020, pp 188–95.

22 Cesare Ripa, *Iconologia* [Rome, 1603], ed. by Erna Mandowsky, Georg Olms Verlag, Hildesheim and New York, 1970, p.404.

23 Juan Luis Vives, *The Education of a Christian Woman. A Sixteenth-Century Manual*, ed. and trans. Charles Fantazzi, University of Chicago Press, Chicago and London, 2000, p.130.

24 Cristina Terzaghi, 'Artemisia Gentileschi a Londra', in Nicola Spinosa et al., *Artemisia Gentileschi e il suo tempo*, exh.cat., Palazzo Braschi, Rome, Skira, Milan, 2017, p.74.

25 Entry of Viviana Farina, cat. no.30, Artemisia Gentileschi's *Cimon and Pero*, in Farina, Viviana (ed.), *Artemisia e i pittori del conte: la collezione di Giangirolamo II Acquaviva d'Aragona*, exh.cat., Conversano, Castle and Church of San Giuseppe, 2018, Area Blu edizioni, Cava de' Tirreni, 2018, pp 262–6.

26 Letter of Artemisia Gentileschi to Don Antonio Ruffo dated 7 August 1649 in Garrard, 1989, p.394; Letter of Artemisia Gentileschi to Don Antonio Ruffo dated 30 January 1649, in Garrard, 1989, p.390; Letter of Artemisia Gentileschi to Don Antonio Ruffo dated 13 November 1649, in Garrard, 1989, p.397; Letter of Artemisia Gentileschi to Don Antonio Ruffo dated 13 November 1649, in Garrard, 1989, p.398.

27 My translation. Letter of Artemisia Gentileschi to Don Antonio Ruffo, 12 June 1649, in Solinas, 2011, letter 55, p.129.

28 Artemisia to Don Antonio Ruffo, 30 January 1649, trans. in Garrard, 1989, p.390.

29 Riccardo Lattuada, 'Unknown Paintings by Artemisia in Naples and New Points Regarding Her Daily Life and Bottega', in Sheila Barker (ed.), *Artemisia Gentileschi in a Changing Light*, Harvey Miller Publishers, London, Turnhout, 2017, p.212.

30 In dating their *Lucretia* (fig.75) to *c.*1627, the Getty Museum follows Jesse Locker's arguments, largely based on a comparison to the *Esther Before Ahasuerus*, which Locker dates to *c.*1628–30 (see Jesse Locker, 'Artemisia Lucretia and Venice', in Patrick Matthiessen and Jesse Locker, *Artemisia Gentileschi: 'A Venetian Lucretia'*, Matthiessen Gallery, London, 2020, pp 51–53). I concur with that comparison, but I follow Ward Bissell, Roberto Contini, Gianni Papi, Mina Gregori and Mauro Natale in dating the *Esther Before Ahasuerus* to the late 1630s, after the *Birth of the Baptist* and the paintings for the Pozzuoli cycle. Moreover, I see connections between the Getty's *Lucretia* and the *David* (fig.60) that Papi dates to the period in England (1638–40), especially in the *pastoso* treatment of David's linen sleeve and the palette of ice-grey and dark olive. The *Lucretia*'s dimensions are close to those of another painting from Artemisia's sojourn in London: the *Self-Portrait as the Allegory of Painting* (fig.61). Notably, in the Getty's painting, Lucretia uses her left arm to bring her heart closer to the knife, a sign of her stoic determination.

31 Averardo de' Medici, 'Memorial to Artemisia Gentileschi', in Artemisia Gentileschi et al., *Lives of Artemisia Gentileschi*, ed. and intro. by Sheila Barker, J. Paul Getty Museum, Los Angeles, 2021, p.184.

32 Riccardo Lattuada and Eduardo Nappi, 'New Documents and Some Remarks on Artemisia's Production in Naples and Elsewhere', in Judy Mann (ed.), *Artemisia Gentileschi. Taking Stock*, Brepols, Turnhout, 2005, pp 79–98.

33 Adelina Modesti, 'A Newly Discovered Late Work by Artemisia Gentileschi: Susanna and the Elders of 1652', in Sheila Barker (ed.), *Women Artists in Early Modern Italy: Careers, Fame, and Collectors*, Harvey Miller Publishers, London, 2016, pp 135–49.

EPILOGUE

1 Michael Levey, 'Notes on the Royal Collection – II: Artemisia Gentileschi's Self Portrait at Hampton Court', *The Burlington Magazine*, vol.104, February 1962, pp 79–80.

Bibliography

ELECTRONIC DATABASES

MIA (www.mia.medici.org)

Memofonte (www.memofonte.it)

MANUSCRIPT SOURCES

Arezzo, Archivio Buonarroti 39

Florence, Archivio di Stato di Firenze, Accademia del Disegno 65, Compagnie soppresse sotto Pietro Leopoldo 1195, Gabelli dei contratti: Scritte matrimoniali condizionati 736, Guardaroba Medicea 309, Mediceo del Principato 998 and 2950

Florence, Biblioteca Nazionale Centrale di Firenze, Magl. Cl. VIII, 1525, vol.II, Cristofano Bronzini, 'Della dignità e della nobiltà delle donne'

PUBLICATIONS

Accademia della Crusca, *Vocabolario degli Accademici della Crusca*, G. Alberti, Venice, 1612

Anonymous, *Leg[g]endario delle Santissime Vergini, Le quali volsero morire per il Nostro Signore Giesu Christo & per mantenere la sua Santa Fede* [*Legends of the Holy Virgins Who Wanted to Die for Our Lord Jesus Christ & to Keep the Holy Faith*], F. Bindoni & M. Pasini, Venice, 1532

Baldassari, Francesca, Judith Mann and Nicola Spinosa (eds), *Artemisia Gentileschi e il suo tempo*, Skira, Milan, 2016

Baldinucci, Filippo, *Notizie dei professori del disegno da Cimabue in qua*, ed. F. Ranalli, V. Batelli e Compagni, Florence, 1846, vol.3, p.713

Banti, Anna, *Artemisia* (1947), SE, Milan, 2015

Barker, Sheila, 'A New Document Concerning Artemisia Gentileschi's Marriage', *The Burlington Magazine*, vol.156, December 2014, pp 803–4

Barker, Sheila, 'Lucrezia Quistelli (1541–94), 'A Noblewoman and Artist in Vasari's Florence', in Sheila Barker (ed.), *Women Artists in Early Modern Italy: Careers, Fame, and Collectors*, Harvey Miller Publishers, London, 2016, pp 47–80

Barker, Sheila (ed.), *Artemisia Gentileschi in a Changing Light*, Harvey Miller Publishers, London, Turnhout, 2017

Barker, Sheila, 'Artemisia's Money: The Entrepreneurship of a Woman Artist in Seventeenth-Century Florence', in Sheila Barker (ed.), *Artemisia Gentileschi in a Changing Light*, Harvey Miller Publishers, London, Turnhout, 2017, pp 59–87

Barker, Sheila, 'The First Biography of Artemisia Gentileschi: Self-Fashioning and Proto-Feminist Art History in Cristofano Bronzini's Notes on Women Artists', *Mitteilungen des Kunsthistorischen Institutes*, vol.60, no.3, 2018, pp 404–35

Barker, Sheila, 'Introduction', in Artemisia Gentileschi et al., *Lives of Artemisia Gentileschi*, ed. and intro. by Sheila Barker, J. Paul Getty Museum, Los Angeles, 2021, pp 9–38

Barker, Sheila, 'Andromeda Unchained: Women and Erotic Mythology in Renaissance Art, 1500–1650', in M. Falomir Faus and A. Vergara (eds), *Mythological Passions: Titian, Veronese, Allori, Rubens, Ribera, Poussin, Van Dyck, Velázquez*, exh.cat., Museo del Prado, Madrid, 2021, pp 57–81

Barker, Sheila, 'Art as Women's Work: The Professionalization of Women Artists in Italy, 1350–1800', in E. Straussman-Pflanzer and O. Tostmann (eds), *By Her Hand: Artemisia Gentileschi and Women Artists in Italy, 1500–1600*, exh.cat., Wadsworth Atheneum and the Detroit Institute of Arts, September 2021–May 2022, Detroit Institute of Arts, Detroit, pp 31–9

Bianchi, Eric and Sheila Barker, '"Upon His Visit to See My Paintings": Artemisia Gentileschi's and Pietro della Valle's Exchanged Sonnets', *The Burlington Magazine*, (forthcoming)

Binaghi Olivari and Maria Teresa, 'I ricamatori milanesi tra rinascimento e barocco', in Paolo Venturoli (ed.), *I tessili nell'età di Carlo Bascapè, vescovo di Novara (1593–1615)*, exh.cat., Interlinea, Novara, 1994, pp 97–123

Bissell, R. Ward, 'Artemisia Gentileschi: A New Documented Chronology', *The Art Bulletin*, vol.50, no.2, June 1968, pp 153–68

Bissell, R. Ward, *Orazio Gentileschi and the Poetic Tradition in Caravaggesque Painting*, The Pennsylvania State University Press, University Park and London, 1981

Bissell, R. Ward, *Artemisia Gentileschi and the Authority of Art: Critical Reading and Catalogue Raisonné*, The Pennsylvania State University Press, University Park, 1999

Bottari, Giovanni Gaetano, *Raccolta di lettere sulla pittura, scultura ed architettura scritte dai più celebri personaggi che in dette arti fiorirono dal secolo XV al XVII*, Pagliarini, Rome, 1757–83, 7 vols

Brown, Jonathan and Richard L. Kagan, 'The Duke of Alcalá: His Collection and Its Evolution', *The Art Bulletin*, vol.69, no.2, June 1987, pp 231–55

Buonarotti, Michelangelo, *Rime di Michelagnolo Buonarroti: Raccolte da Michelagnolo suo Nipote*, Giunti, Florence, 1623

Christiansen, Keith, 'Becoming Artemisia: Afterthoughts on the Gentileschi Exhibition', *Metropolitan Museum Journal,* vol.39, 2004, pp 101–26

Christiansen, Keith and Judith W. Mann, *Orazio and Artemisia Gentileschi*, exh.cat., Rome/New York/Saint Louis 2001–2, The Metropolitan Museum of Art, New York, Yale University Press, New Haven and London, 2001

Cohen, Elizabeth S., 'The Trials of Artemisia Gentileschi: A Rape as History', *Sixteenth Century Journal*, vol.31, no.1, Spring 2000, pp 47–75

Cole, Janie, *Music, Spectacle and Cultural Brokerage in Early Modern Italy: Michelangelo Buonarroti il Giovane*, Leo S. Olschki, Florence, 2011, 2 vols

Contini, Roberto, 'L'indotto fiorentino di Artemisia Gentileschi', in *Orazio e Artemisia Gentileschi*, exh.cat., Florence, 2001, pp 313–19

Contini, Roberto and Francesco Solinas, *Artemisia Gentileschi: Storia di una passione*, exh.cat., Palazzo Reale, Milan, 2011–12, 24 ORE Cultura, Pero, 2011

Contini, Roberto and Francesco Solinas (eds), *Artemisia la musa Clio e gli anni napoletani*, exh.cat., De Luca, Rome, 2013

Crinò, Anna Maria, 'Due lettere autografie inedite di Orazio e Artemisia Gentileschi de' Lomi', *Rivista d'arte*, vol.29, ser.3, no.4, 1954, pp 202–6

Crinò, Anna Maria, 'More Letters from Orazio and Artemisia Gentileschi', *The Burlington Magazine*, vol.102, 1960, pp 264–5

Cropper, Elizabeth, 'New Documents for Artemisia Gentileschi's Life in Florence', *The Burlington Magazine*, vol.135, 1993, pp 760–61

Cropper, Elizabeth, 'The Place of Beauty in the High Renaissance and its Displacement in the History of Art', in Alvin Vos (ed.), *Place and Displacement in the Renaissance*, State University of New York Press, Binghamton, New York, 1995, pp 159–205

Cropper, Elizabeth, 'Life on the Edge: Artemisia Gentileschi, Famous Woman Painter', in Keith Christiansen and Judith W. Mann (eds), *Orazio and Artemisia Gentileschi*, exh.cat., The Metropolitan Museum of Art, New York, Yale University Press, New Haven and London, 2001, pp 263–81

Cropper, Elizabeth, 'Galileo Galilei e Artemisia Gentileschi tra storia delle idee e microstoria', in Lucia Tongiorgi Tomasi and Alessandro Tosi (eds), *Il cannocchiale e il pennello: Nuova scienza e nuova arte nell'età di Galileo*, exh. cat., Giunti, Milan, 2009, pp 194–213

Cropper, Elizabeth, 'Artemisia Gentileschi: La Pittora', in Letizia Treves (ed.), *Artemisia*, exh.cat., National Gallery, London, 2020, pp 10–31

Cusick, Suzanne G., *Francesca Caccini at the Medici Court: Music and the Circulation of Power (Women in Culture and Society)*, University of Chicago Press, Chicago, 2009

DaCosta Kauffmann, Thomas, '*Esther before Ahasuerus*: A New Painting by Artemisia Gentileschi in the Museum's Collection', *Metropolitan Museum of Art Bulletin*, vol.29, no.4, December 1970, pp 165–9

De Dominici, Bernardo, *Vite dei pittori scultori ed architetti napoletani*, Francesco e Cristoforo Ricciardi, Naples, 1742–43, 3 vols

De Nicolay, Nicolas, *Les quatres premiers livres des navigations et peregrinations orientales*, Guillaume Roville, Lyon, 1568

Farina, Viviana (ed.), *Artemisia e i pittori del conte: la collezione di Giangirolamo II Acquaviva d'Aragona*, exh.cat., Conversano, Castle and Church of San Giuseppe, 2018, Area Blu edizioni, Cava de' Tirreni, 2018

ffolliott, Sheila, 'Artemisia Gentileschi', *Oxford Bibliographies in Art History*, ed. Thomas DaCosta Kaufmann, Oxford University Press, New York, 2021

Fonte, Moderata, *The Worth of Women, Wherein Is Clearly Revealed Their Nobility and Their Superiority to Men* [1600], ed. and trans. Virginia Cox, University of Chicago Press, Chicago and London, 1997

Fuda, Roberto, 'Un'inedita lettera di Artemisia Gentileschi a Ferdinando II de' Medici', *Rivista d'Arte*, vol.41, ser.4, no.5, 1989, pp 167–71

Fumagalli, Elena, 'Florence', in Richard E. Spear and Peter Sohm (eds), *Painting for Profit: The Economic Lives of Seventeenth-Century Painters*, Yale University Press, New Haven and London, 2010, pp 172–203

Gabbarelli, Jamie, 'Cornelis Galle I between Genoa and Antwerp', *Print Quarterly*, vol.34, 2017, pp 18–31

Galilei, Galileo, *Le opere*, ed. by Antonio Favaro, Barbèra, Florence, 1968, 20 vols

Gallonio, Antonio, *Historia delle Sante Vergini romane* [*History of the Roman Holy Virgins*], Ascanio e Girolamo Donangeli, Rome, 1591

Garrard, Mary D., 'Artemisia Gentileschi's Self-Portrait as the Allegory of Painting', *The Art Bulletin*, vol.62, no.1, March 1980, pp 97–112

Garrard, Mary D., *Artemisia Gentileschi: The Image of the Female Hero in Italian Baroque Art*, Princeton University Press, Princeton, 1989

Garrard, Mary D., 'Artemisia Gentileschi's "Corisca and the Satyr"', *The Burlington Magazine* , vol.135, January 1993, pp 34–8

Garrard, Mary D., *Artemisia Gentileschi Around 1622: The Shaping and Reshaping of an Artistic Identity*, University of California Press, Berkeley, 2001

Garrard, Mary D., *Artemisia Gentileschi and Feminism in Early Modern Europe*, Reaktion Books, London, 2020

Gentileschi, Artemisia, et al., *Lives of Artemisia Gentileschi*, ed. and intro. by Sheila Barker, J. Paul Getty Museum, Los Angeles, 2021

Gerard, Véronique, 'Philip IV's Early Italian Commissions', *Oxford Art Journal*, vol.5, no.1, 1982, pp 9–14

Harness, Kelley Ann, 'Amazzoni di dio: Florentine Musical Spectacle Under Maria Maddalena d'Austria and Cristina di Lorena (1620–1630)', PhD Dissertation, University of Illinois at Urbana-Champaign, 1996

Harness, Kelley Ann, *Echoes of Women's Voices: Music, Art, and Female Patronage in Early Modern Florence*, University of Chicago Press, Chicago, 2006

Harris, Ann Sutherland, 'Artemisia Gentileschi: The Literate Illiterate or Learning from Example', in *Docere Delectare Movere: Affetti, devozione e retorica nel linguaggio artistico del primo barocco romano*, Instituto Olandese and Bibliotheca Hertziana, Rome, 1998, pp 105–20

Harris, Ann Sutherland, 'Artemisia Gentileschi and Elisabetta Sirani: Rivals or Strangers?' *Woman's Art Journal*, vol.31, no.1, Spring/Summer 2010, pp 3–12

Harris, Ann Sutherland and Linda Nochlin, exh.cat., *Women Artists: 1550–1950*, Los Angeles County Museum of Art and Alfred A. Knopf, Los Angeles and New York, 1976

Hofrichter, Frima Fox, 'Artemisia Gentileschi's Uffizi *Judith* and a Lost Rubens', *The Rutgers Art Review*, vol.1, January 1980, pp 9–15

Jacobs, Fredrika H., 'Woman's Capacity to Create: The Unusual Case of Sofonisba Anguissola', *Renaissance Quarterly*, vol.47, no.1, Spring 1994, pp 74–101

Lapierre, Alexandra, *Artemisia: Un duel pour l'immortalité*, Robert Laffont, Paris, 1998

Lapierre, Alexandra, *Artemisia: A Novel*, trans. Liz Heron, Grove Press, London and New York, 2000

Lattuada, Riccardo, 'Artemisia in Naples, Naples and Artemisia', in Keith Christiansen and Judith W. Mann (eds) *Orazio and Artemisia Gentileschi*, exh.cat., The Metropolitan Museum of Art, New York, Yale University Press, New Haven and London, 2001, pp 379–91

Lattuada, Riccardo, 'Unknown Paintings by Artemisia in Naples and New Points Regarding Her Daily Life and Bottega', in Sheila Barker (ed.), *Artemisia Gentileschi in a Changing Light*, Harvey Miller Publishers, London, Turnhout, 2017, pp 187–216

Lattuada, Riccardo and Eduardo Nappi, 'New Documents and Some Remarks on Artemisia's Production in Naples and Elsewhere', in Judy Mann (ed.), *Artemisia Gentileschi: Taking Stock*, Brepols, Turnhout, 2005, pp 79–98

Levey, Michael, 'Notes on the Royal Collection – II: Artemisia Gentileschi's Self Portrait at Hampton Court', *The Burlington Magazine*, vol.104, February 1962, pp 79–80

Locker, Jesse, '"Con pennello di luce": Neapolitan verses in praise of Artemisia Gentileschi', *Studi Secenteschi*, vol.48, 2007, pp 243–62

Locker, Jesse, 'An Eighteenth-Century Biography of Artemisia Gentileschi', *Source: Notes in the History of Art*, vol.29, no.2, Winter 2010, pp 27–37

Locker, Jesse, *Artemisia Gentileschi: The Language of Painting*, Yale University Press, New Haven and London, 2015

Locker, Jesse, 'Artemisia Gentileschi: The Literary Formation of an Unlearned Artist', in Sheila Barker (ed.), *Artemisia Gentileschi in a Changing Light*, Harvey Miller Publishers, London, Turnhout, 2017, pp 89–101

Lomazzo, Gian Paolo, *Idea del tempio della pittura*, Paolo Gottardo Pontio, Milan, 1590

Lomazzo, Gian Paolo, *Idea of the Temple of Painting* [*Idea del tempio della pittura*] [1590], ed. and trans. Jean Julia Chai, Pennsylvania State University Press, University Park, Pennsylvania, 2013

Longhi, Roberto, 'Gentileschi padre e figlia', *L'Arte*, vol.19, 1916, pp 235–314

Mann, Judith W., 'Caravaggio and Artemisia: Testing the Limits of Caravaggism', *Studies in Iconography*, vol.18, 1997, pp 161–85

Mann, Judith W. (ed.), *Artemisia Gentileschi: Taking Stock*, Brepols, Turnhout, 2005

Marinella, Lucrezia, *The Nobility and Excellence of Women and the Defects and Vices of Men* [1601], ed. and trans. Anne Dunhill, intro. Letizia Panizza, University of Chicago Press, Chicago, 1999

Marshall, Christopher R., '"The Spirit of Caesar in this Soul of a Woman": Artemisia Gentileschi and the Will to Succeed, 1629–1654', *Melbourne Art Journal*, vol.8, 2005, pp 4–27

Medici, Averardo de', 'Memorial to Artemisia Gentileschi', in Artemisia Gentileschi et al., *Lives of Artemisia Gentileschi*, ed. and intro. by Sheila Barker, J. Paul Getty Museum, Los Angeles, 2021, pp 161–84

Modesti, Adelina, 'A Newly Discovered Late Work by Artemisia Gentileschi: Susanna and the Elders of 1652', in Sheila Barker (ed.), *Women Artists in Early Modern Italy: Careers, Fame, and Collectors*, Harvey Miller Publishers, London, 2016, pp 135–49

Moir, Alfred, *The Italian Followers of Caravaggio*, Harvard University Press, Cambridge, Massachusetts, 1967

Morucci, Valerio, *Baronial Patronage of Music in Early Modern Rome*, Routledge, New York and London, 2018

Nicolson, Benedict, 'Caravaggesques in Florence', *The Burlington Magazine*, vol.112, 1970, pp 636–41

Nicolson, Benedict, *The International Caravaggesque Movement: Lists of Pictures by Caravaggio and His Followers Throughout Europe from 1590 to 1650*, Phaidon, Oxford, 1979

Orlando, Anna, 'I Gentileschi a Genova: Dati certi e incerti per Orazio, Artemisia, Francesco e Giulio', in Anna Orlando (ed.), *Caravaggio e i genovesi: Committenti, collezionisti, pittori*, Sagep Editori, Genoa, 2019, pp 150–73

Orso, Steven N., *Philip IV and the Decoration of the Alcázar of Madrid*, Princeton University Press, Princeton, 1986

Papi, Gianni, 'Un David e Golia di Artemisia Gentileschi', *Nuovi Studi*, vol.1, 1996, pp 157–60

Papi, Gianni (ed.), *Caravaggio e caravaggeschi a Firenze*, Sillabe, Pisa, 2010, pp 154–70

Papi, Gianni, 'Artemisia ritrovata', in Gianni Papi, *Spogliando modelli e alzando lumi*, Edizioni Paparo, Naples, 2014, pp 207–15

Papi, Gianni with Tracey D. Chaplin and Simon Gillespie, 'A *David and Goliath* by Artemisia Gentileschi Rediscovered', *The Burlington Magazine*, vol.162, March 2020, pp 188–95

Ripa, Cesare, *Iconologia* [Rome, 1603], ed. by Erna Mandowsky, Georg Olms Verlag, Hildesheim and New York, 1970

Ruffo, Vincenzo, 'Galleria Ruffo nel secolo XVII in Messina con lettere di pittori ed altri documenti inediti', *Bollettino d'arte*, vol.10, 1916, pp 21–64, 95–128, 165–92, 237–56, 284–320, 369–88

Ruffo, Vincenzo, 'La Galleria Ruffo (Appendice)', *Bollettino d'arte*, vol.13, 1919, pp 43–56

Sarrocchi, Margherita, 'Margherita Sarrocchi and the Writing of the *Scanderbeide*', in Rinaldina Russell (trans.), *Scanderbeide: The Heroic Deeds of George Scanderbeg, King of Epirus (The Other Voice in Early Modern Europe)*, University of Chicago Press, Chicago, 2007, pp 1–43

Schutte, Anne Jacobson, 'Irene di Spilimbergo: The Image of a Creative Woman in Late Renaissance Italy', *Renaissance Quarterly*, vol.44, no.1, Spring 1991, pp 42–61

Simons, Patricia, 'Artemisia Gentileschi's *Susanna and the Elders* (1610) in the Context of Counter-Reformation Rome', in Sheila Barker (ed.), *Artemisia Gentileschi in a Changing Light*, Harvey Miller Publishers, London, Turnhout, 2017, pp 41–57

Solinas, Francesco (ed.), with Michele Nicolaci and Yuri Primarosa, *Lettere di Artemisia: Edizione critica e annotata con quarantatre documenti inediti*, De Luca Editori d'Arte, Rome, 2011

Spear, Richard E., *Caravaggio and His Followers*, Cleveland Museum of Art, Cleveland, 1971, revised ed. Harper and Row, New York, 1975,

Spear, Richard E., 'Artemisia Gentileschi: Ten Years of Fact and Fiction', *The Art Bulletin*, vol.82, no.3, September 2000, pp 568–79

Spear, Richard E., '"I have made up my mind . . . to take a short trip to Rome"', in Keith Christiansen and Judith W. Mann (eds) *Orazio and Artemisia Gentileschi*, exh.cat., The Metropolitan Museum of Art, New York, Yale University Press, New Haven and London, 2001, 335–43

Spike, John T., 'Artemisia Gentileschi. Florence, Casa Buonarroti', *The Burlington Magazine*, vol.133, 1991, pp 732–34

Spike, John and Barbara Rose, 'The Gentileschi Papers', *The Journal of Art*, November 1991, pp 12–13

Spinosa, Nicola, 'Artemisia Gentileschi e Onofrio Palumbo: insieme o "separati"?', in Pietro Di Loreto (ed.), *Una vita per l'arte: Scritti in memoria di Maurizio Marini*, Etgraphiae, Rome, 2015, pp 379–88

Spinosa, Nicola, et al., *Artemisia Gentileschi e il suo tempo*, exh. cat., Palazzo Braschi, Rome, Skira, Milan, 2017

Stagno, Laura, 'Modelli iconografici per l'Immacolata a Genova nel Cinquecento', in Alessandra Anselmi (ed.), *L'Immacolata nei rapporti tra l'Italia e la Spagna*, De Luca Editori d'Arte, Rome, 2008, pp 303–26

Tasso, Torquato, *Discorso della virtù feminile e donnesca*, Bernardo Giunti e fratelli, Venice, 1582

Terzaghi, Cristina, 'Artemisia Gentileschi a Londra', in Nicola Spinosa et al., *Artemisia Gentileschi e il suo tempo*, exh.cat., Palazzo Braschi, Rome, Skira, Milan, 2017, pp 69–77

Terzaghi, Cristina, *Orazio and Artemisia Gentileschi: Between Paris and London*, Officina Libraria, Rome, 2017

Toesca, Ilaria, 'Versi in lode di Artemisia Gentileschi', *Paragone*, vol.251, January 1971, pp 89–92

Topper, David and Cynthia Gillis, 'Trajectories of Blood: Artemisia Gentileschi and Galileo's Parabolic Path', *Woman's Art Journal*, vol.17, no.1, Spring/Summer 1996, pp 10–13

Treves, Letizia (ed.), *Artemisia*, exh.cat., National Gallery, London, 2020

Treves, Letizia, 'Venice, Naples and London', in *Artemisia*, exh.cat., National Gallery, London, 2020

Vicioso, Julia, *Costanza Francini tra Artemisia Gentileschi e le committenze della Compagnia della Pietà in San Giovanni dei Fiorentini a Roma*, Ginevra Bentivoglio Editoria, Rome, 2014

Vives, Juan Luis, *The Education of a Christian Woman: A Sixteenth-Century Manual*, ed. and trans. Charles Fantazzi, University of Chicago Press, Chicago and London, 2000

Vodret, Rossella, *Alla ricerca di 'Ghiongrat': Studi sui libri parrocchiali romani (1600–1630)*, 'L'Erma' di Bretschneider, Rome, 2011

Von Tippelskirch, Xenia, 'Die indexkongregation und die würde der frauen: Cristofano Bronzini, "Della dignità e nobiltà delle donne"', in Anne-Marie Bonnet and Barbara Schellewald (eds), *Frauen in der Frühen Neuzeit: Lebensentwürfe in Kunst und Literatur*, Böhlau Verlag, Cologne, 2004

Whitfield, Clovis and Jane Martineau (eds), *Painting in Naples: From Caravaggio to Giordano*, Royal Academy of Arts/Weidenfeld & Nicolson, London, 1982, pp 165–8

Wilbourne, Emily, 'A Question of Character: Artemisia Gentileschi and Virginia Ramponi Andreini', *Italian Studies*, vol.71, no.3, 2016, pp 335–55

Zarri, Gabriella (ed.), *Donna, disciplina, creanza cristiana dal XV al XVII secolo: studi e testi a stampa*, Edizioni di Storia e Letteratura, Rome, 1996

Image credits

1 Patrimonio Nacional 10045145-ICD002; 2 Fundación Casa de Alba; 3 The Metropolitan Museum of Art, New York; 4 Rijksmuseum, Amsterdam; 5 Courtesy of the Ministero per i Beni e delle Attività Culturali e del Turismo – Galleria Nazionale d'Arte Antica, Galleria Corsini; 6 National Gallery of Art, Washington; 7 The Morgan Library & Museum; 8 Courtesy of the Ministero per i Beni e delle Attività Culturali e del Turismo – Biblioteca Nazionale Centrale di Firenze, photo: author; 9 The Metropolitan Museum of Art, New York; 10 Courtesy Gallery Moshe Tabibnia, Milan; 11 Courtesy of the owner. Photo Mauro Coen Studio Fotografico; 12 Bridgeman Images; 13 Harvard Art Museums/Fogg Museum. Gift through William A. Coolidge in memory of Marian Lady Bateman. Photo © President and Fellows of Harvard College; 14 Chiesa di Sant'Agostino, Rome, Italy. Photo: © Electa / Bridgeman Images; 15 Courtesy of the Ministero per i Beni e delle Attività Culturali e del Turismo – Galleria Nazionale d'Arte Antica di Palazzo Barberini; 16 © Vanni Archive/Art Resource, NY; 17 Rijksmuseum, Amsterdam; 18 Courtesy of the Ministero per i Beni e delle Attività Culturali e del Turismo – Galleria Spada; 19 Courtesy of the Ministero per i Beni e delle Attività Culturali e del Turismo – Galleria Spada; 20 By permission of the Ministero per i beni e le attività culturali e per il turismo, Soprintendenza Archeologia, Belle Arti e Paesaggio per la città metropolitana di Genova e la provincia di La Spezia. Reproduction prohibited; 21 Photo: Allen Phillips / Wadsworth Atheneum; 22 photo © President and Fellows of Harvard College; 23 Galerie Bassenge, Berlin; 24 Courtesy Casa Buonarotti; 25 Courtesy of the Ministero per i Beni e delle Attività Culturali e del Turismo – Archivio di Stato di Firenze. Photo: author; 26 Courtesy of the Ministero per i Beni e delle Attività Culturali e del Turismo – Gallerie degli Uffizi; 27 Courtesy of the Ministero per i Beni e delle Attività Culturali e del Turismo – Museum and Real Bosco di Capodimonte; 28 Courtesy of the Ministero per i Beni e delle Attività Culturali e del Turismo – Gallerie degli Uffizi; 29 The Metropolitan Museum of Art, New York; 30 © Dario Grimaldi/ Bridgeman Images; 31 Archivio Fotografico Museo Stibbert, Florence; 32 Photo: Nicolo Orsi Battaglini/Art Resource, NY; 33 The Metropolitan Museum of Art, New York; 34 Flint Museum of Art; 35 Szépművészeti Múzeum/Museum of Fine Arts, Budapest; 36 Photo: author; 37 Courtesy of The Burghley House Collection. Image: Bridgeman Images; 38 Photo: Scala/Art Resource, NY; 39 Detroit Institute of Arts; 40 Courtesy of the owner; 41 Courtesy of the Ministero per i Beni e delle Attività Culturali e del Turismo – Galleria Nazionale d'Arte Antica di Palazzo Barberini; 42 Szépművészeti Múzeum/Museum of Fine Arts, Budapest; 43 Courtesy of Fondazione Pisa; 44 Courtesy of the Ministero per i Beni e delle Attività Culturali e del Turismo – Museum and Real Bosco di Capodimonte; 45 Photo: Scala/Art Resource, NY; 46 Photo: Mauro Coen Studio Fotografico; 47 The Metropolitan Museum of Art, New York; 48 Courtesy of the Ministero per i Beni e delle Attività Culturali e del Turismo – Museum and Real Bosco di Capodimonte; 49 © Archivo Fotografico Museo Nacional del Prado; 50 Patrimonio Nacional. 10010009-DG058165; 51 Photo: author; 52 Photo: author; 53 Gabinetto fotografico Museo Civico, Padua; 54 Photo: Katherine Wetzel © Virginia Museum of Fine Arts; 55 Courtesy of the Ministero per i Beni e delle Attività Culturali e del Turismo – Gallerie degli Uffizi; 56 Courtesy of the Ministero per i Beni e delle Attività Culturali e del Turismo – Galleria Nazionale d'Arte Antica di Palazzo Barberini; 57 Photo: author; 58 Royal Collection Trust/© Her Majesty Queen Elizabeth II 2021; 59 Royal Collection Trust/© Her Majesty Queen Elizabeth II 2021; 60 Courtesy the owner; 61 Royal Collection Trust/© Her Majesty Queen Elizabeth II 2021; 62 The Metropolitan Museum of Art, New York; 63 Photo: Gérard Blot. © RMN-Grand Palais/Art Resource, NY; 64 Archivio Fotografico Museo Stibbert, Florence; 65 Royal Collection Trust /© Her Majesty Queen Elizabeth II 2021; 66 © San Diego Museum of Art / Gift of Anne R. and Amy Putman/ Bridgeman Images; 67 © National Portrait Gallery, London 68. Royal Collection Trust/© Her Majesty Queen Elizabeth II 2021; 69 Toledo Museum of Art; 70 Courtesy the owner; 71 Photo: A. De Gregorio / Art Resource, NY; 72 Courtesy of the owner; 73 Columbus Museum of Art, Ohio; 74 Courtesy of Cesare Lampronti Gallery; 75 The J. Paul Getty Museum, Los Angeles, California; 76 Photo © Christie's Images / Bridgeman Images; 77 Collection of The John and Mable Ringling Museum of Art; 78 Courtesy of the Ministero per i Beni le Attività Culturali e per il Turismo – Pinacoteca Nazionale di Bologna; 79 Courtesy of the owner; 80 National Gallery of Art, Washington

Index

Note: Page numbers in italics refer to illustrations.